Paul Stewart is best  children's books. The with Chris Riddell h two million copies worldwide.

TREK

Paul Stewart

CORGI BOOKS

TREK
A CORGI BOOK: 9780552154598

Originally published in Great Britain by Jonathan Cape,
a division of The Random House Group Ltd.

PRINTING HISTORY
Jonathan Cape edition published 1991
Corgi edition published 2007

3 5 7 9 10 8 6 4 2

Set in 11/12.5 pt Palatino by
Falcon Oast Graphic Art Ltd.

Corgi Books are published by Transworld Publishers,
61–63 Uxbridge Road, London W5 5SA,
a division of The Random House Group Ltd,
in Australia by Random House Australia (Pty) Ltd,
20 Alfred Street, Milsons Point, Sydney, NSW 2061, Australia,
in New Zealand by Random House New Zealand Ltd,
18 Poland Road, Glenfield, Auckland 10, New Zealand
in South Africa by Random House (Pty) Ltd,
Isle of Houghton, Corner of Boundary Road & Carse O'Gowrie,
Houghton 2198, South Africa,
and in India by Random House Publishers India Private Limited,
301 World Trade Tower, Hotel Intercontinental Grand Complex,
Barakhamba Lane, New Delhi 110 001, India.

Printed in Great Britain by
Cox & Wyman Ltd, Reading, Berkshire.

Papers used by Transworld Publishers are natural, recyclable
products made from wood grown in sustainable forests. The
manufacturing processes conform to the environmental
regulations of the country of origin.

For Julie, Joseph and Anna

Contents

Illustrations

PLATE SECTION:
A collection of snapshots taken on the journey
   with Peter Barnes's Kodak Box Brownie camera

Acknowledgements

This book would not have been possible without the help, both intentioned and inadvertent, of several people.

I would like to thank those who played their part in the series of coincidences which first drew me to the story: Julie for 'What about Kenya?'; Jonathan Richards for 'You must stay at Mrs Simpson's' and Frank Reid for the edition of the *Daily Sketch* he sent me as a birthday present.

Thanks also to those whose invaluable information helped me to flesh out the bones of the tale. To Jill and Duncan Scroggie and Maurice Frost for taking the trouble to visit me at my hotel in Nairobi. To Barbara Simpson for showing me the cine-film and offering such an insight into the characters. But most of all to Peter Barnes who generously allowed me access to his personal diaries, journals and albums.

In addition I must express my gratitude to my editor at Cape, the late Tony Colwell, for his patient advice.

Most of all, I wish to acknowledge the help of my friend, Barry Tombs, who steered me through my growing obsession with the trek, and whose sudden death in 2006 was a tragedy to all who knew him.

Author Note

When I first stumbled across the events that became the subject of this book, I knew that it was a story that needed to be told. It was a rip-roaring adventure, full of grit, grime and grim determination which, while in the tradition of the type of *Boy's Own* fiction I devoured as a boy, had the added advantage of being all true.

The hardback book was published to critical acclaim, sold its print run and promptly disappeared; this, despite considerable film interest, from independent documentary makers to major studios – interest which has continued to this day. Now at last, 16 years after it first appeared on the shelves, the book is available in paperback – freshly packaged and updated – so that details of the remarkable events can reach a whole new audience.

Since those events occurred in 1955, the story was already a snapshot of a bygone British eccentricity when I first wrote it up. Yet at the same time, it is also a timeless recounting of human endurance in the face of terrible adversity – a tale of loyalty, endurance and wilful deception which, though it has aged still further, will never date.

PART ONE

A Rash of Coincidences

Alan Cooper, Barbara Duthy,
Freda Taylor and Peter Barnes

ONE

Home Movies Away

L OOKING around the room at the assortment of loose-cover furniture, dusty bookshelves crammed with reference books and whodunnits, tasselled lampshades and the sundry collection of framed etchings and water-colours, I realized that had Mrs Simpson decided to establish her guest-house in England, it would have looked no different. The sound of a bone china teacup coming to rest on its floral saucer reinforced the impression of rural gentility. Sticky humidity, smarting shoulders and the constant whine of dive-bombing mosquitoes indicated an altogether more raw tropical setting. The moon-rippled sea we could hear lapping at the bottom of her garden was the Indian Ocean.

Julie and I had decided to break our journey along the coast with a few days of snorkelling and sunbathing and, following a friend's recommendation, we had made our way to this displaced slice of Britain, sandwiched between Mombasa and Malindi on the eastern seaboard of Kenya.

I watched Mrs Simpson herself offering advice on how to get the antiquated film-projector to work. Two of her guests – a Canadian forester and a middle-aged English computer expert – were attempting to make sense of the mildewed instructions. All too aware that the contraption could deliver a vicious shock, they were gingerly winding the fiddly cine-film round the maze of reels, cogs and sprockets.

'I hope to God it still plays,' Mrs Simpson said quietly, and sipped at her coffee.

We all did. At dinner that evening, she had teased us with tantalizing titbits about the trek she had undertaken in 1955. It appeared that four of them had attempted to travel from Kenya to England in an 8 h.p. Morris Traveller. Something, it seemed, had gone wrong in the middle of the Sahara, though she hadn't said what. On learning that she had kept a cine version of the entire journey, her nine guests had pestered and pleaded to be allowed a viewing. It would be frustrating if, having persuaded her, we were now to be thwarted by oxidation and decay.

Mrs Simpson turned to me. 'The trouble is that damp gets into everything,' she said, almost apologetically.

She had intended no irony, but as she awkwardly replaced her cup I saw how the moist climate had invaded even her own body. Her joints were swollen, her fingers arthritic. It occurred to me that my first impression of the old woman had been wrong. The previous week I had phoned her from Nairobi to book a room.

'Hello, yes?' I heard.

'Hello, my name's Stewart and I was . . .'

'You'll have to speak up, I can't hear you,' she had interrupted. The peremptory nature of her tone belied the frailty in her voice and I knew I was talking to an elderly, British expat. The clipped vowels suggested decades of colonial service and I began to wonder whether our plan to stay with her might be a mistake. In the event, I didn't have to make a decision: all the rooms were taken. I was instantly disappointed.

'There is the garage,' she continued.

'The garage,' I repeated flatly.

'Yes, I mean, it's got beds and mosquito nets and everything. And a hurricane lamp.'

There was an almost childlike enthusiasm to her voice. I knew that I wanted to go.

From our brief conversation, I had built up an image of a hearty, tweedy woman who deplored the demise of the Empire and addressed her servants only in the imperative. I was wrong. Although she had indeed spent the majority of her seventy-four years in the colonies, Mrs Simpson was far from the blimpish stereotype.

One of the brightly patterned local kangas she would wrap around herself for her early morning dip in the sea had the word *Harambee* repeated around the hem. Roughly translated, it means 'pull together': it was Jomo Kenyatta's rallying cry for the modern Kenya which emerged on 12 December 1963. Not only had he been referring to the Kikuyu, Maasai, Turkana and numerous other tribes living within the arbitrary borders which marked out the old Kenya Colony, but the Europeans too were being invited to stay and help build the new Kenya Republic.

Mrs Simpson had stayed. She had 'pulled together'. She speaks Swahili, and though one of the men who works for her smiled wryly when I asked him about her accent (which, to my ear, sounded peculiarly Home Counties for an African tongue), he conceded that she could get by well enough, even if her grammar was a bit shaky.

It wasn't only her willingness to master the language which singled her out. Instead of the peremptory ring of a silver bell, Mrs Simpson had her own method of announcing to the kitchen that it was time for her next course. She would lean towards the door and, in her high, quavering voice, call out.

'Samp-son!' – the notes of a train entering a tunnel.

19

'Yo!' came the deep, resonating acknowledgement.

And while we were waiting, she would continue with whichever episode of her life she was reliving: an incident from her time with the FANIs, or perhaps a particularly tricky tribal dispute her late husband, Sandy, had been called to deal with in his capacity as District Commissioner. A favourite anecdote concerned the time she had to make an emergency landing in a light aircraft in the Ugandan bush.

Time has dealt harshly with her body. A bicycle accident when she was a girl left her right arm twisted and one side of her face disfigured. The arthritis has caused her knees and ankles to swell, and rendered a once confident stride unsteady. However, fixed by the piercing brown eyes and listening to her account of the past, analysis of the present and hope for the future, I soon became unaware of her physical frailty. She is a woman who, despite, or perhaps because of, her early brush with death, has decided to treat life as an adventure. None of her stories failed to hold us spellbound. Yet when something someone said triggered off her recollections of the desert, I instinctively knew that whatever had taken place in the Sahara was different. From the way her eyes had narrowed and her lips had tightened, it was clear that those particular memories were painful, and it made me all the more eager to hear the story. I waited, with increasing impatience, for the projector to be declared workable.

'That ought to do the trick,' said the computer expert.

'Lights!' Mrs Simpson called out.

Action, I thought – or rather hoped. As a child, I had learnt that an evening of someone else's slides had the potential for unparalleled tedium. For all the advances of technology, cine-films in the hands of the amateur could be worse. My memories of cine evenings are of interminable shaky panoramas of harbours and hillsides, interspersed by unknown people doing something altogether mundane – turning a barbecue sausage or towelling down, followed inevitably by embarrassed grinning and shooing away as the subject matter became aware of the peeping camera. I kept my fingers crossed that Mrs Simpson's eye behind the lens would have seen more than this.

Whirring and ticking, the projector cast a bright beam against the creamy wall selected as the screen. Everyone in the room paused in mid-conversation and turned towards the dazzling square of light. For a few seconds we watched an intermittent display of numbers, asterisks, obliques; stray hairs. Someone giggled. Mrs Simpson leant forward in her chair and stared expectantly at the wall.

'That's Alan,' she said as the grinning figure of a stocky, middle-aged man appeared. He was leaning against a Morris Traveller, that curiously British half-timbered bungalow on wheels.

I needn't have worried about the quality of the film. Not only was the image sharp, it became apparent immediately that this 'home' movie had been put together more professionally than most. Mrs Simpson confirmed that she and her husband had owned their own splicing equipment.

'There's Peter. And Freda,' she continued, as two more figures appeared with armfuls of luggage. 'And that's me.'

Projected against the wall was a version of Mrs Simpson thirty-four years her junior. The bob and wide skirts made her look curiously girlish for a woman of forty. Clearly visible was the badly set arm, but the injuries to her cheek looked far less serious. As she has aged, the facial muscles which were so painstakingly rebuilt by plastic surgeons must have slowly relaxed. I turned to the older woman. In the silvery shadows her

21

face had become a steely mask. I wondered whether I was the only one to recognize the combination of horror and resignation in her expression, knowing what was to follow.

There was something oddly touching about the obvious enthusiasm of the four adventurers. The knee-length baggy shorts and modest blouses made both the men and women appear charmingly naive. The Morris looked horribly small for a crossing of the Sahara. The word 'street-wise' sprang to my mind. Whatever else the small team of British eccentrics might look, it certainly was not street-wise.

Mrs Simpson verbally annotated the moving pictures as their journey progressed through Kenya and into Uganda. The Protectorate, she called it, automatically lapsing into the pre-Independence names of the countries they crossed. Sometimes her memory failed her.

'This must be Mambasa, no, I mean Beni. Well, somewhere in the Belgian Congo, definitely. Unless this is just before the border . . .'

Sometimes her recollections were crystal clear.

'Alan,' she muttered bitterly, as we watched three of them trudging through the undergrowth. 'No attention to detail,' she added. 'He could have brought a primus, but no. So we had to collect wood every time we wanted a cup of tea. And it was the wet season!'

I couldn't help wondering what had happened in the desert. Not that their journey across Africa was anything less than captivating in itself: the dusty game parks, the succulent rainforests, the turquoise glades of giant bamboo – but this was all on recognizable roads. How would the expedition fare in the vast, featureless tracts of desertland, led by a man who scorned the intricate planning essential for a safe, if uneventful, crossing of the Sahara?

Every stop became a photo opportunity. The same guileless smiles, the same artless movements as the four travellers posed on datelines, at the resthouses, climbing into the car time and again to complete a further stretch of their monumental journey. I felt my pulse quicken, not only in fearful anticipation of what was to come, but also because of a rising sense of familiarity.

The names. The Morris. An incident in the desert. Bells were ringing but I didn't know why. If it was *déjà vu* it was persisting more stubbornly than ever before.

'I'm sure I've heard about all this,' I said at one stage.

'You may have,' Mrs Simpson said. 'It made the newspapers at the time.'

But I was scarcely even a baby then. I couldn't have remembered. Yet, as their journey progressed up into the arid scrub at the southern edge of the Sahara and Mrs Simpson continued to reminisce, analysing the reasons why things had gone so terribly wrong, the hairs at the back of my neck tingled. I was positive that I knew how the story would end.

'If only Alan hadn't been so stupid . . . so arrogant,' she was saying. 'I mean, afterwards, Peter agreed with me that the crossing had been perfectly feasible, but Alan simply . . .'

'Alan Cooper,' I interrupted. 'His name was Cooper, wasn't it?'

The blood was pounding in my head. I was willing her to say – no, Smith actually.

But she didn't. Without even looking in my direction, she confirmed that, yes, Cooper had indeed been the surname of the expedition's leader. In the shadowy darkness of the room I noticed Julie staring at me.

'How did you know?' she whispered.

'I've no idea,' I said quietly, as anxious shivers continued to shoot up and down my spine.

TWO

READING THE SIGNS

SEVERAL years ago, a friend sent me a copy of a newspaper from the day I was born. He had tried to get *The Times*, but could find only the now defunct *Daily Sketch*. On that day – 4 June 1955 – the newspaper had cost two old pence, but despite the lower price, the format and bias were all too familiar. I remember thinking as I read it through that nothing ever changes; a fact which is at once depressing yet curiously reassuring.

The headline news was of a crippling rail strike which was going into its second week. At the foot of the back page was an early Peanuts strip cartoon. It was, however, neither the cyclical nature of news nor the unintentional bathos created by the juxtaposition of Charlie Brown and 'the enemy within' which interested me. I had mounted the paper in a frame so that both back and front were on display, and it was an article at the top of the back page that I hurried to reread.

They were trying to cross West Africa by car.

A third Briton in the party is in hospital.

Miss Muriel Taylor, a 48-year-old teacher from Capenhurst, near Chester, who was given leave from school to tour Africa, set out with two men in a Morris

24

Minor car from Agades in the Niger province of French West Africa for Algiers.

A week later a French military patrol picked up Mr Peter Barnes, one of the men, on a desert road.

He was suffering from extreme thirst and exposure to the sun.

After a search the patrol found Miss Taylor and the other man, Mr Alan Norman Cooper, in the car.

They were given water and first aid and told to follow the patrol to safety.

But Miss Taylor and Mr Cooper lost touch with the patrol.

There were discrepancies between what I had heard from Mrs Simpson and what the newspaper reported, not least the fact that they had failed to mention her at all. But I was in no doubt that this was the journey recorded on the cine-film. The events had lodged in the back of my mind simply because the news had broken in England on the day I was born. Had I not been sent that day's issue of the newspaper I would not have known.

I have never been one to listen to omens or portents, but if the chances of stumbling upon the story at all had been remote, then the coincidence of the dates was astonishing. Whereas before it had been a quirky little tale of four barmy Brits going on a chaotic trek, now it had become personalized. I felt somehow possessed by these people, who had come to belong to me. As if they were lost relatives, I was bound to pursue the story, to find out for myself precisely what had gone wrong in the desert.

Mrs Simpson had mentioned in passing that, as far as she knew, Barnes was still living in Kenya. International Enquiries came up with an address and I wrote to him the following day. It was my best lead and I could only hope that this was the Barnes I was looking for. Trying to track down a Barnes, Cooper or Taylor in England would be a nightmare.

While I was waiting for a reply, I carried out some research of my own. On a wet morning in mid-March I visited the rectangular, brown-brick newspaper library at Colindale. As I knew the exact dates of the events the articles were easy to locate. The account I had read in the *Daily Sketch* was also covered by the other national dailies. Even in those first reports of Saturday, 4 June, minor differences had arisen between the various papers. The spelling of the travellers' names was not consistent. Their ages varied.

I decided that I would have to confirm the facts at the General Register Office – the official centre of 'hatch, match and dispatch' records. Working alphabetically, it proved to be a simple enough matter checking Barnes's and Cooper's details and, having ascertained from the *Sunday Express* of 5 June 1955 that Mrs Simpson was then an unmarried woman called Barbara Duthy, I succeeded also in noting down her particulars.

When I got to Freda Taylor – or to be more precise Muriel Freda Taylor – I drew a blank. The newspapers had given her age as '38' and '48', but despite going through all the volumes covering these two possibilities, I could find no record of her being born. I considered the reasons for this. Perhaps she was illegitimate and adopted. Perhaps she had been married and divorced, and Taylor was her married name. More likely I had simply missed the entry, but it was too late in the afternoon to begin all over again.

I would not return to St Catherine's House to continue my search for a fortnight. When I did, and finally established Freda's actual date of birth, it threw up more questions than it answered. In fact, the further into the story I was delving, the more mysterious the circumstances seemed to be.

The *Sunday Dispatch* had noted that, 'An inquiry has been opened to find out why they were allowed to set out alone, contrary to rules which say that Sahara travellers must go in convoy.' It had occurred to me that since the story involved British nationals in Africa, the Foreign Office might have been involved. The mention of an inquiry strengthened this possibility.

Situated at the end of a cul-de-sac in suburban Kew, the Public Records Office is a large, squat, concrete and glass affair, notorious for being one of the first 'sick' buildings reported in London. It took two days to find an entry in the reference books which might lead me to the documents I needed. 1955: *Welfare of British Commonwealth Citizens in French Africa* – F.O. 369; 5217 and 5218. I tapped my request into the computer and waited.

When they arrived, the two buff envelope-folders were fatter than I had dared to hope. With fingers trembling, I fumbled with the string, whispering over and over, 'let them be the right ones'.

As the knot slipped and the front cover sprang open, I saw that I'd hit the jackpot. The files were exactly what I had been looking for; they contained pages and pages of letters, military accounts, police reports, departmental memos, governmental briefs. As I looked closer, I found myself reading the four names that had already become so familiar: Muriel Freda Taylor, Alan Norman Cooper, Barbara Lois Duthy and Peter Bruce Robert Barnes. My eyes lingered on the final name, and I wondered once again whether I'd written to this Barnes, or to someone who would be unable to make head or tail of my letter.

On Wednesday, 19 April, a pale-blue airmail envelope came through my letter-box. It had five Kenyan stamps on it, each decorated with a representation of the Gedi Ruins we had visited while staying with Mrs Simpson.

The lost city of Gedi, as it is known, was established as

a port by Arab traders in the thirteenth century. Today it is stranded, miles back from the sea and almost lost in the centre of dense forest. We visited it one late afternoon as the shadows were lengthening and the silky Sykes monkeys were leaping irreverently about the walls and archways of the crumbling Palace and Great Mosque. Mrs Simpson pooh-poohed the idea of an entire population mysteriously abandoning the city.

'There was nothing mysterious about it at all,' she had said. 'An extended period of low rainfall led to a dropping of the water table and so, when the wells dried up, the people were forced to move.'

And yet Gedi is mysterious. It is impossible to walk around the eerie, shadowy ruins without feeling you are being watched. As I took a knife to the envelope, the same shivers of apprehension tingled ominously. I pulled out the letter.

It was written on pale-grey paper with a dark-red letterhead consisting of an address and a small bearded man holding an enormous pencil. The impression the sketch gave was that this particular Peter Barnes was a draughtsman, or perhaps an advertising copywriter. It did not tally with Mrs Simpson's description of the man and I was suddenly convinced that this was the wrong Peter Barnes.

I read the letter. Certain phrases stood out as if highlighted with a fluorescent marker. Wonderful phrases; phrases like 'I have no objection to your suggestions'; 'I did keep a comprehensive set of diaries at the time which I now have'; 'I doubt if better material is available, and there is plenty of it.' And the generous '. . . you could stay here with us – no problem.'

Instead of attempting to chase up other slender leads in England, I took him up on his offer and on Saturday, 21 October, I arrived back in Kenya to continue with my investigation. Because of a national holiday, Barnes and his wife had taken a long weekend on the coast. He had left a note at my hotel that he would be picking me up on the Wednesday.

* * *

Mrs Simpson had mentioned that those on the trek had not been friends, but had come together through an announcement Cooper placed in the *East African Standard*. I knew he hadn't been well off. I knew that he wouldn't have wasted money on a flamboyant advertisement. So I went straight for the small ads in the personal column. And there it was, in the edition of Saturday, 15 January 1955.

> Car crossing Africa, Sahara, Spain, France for England, leaving Kenya last fortnight April, has room for six passengers. Full particulars from Voucher X905.

The advertisement was repeated on Friday, 21 January. I had heard that Alan Cooper's original plans for the African crossing had been more grandiose than the party of four which finally departed, and by uncovering the original announcement in the McMillan Memorial Library in Nairobi, I had the proof I needed.

Continuing through the papers, I found a second version of the proposed trip which appeared first on Friday, 11 February, and again the following day.

> Car safari leaving Kenya 15th April for England via Congo, Sahara, Spain, France. Still two seats available. Apply Voucher X053.

From the two advertisements, it is impossible to tell how radically Cooper's proposed trip had altered. It appeared as if he had accepted four passengers who had answered the first ad, and now needed only two more to complete the party.

29

The truth was quite different. In the three weeks that elapsed between the January and February advertisements, Alan Cooper had been forced to rethink his entire plan.

* * *

As arranged, Peter Barnes picked me up from the hotel and took me to his home in Nakuru. He had put a desk into the bedroom I would occupy for the next month, and there, neatly stacked, was a pile of journals, diaries, scrap-books and albums waiting for my eager inspection. He had written that the information he had was comprehensive, but I was nevertheless overwhelmed with the wealth of material he had saved.

'I hope you can read my writing,' he said with an embarrassed smile.

Reverently I picked up the first of his diaries and turned to the first page.

'No problem.'

THREE

CUTTING ONE'S COAT

Aᴸᴬᴺ Cooper had left his home in Beaconsfield, England, in 1928. He was twenty-one at the time. Hoping to find his fortune, if not fame, on the rich and fertile land in the Kenya Colony, he went to work for Conway Hervey on his farm at Songhor. Like so many young men in those days, Cooper had been toying with the idea of emigration to the new African colony for some time. His married sister was already living there and had sent encouraging letters home to her younger brother. The worsening economic crisis in America and Europe, culminating in the Wall Street Crash, seems to have given him the necessary impetus to make that break.

He soon bought his own land near Kapsabet on the Nandi Escarpment, and set about farming coffee. It was a bad time for his new enterprise. The collapse of money markets at home had a dire effect on the new settlers. At that time, apart from Algeria and South Africa, there were some 60,000 Europeans scraping a living in the African continent. All of them were in serious financial trouble.

As Maurice Frost, an old friend of his, pointed out to me, life then was harsh. 'It wasn't all garden parties and hunting safaris, by any means. Most of the farmers were incredibly hard up. We were literally struggling to stay alive.'

Undoubtedly some well-to-do aristocrats were living there too, and it is primarily these who are remembered now. There was Lord Delamere and his 'Kenya Cowboys', whose rowdy and excessive behaviour is well documented, and Lord Errol, whose unsolved murder became the subject of James Fox's *White Mischief*. In her book *Out of Africa*, the Baroness Karen Blixen perhaps did more to romanticize the lifestyle of the upper-class élite than anyone else. The interest in these aristocrats is out of all proportion to their number however. The vast majority of the settlers were ordinary Europeans attempting to carve out a new life for themselves in an unfamiliar country.

The difficulties they would have to face were soon made manifest. Far from escaping the slump, the new farmers found the worldwide economic problems following them. Kenya had been a colony for some thirty years, and was dependent on the mother country buying its produce. In the wake of the crash, Britain cut back on imports, and those she did take were on her own terms. Prices were fixed artificially low and there was nothing the Kenyan farmer could do about it.

Alan Cooper diversified. He tried breeding cattle and pigs for meat and opened his own farm butchery. He experimented with other crops: sisal, tea, oats, wheat, passion-fruit. It was all a matter of trial and error, and like so many other farmers he made mistakes. The soil was too dry for this, the indigenous insects destroyed that. Lean years followed, but he managed to keep his head above water, and in 1933 decided to take a trip back to England.

The cheapest way to return at that time was a complicated, though established, journey by train, ferry and coach up through the Sudan, into Egypt and across the Mediterranean. Alan Cooper devised an altogether more exciting way of getting back. It was also to prove even less expensive.

On Thursday, 13 April 1933, *The Times* reported his arrival in England.

A two-seater 8 h.p. Morris Minor has crossed the Sahara. This is the first time that a car of so low engine capacity has completed this arduous journey.

Mr Alan N. Cooper, a Kenyan coffee planter, has arrived in England on the completion of the last stage of an 8,000 mile journey from Nairobi to London. His car – a 1931 side-valve model – was purchased second-hand with a considerable mileage already to its credit. He set out some seven weeks ago with one companion, Mr Walsh, and travelled through Uganda, the Sudan, the Congo, the Cameroons, Nigeria, the Sahara, Algeria, Morocco, Spain and France. The trip across the desert between Gao and Reggan, a distance of more than 800 miles, was accomplished in 4 days.

That trip, twenty-two years earlier, was the last time that Cooper had seen his mother. In 1955, she had reached the age of eighty-four and Cooper knew that if he left it much longer he would never see her alive again.

By this time, the economic situation of the white settlers had improved considerably. From 1938 onwards, the price of coffee had been steadily rising. The fact that Alan Cooper was still experiencing financial difficulties was attributable now as much to his character as to external factors.

He was, as his friend Maurice Frost put it, 'a fun man, not a great worker'. He would throw all his energy into each new venture that caught his imagination. He built a tennis court and a swimming pool on his farm. He helped to establish the Nandi Bears Club to which, Frost explained, all the local expats belonged. He had a spell running a hotel. The daily grind of looking after a successful farm was irksome to him. It took too much of his time; time he would far rather spend playing tennis with his friends.

It became a vicious circle. Because he did the minimum amount of work, the farm never realized its full potential. And because it was comparatively unsuccessful, it never made Cooper enough money for him to free himself from it. In 1955, when he decided to make a second trip back to England, he was in precisely the same financial situation as in 1933. Circumstances once more dictated the cheapest mode of travel, and though he was by now forty-eight, he decided in favour of another overland trek. It was then that he contacted the *East African Standard*.

Fifty-six people replied to the first advertisement. This must have heartened Cooper and he wrote back immediately, enclosing typed details of his proposed itinerary. Of the three who finally travelled with Cooper, Freda Taylor was the only one who had responded to this initial ad. She was impressed enough by his reply to write to her school, Capenhurst Primary, near Chester, to ask for a six-week extension to the long leave she had already taken to visit relatives in Rhodesia and South Africa. She wanted, in her own words, 'to go on a safari in the Sahara on my way home'.

A more powerful Morris Oxford estate car for four people and a half-ton Morris commercial truck for a further three, plus all the baggage, equipment and provisions, were to form the mini-convoy that Cooper would lead through Central Africa and across the Sahara. Each person was allowed to bring luggage weighing up to 80 pounds. Later Freda Taylor told Barbara Duthy she had been promised that two Africans would also be accompanying them to do all the day-to-day work on the trip. It was this fact that was to lead to so much confusion later when the newspapers took up her relatives' questions about the 'two missing porters'.

The trip was to cost each person £175. Alan Cooper had estimated that if the journey was accomplished at an average speed of 200 miles per day, the sum of money his passengers paid should subsidize his own fare. If his calculations were correct, he would make it back to England at no cost to himself.

Jill Scroggie, another friend of Cooper's whom I met in Nairobi, laughed when I asked her how those who knew him well had reacted to his planned trek.

'None of us would have gone with him.' On being pressed for reasons, she explained that he had an almost childlike disbelief in anything ever going wrong.

Maurice Frost disagreed with her assessment of Alan. 'Oh, I think we all had enough faith in "Sweetie" Cooper,' he said, 'but certainly not in the vehicle.'

'Sweetie?'

'His nickname,' he said, and chuckled. 'Not that he was one of those. There was nothing feminine about him. It was simply that, well, some people say that's rather nice, or chic, or splendid, or whatever. Alan always used to say "that's rather sweet". You know, a lovely view, a good tennis shot. Always sweet. And it caught on.'

I nodded. 'The car wasn't good enough, in your opinion?'

'Eight horse-power for the Sahara?' he said. 'I know he'd done it before, but you wouldn't have got me to try it.'

Of those who responded to Cooper's first advertisement, very few followed up his reply. Some were put off by the relatively high cost, some by the means of transport, and some, when they discovered who was behind the anonymous notice, must have been deterred by Alan

Cooper himself – he was not unknown among the European population of Kenya. One cheeky couple contacted him to get advice for their own proposed journey.

Eventually circumstances forced him to abandon the idea of two vehicles. One would have to suffice. This, of course, meant a reduction in the baggage allowance: instead of 80 pounds, each person was limited to one small suitcase. More dropped out.

In addition, Cooper himself turned down a few of the applicants. An old woman of seventy-five was informed politely that the trek would not be suitable for her. An Indian couple was rejected, not it seems because he disliked them, but, according to Barbara Simpson, 'because they might cause unpleasantness on the way.' It is not clear what he meant by this.

Cooper finally managed to assemble a party of four with which he was content. Then two of them got amoebic dysentery and cancelled. Apart from Freda Taylor, the first person to have replied, he was back to square one. It was at this point that he drafted the second advertisement, yet it was to be word of mouth and coincidence that finally filled those two extra seats. Peter Barnes was next to pay his £175.

There was nothing in the Barnes diaries to tell me how he heard about the trek, merely a note in a journal that he had applied through Miss Taylor, whom he knew was going. I discovered that by this time he had left school and was working for the Mowlem Construction Company (a subsidiary of Lever Brothers), so I asked him how he had heard about the proposed journey.

'I must have been about seventeen-and-a-half when the trip came up and I decided – or rather my mother decided – that I should go on it.'

'Your mother?'

'Yes.'

'She was quite happy about you going?'

'She wanted me to go on the trip because, you know, young men suddenly feel the urge for independence, they think they can look after themselves and want to go off and be on their own. But mothers tend to hold them back and say, "You'll do what Mummy tells you to do." That sort of thing. So I rebelled; became a bit of a nuisance. I even ran away from home for a few days. I think my mother decided that a trip like this would toughen me up and make me a bit more sensible. When she first mentioned it I was totally against the idea. I refused to go anywhere. But then the situation reversed. She got more and more worried, and thought maybe she'd made a mistake; maybe it was much too dangerous. But by this time I'd got all keen. I decided I wanted to go. We had a number of rows about it, but in the end I went.'

'So it was definitely your mother who saw the advertisement? Not you.'

'No, it was her.'

I asked Evelyn Barnes, his mother. A small wiry woman with her northern English accent still intact, she was equally sure who had first read the advert.

'It was Peter.'

A third version was offered by Barbara Duthy. In 1955, shortly after the trip, she noted down that Evelyn Barnes had a friend who worked at the Salisbury Hotel, and it was she who had told her about Freda Taylor's planned trip to England. At first she had thought it would be a wonderful opportunity for her son. He was due to be called up for two years' National Service in the Kenya Regiment that September. What better way of spending his last few months of freedom than going on a long African trek? It would also enable him to see his grandparents, Robert and Ethel Hogg, who lived in Derbyshire.

Whoever had instigated the scheme, it was decided that Peter Barnes would join the Cooper entourage. They shared the costs between them. Evelyn put forward some money she herself had been intending to use for a trip to England and she persuaded Peter to sell his stamp collection and train set so that he would feel more committed to the venture.

'Yes, I sold the stamp collection I'd been building up,' he told me. 'It was a very good one, actually. I got quite a lot of money for it – in those days. And I sold my train-set, which was my absolute love in life. Beautiful Hornby dublo gauge train-set. Super thing. All electric.'

Barbara Duthy never saw the second advertisement either. She heard about the trip through a friend of hers – a veterinary surgeon called John Wood. While in hospital with a broken femur in February 1955, he had found himself in the bed next to Alan Cooper.

Erica Boswell, whose parents had owned the farm adjacent to Alan Cooper's land, told me how she, as a teenager, had viewed her neighbour.

'Oh, he was a lovely man. Fun. Superb piano player. Loved tennis. He had these hooded eyes that would look at you so deeply, and beautiful long eyelashes. Always making people laugh, that's my main memory of him. In fact, there was only the one time when I remember him depressed.'

'When was that?'

'He thought he had cancer. Thought he was going to die. I remember he used to smoke these cigarettes. Black ones – Bastos, I think they were called. From Uganda. Always had one in his mouth. I think he must have thought they made him look chic. And then suddenly he found he had this lump on his tongue. Absolutely convinced it was cancer.'

Cooper was rushed into hospital in Nairobi to be

operated on, and the growth, which proved not to be malignant, was removed. It was while he was recuperating that he outlined his ideas for the overland trek to John Wood.

Barbara Duthy, meanwhile, had been making her own plans for getting back to England. She worked as a zoologist for the Kenya Government at Kabete. Her specialist field was helminthology – the study of worms – and she would often accompany vets to isolated farms where they would deal with the problem of worms in livestock. Access to these farmsteads was no problem, for Barbara Duthy was a qualified pilot.

In 1947 the father of Audrey Watts, a close friend, offered to pay two-thirds of the cost of her learning to fly if she would agree to take his daughter with her. She leapt at the opportunity. 'Since that time,' she was to write, 'flying has been one of the great things in my life.' Drawing out all her savings, she bought her first plane – a Piper Cub – and by using it partly while working for the Veterinary Department, she managed to afford to keep it in the air.

In 1955 she was owed a few months' leave and thought about a return to England. Having already flown there and back in 1949, she was keen to travel a different way.

'I didn't hold with coming home the ordinary way – that anyone can do, and that I could do when I was sixty or more,' she told me.

She answered an advertisement for passengers wishing to crew their way home on a yacht, and was accepted. She and a friend of hers, Elizabeth Lutley, went down to Mombasa to inspect the boat and its owner, Channing Pierce.

'The yacht,' she explained, 'was a honey, but the voyage was utterly unprepared.'

There was no sextant, an insufficient supply of

drinking water, no charts and no spare sails. What was more, Channing Pierce himself appeared not to know anything about ocean navigation.

'No need for charts,' he told them, on being asked, 'we'll just follow the coast round.'

Even if they had still been tempted to go, a friend's comment that Pierce had 'had something done' to the bottom of the boat convinced them that, sadly, they would have to turn down their places on board. Subsequently they heard that Channing Pierce had set off undaunted. Without the charts, however, he had no idea of the ocean depths and ran aground in the shallow water off Mogadishu. He had covered barely 500 miles.

When John Wood told her of the proposed crossing of Africa – which he considered Cooper had planned fairly thoroughly – she wrote immediately, expressing her interest in a seat. Alan Cooper finally had the three passengers he needed.

In her 1933 book, *Out in the Midday Sun – My Kenya*, Elspeth Huxley describes the atmosphere of the Torr's Hotel.

> Torr's was Nairobi's grandest building . . . It had become the rendezvous for Nairobi's café society and for safari parties and others who gathered there for eleven o'clock coffee, pre-lunch drinks and, in the evening, epicurean meals produced by a Swiss chef, and dancing to a fashionable band.

Today, dwarfed by the modern multi-storey buildings which line Kenyatta Avenue, the Torr's days as a hotel are over. It is now a bank. In 1955, although it was no longer the grandest building in the capital and without its Swiss chef, it was still a popular meeting-place.

Over tea Cooper outlined his long-term plans to

Barbara and Peter. He said that he wished to go to England to float his farm as a company for £10,000, eventually growing tea rather than coffee. If the farm ran as a company, he explained, he would not be solely in charge. This would leave him with more time for his second venture: the establishing of a regular tourist trip across the Sahara. He intended to collect information on this journey which subsequently he would be able to put to use.

Barbara Duthy was less concerned with his future ambitions than in the practicalities of the journey at hand. After her experience with Channing Pierce, she was eager to discover how well everything had been planned, and she questioned Cooper closely on equipment, tools, spares, maps, and provisions for taking extra water and fuel across the desert areas. Cooper assured her, with increasing impatience, that he had done all that was necessary. The car had been dust-proofed, the roof painted white to minimize the heat of the sun and special brackets had been fitted to the rear bumper to take two 4-gallon tins. As for spares, he had sufficient for every eventuality: petrol pump, fan belts, inner tubes, you name it.

'And a primus stove?'

'We don't need a primus.'

'Of course we do. We can't go hacking down trees to make a fire every time we want a cup of tea. And what about the desert, where there's no vegetation?'

'All right, all right,' Cooper said. 'I'll get a primus.'

As she explained to me later, the problem was that, unlike in a boat, you can't really check what a driver's taking because it's not in the car beforehand. They had to take it on trust that Alan Cooper was honest and would keep to all he had promised.

That evening there was a small party. Freda Taylor had decided to have a farewell get-together at a friend's home in the grounds of Government House and, for the first time, the four travellers met up. Again, questions concerning equipment arose. Again, Cooper assured everyone that everything was under control. Even at this stage, Barbara admitted that she was not entirely happy with Cooper's apparent lack of attention to small detail. She had noticed the irritation in his voice when pressed for specific information.

'Yes, I do realize how important they are,' he snapped at one guest who was stressing the value of sand-mats in the desert.

It seems that, in the end, Barbara – like everyone else – was won round by Cooper's boundless energy and enthusiasm, and the evening ended on an optimistic note. Someone proposed a toast:

'To Alan, Freda, Barbara and Peter – a safe and successful trip!'

The four of them left the party in high spirits, eager now to get underway. The departure date was fixed for 15 April, leaving from Alan Cooper's farm.

PART TWO

ACROSS AFRICA

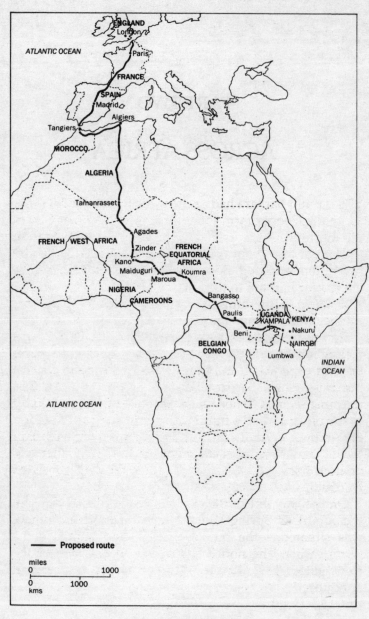

From a map of the period

FOUR

A STATE OF EMERGENCY

PETER and Barbara had arranged to travel the 200 miles to the Cooper farm together by coach and, at 8.30 in the morning, Peter arrived at the Grey Line Bus Station in Nairobi with plenty of time to spare. Accompanied by his mother and dog, Bonzo, a huge shaggy mongrel, he waited for Barbara to turn up. She didn't.

'I knew something like this would happen,' his mother was fretting. 'I just knew it.'

By the time of Peter's departure Evelyn Barnes was feeling uneasy about her son going on such a hare-brained expedition, and though she had tried to conceal her misgivings, Barbara Duthy's absence on the first morning seemed to her a hideous portent. She rushed off to the office and sent frantic telegrams to the bus station at Lumbwa, to Alan's farm and to Kabete, where Barbara lived. She insisted that the bus wait, but when after half an hour there was still no sign of her, the driver insisted he could wait no longer.

On the way out of the city, the coach passed through the suburb of Spring Valley where his mother's school was situated – the school that he had named some years earlier. The notice board was to one side of the front gates: 'M.E. Barnes – Junior House Nursery,' it announced.

I asked Peter if he had felt particularly sad on that morning. He pondered over the question for some while.

'I think I was too excited to feel really sad,' he said finally. 'It was the beginning of a huge adventure.'

Kabete is 8 miles north of Nairobi. In 1955 it wasn't really a town so much as the centre of agricultural research and training. Amongst many of its works and projects, the Government Veterinary Laboratories had been set the task of finding cures for sleeping sickness (trypanosomiasis) and rinderpest.

As the coach was making its way along the dusty main street, a European woman suddenly leapt out of a parked car, rushed into the middle of the road and held up both hands. It was Kabete's helminthologist, Barbara Duthy. The coach stopped.

'Why is the bus so late?' she demanded to know.

'We were waiting for you,' Peter answered. Relief that she had turned up was rapidly becoming irritation – she might at least apologize.

'But I told them,' she said. 'It would have been ridiculous going all the way to Nairobi, just to come back again, so I phoned the coach company to tell you. I knew your mother would be worried.'

'Well, the message didn't get through.'

'Evidently,' she said. 'Can you help me with this?'

Peter took hold of the heavier of the two grips and swung it up on to the rack. He looked round for the suitcases. Apart from the grips all he could see was an African basket (a kikapu), with knitting needles sticking out from it.

'Is this all there is?' he asked, genuinely surprised, and proceeded to interrogate her on what she had remembered to bring. To each item he raised, she answered in the affirmative.

'How have you got it all in such a small space?'

'A woman's secret,' Barbara said, and smiled.

46

The journey up-country took eight hours. For much of that time Peter gazed out of the window, sadly aware of the fact that the country he had grown up in was in a state of violent change. The evidence was everywhere. In his diary he noted the presence in Nairobi of 'armed native policemen who patrol the city in pairs'. High up above the Rift Valley he described how the vegetation had been cut back 50 feet on each side of the road, to deter rebels from lurking in wait. A particularly fine panorama was obscured by a sign warning anyone who might have been tempted to stop there: 'No picnicking! Terrorist gangs in the vicinity!'

Born in British Guyana, toddling in Zanzibar and raised in Kenya, the education Peter received was inevitably weighted heavily in favour of the colonial powers. They, after all, had written the history books. History books which at that time promulgated the belief that before the white man came to East Africa to save and civilize, the black inhabitants had been the victims of disease, of tribal war, and of slave traders who would make deep forays inland from the coast, seize the villagers and sell them to the highest bidders in the markets of Mombasa or Zanzibar.

By 1955, however, when Peter was about to embark on his adventure, even a report written that year by the British Royal Commission on East Africa could no longer claim that the British presence had unreservedly improved the lot of the indigenous populations. It detailed the 'noisome and dangerous' conditions Africans were now living under, and pointed out that the combination of low wages and high cost of food and accommodation had made 'family life impossible for the majority'. Despite the introduction of wheat, the railway, the labour tax and other symbols of a civilized society, sixty years of colonial rule had severely worsened the situation of the peoples of Kenya. Many in Britain recognized this fact. Yet, as those at home began to relax their grip on the colonies (or at least contemplate doing so), the attitude of the European settlers themselves was hardening.

On Monday, 26 January 1953, over a thousand white settlers had marched through Nairobi to Government House, demanding to see the Governor of Kenya, Sir Evelyn Baring. The demonstration had been sparked off by the weekend murder of a white farming family, the Rucks, who lived up on Kinnon Kop, the plateau near Nakuru. Increasingly the settlers felt they were being sacrificed to the changing mood at Westminster and they insisted both on tougher action against the Mau Mau and more say in the running of the colony.

'Do you remember much about the march?' I asked.

'Oh yes,' Peter replied. 'I was there. I was supposed to have been sick from school, but instead my mother said, "you're coming up," and we all went marching. I remember the whole of Government House was lined with police, black and white, all linking hands. And we just charged it, broke through and demanded someone come out. I was in the front row – there was a picture of me somewhere. I could only have been fifteen at the time.'

A popular double-edged misconception is that 'Mau Mau' actually translated as 'black Kenyan freedom fighter', or some such, and that back in the fifties, the entire country had risen up in revolt against the colonialists. The truth was quite different. No one knows where the term 'Mau Mau' originates; what is certain is that it was never used or accepted by the rebels. They called themselves 'the Land and Freedom Armies'. Furthermore, of all the many peoples of Kenya, it was only the Kikuyu who joined these liberation armies – and even amongst them there was conflict. Many were against the rebellion, and this led to a further complication in the situation. As well as being a struggle to regain the land they had lost to the settlers, the Kikuyu uprising became a civil war between rebels and those remaining loyal to the British crown. It was these loyalists whom Peter saw from the bus window, housed in their model villages, protected by guards, enclosed by barbed wire and bamboo stakes.

Evelyn Barnes told me that, for her, perhaps the worst aspect of the entire emergency was not knowing whom to trust. Her school had British soldiers guarding the front and back entrances and, as she was in charge of children, she had been equipped with a siren and given permission to carry firearms. At night, despite the presence of Bonzo, she couldn't allow any of the servants or helpers to sleep in the house. Just in case. One night Peter was woken by the sound of someone tapping on the window. It was the Kikuyu cook, evidently distressed.

'I am not rebel. I am loyal,' he insisted in a loud whisper. 'You tell.'

The coach continued north, climbing up into the misty altitudes of cloud, past Lake Naivasha, through Gilgil and Nakuru, and on to Molo where they stopped for lunch. The surrounding landscape was green and lush, with fields of wheat and vegetables, and meadows full of grazing cows.

In his diary, Peter wrote: 'A very beautiful area, just like England.'

Although parts of the landscape might have resembled Britain, there was little other similarity. On 21 April 1955, it was reported in the press that two English schoolboys had been found murdered by Mau Mau terrorists. Peter had known them, had been at the same school. By October 1955, the death toll had risen to more than 13,000 – amongst whom must have been many more schoolboys. Kenya, in 1955, was a bad place for schoolboys, black or white.

After a substantial lunch, Barbara and Peter continued on the last stretch of their journey to Lumbwa. It was cold and misty and Barbara put names to some of the trees and shrubs that Peter merely recognized. He committed the word *agapanthus* to memory as she pointed to a lily crowned with a cluster of blue flowers.

'From the Greek,' she had explained, '*agape* meaning "love", and *anthus* "flower".'

It was after five o'clock and getting dark as they approached their destination. Lumbwa is set in a crater. Steep walled valleys radiate away from it. The sun had already disappeared behind the mountain tops.

'I hope this isn't an omen,' Barbara said irritably.

'What?' Peter asked.

'Well, where is he?' she said, looking up and down the street. 'He must have got one of the telegrams. I sent three.'

They asked at a nearby store whether there was any message waiting for them. The store-keeper shook his head. A European farmer, overhearing their plight, offered to take them to the railway station. 'Perhaps your telegram is waiting for you there.' It wasn't, but he insisted on buying them tea and arranged with the station-master to let them sleep in the waiting room for the night, or until they were collected.

Barbara looked at Peter, shrugged and giggled. It was looking ominously chaotic.

Fortunately they did not have to make use of the blankets the station-master had offered. A telegram came through from Alan Cooper informing them that he was on his way. There had, it transpired, been misunderstandings about the time and place they were to arrive. Lumbwa or Mubonsoni; a.m. or p.m.; fifteenth or sixteenth – the amount of confusion a telegram can generate is altogether disproportionate to its value. At best it translates tragedy or joy into staccato gobbets of dispassionate fact, at worst it is little more than a game of Chinese whispers.

When the car finally pulled up beside them, Barbara and Peter exchanged glances but said nothing. Cooper had talked of a Morris Oxford shooting brake. The car he was now driving was the considerably smaller Morris Traveller: registration number KBY 779.

'Wonderful little car,' he offered, unprompted. 'Really lively performance.'

He explained that it had the new A-30 engine, did 35 to 40 miles to the gallon and had a top speed of 75 miles per hour. He was so obviously enthusiastic that neither Barbara nor Peter questioned how four people and their luggage, equipment and provisions for six weeks would fit into so small a vehicle.

'Let's get a move on, then. The road's awful and there's more rain forecast.'

Alan Cooper introduced his Nandi driver, sitting in the next seat. 'He takes over when I fall asleep,' he said. 'Drives it like a tractor, but at least he makes it go.' He laughed.

'You fall asleep at the wheel?' Peter asked.

'It has been known,' Cooper admitted and, letting his head slump forward, he snored loudly.

Even through the thick fog, Barbara could see the side of the road speeding towards them.

'Alan!' she shouted.

Instantly alert again, he flicked the wheel round.

'Feel that pull?' he said, and Peter had to admit that the little Morris was much more powerful than it looked. It took the road out of the valley and up the steep embankment with no difficulty at all.

It was by now dark. This, combined with the torrential

rain and thick fog, had reduced visibility to almost nil. Rather than penetrating the gloom, the light from the headlamps was reflected back into the eyes of passengers and driver who nevertheless kept his foot down on the accelerator. The somewhat predictable result was recorded in Peter's diary.

He drove furiously along the wet, slippery road, and once, rounding a bend at 40 miles per hour, we went sideways into the bank. Everyone was thrown into a heap at the side. Fortunately, the car did not turn over.

This was hardly guaranteed to inspire confidence and yet Peter's trust in Alan Cooper's ability to get them back to his farm and across Africa remained unabated. Further down the page I read 'Mr C must have known the road like the back of his hand'.

His farmhouse was large, comfortable, but, as Barbara was later to comment, 'had seen better days'. As well as Freda, who was nursing a sprained ankle, three other Europeans were staying there. There was the couple who would look after the farm during Cooper's absence, and an old friend who boarded at the Nairobi Club, but who had come up to the farm to wish them all well on their departure.

Alan Cooper, the perfect *mine host*, wined and dined his guests and played a selection of pieces on the piano. Barbara was evidently impressed by the quality of his playing. 'He was a pianist of no mean order and had a grand piano in his lounge in which he took great pride,' she was later to write.

'Right,' said Alan at ten o'clock. 'We've got an early start tomorrow . . .'

'Oh, yes,' Freda said dutifully. 'Must have my beauty sleep.'

The guests were all shown to their rooms. Alan, who

never slept in the house, lit a hurricane lamp and took Peter down to the open bungalow he had built next to the swimming pool. As they were all bidding one another goodnight, Barbara asked what she had been meaning to ask all evening.

'What *is* the matter with those dogs?'

The two dogs had been cowering, whimpering and trembling with obvious terror ever since they had arrived. Alan remained unforthcoming and it was his friend who told them what had happened. The night before, at midnight, they had heard an awful row coming from the veranda. Barking, yelping, screeching. Alan had grabbed his rifle, but it was already too late. A leopard had carried off his third and favourite dog.

Peter lay awake in the open bungalow. It should have been idyllic. The trees were rustling, the frogs in the swimming pool were croaking and now that the storm had passed, the stars were dazzlingly bright. But the thought of the leopard was turning the whole experience into a waking nightmare. What if it came back?

'Night, Peter,' Alan called over from his mattress. 'Frogs not too loud for you, eh?'

'No,' he replied. 'But what about the leopard?'

'They don't like the smell of humans,' Alan reassured him.

Peter remained unconvinced, and when sleep did at last come it was fitful and troubled. The sound of the frogs, the thought of the leopard and the memory of Barbara's comment on the story repeatedly dragged him back to a light and dream-filled sleep. For the second time that day she had muttered:

'I hope it's not an omen.'

It was probably just a phrase, a saying, a little snippet of her idiolect that had caused Barbara Duthy to mention omens. She was, after all, a scientist. Her studies at London University had taught her to revere the empirical, not the irrational, the illogical, the suppositional. The composition of a worm had been discovered by dissection, not intuition. And yet, so far away from the bright unequivocality of stainless steel and strip lighting, even the most sceptical of Europeans could be sucked into the local superstitions. Not for nothing was Africa still known to many as 'the dark continent'. And certainly, to anyone looking for them, there had been omens enough which indicated that the proposed African trek might end in disaster.

FIVE

MORE THAN A STRING OF BEADS

ALAN Cooper was very popular with the people who worked for him. Several of the anecdotes I heard from his old friends testified to this.

On one occasion, he had aroused the wrath of the stuffier members of the colonial élite at the Nyanza Open Handicap Tennis Tournament at Kisumu. Situated on the banks of Lake Victoria, Kisumu was at that time the administrative centre of the area, and the annual championships attracted all the local bigwigs; Provincial Commissioners, District Commissioners, the Provincial Commissioner of Police – the type of arrogant bureaucrats Alan Cooper instinctively despised.

'Of course, he'd given him a clean pair of shorts,' Maurice Frost explained to me, 'but as he played so much better without shoes Alan had said he could play barefoot.'

'They were allowed to play, then?'

'There was nothing in the rules to stop them,' Frost said with a smile, 'nobody had ever thought it might be necessary.'

Frustrated by the fact that there were occasions when none of his neighbours were free for a game of tennis, Alan had taught his houseboy the rudiments. He had proved to have a natural ability and, when the time came, Alan hadn't hesitated to enrol him as his partner in the Kisumu championships. 'It says "open", after all,' he'd said in defiant justification.

They made it to the finals.

Another incident occurred shortly before the trip began. One of his men claimed that the men on the neighbouring farm had beaten him up. Rather than sorting the problem out through the courts, Alan had taken the law into his own hands. He had assembled his aggrieved men, led them back on to the farm and organized the burning down of a number of their huts. A lawsuit was pending.

Neither event endeared him to the white authorities, who considered him something of a maverick. But they did instil a great deal of loyalty and affection in his own workforce.

On hearing of the proposed trip, his cook became worried. As the time for departure approached he grew even more convinced that his boss would need some kind of spiritual protection. The man came from the Baluya tribe and, as was customary amongst his own people, he gave Alan a *mchanga* to ward off evil and misfortune. It was a necklace made of beads and a variety of seeds.

Three days before he was due to leave, Alan caught the string and it broke. The beads went everywhere.

The cook was beside himself. It was bad enough that Alan was leaving at an inauspicious time, but breaking the charm that was to have protected him on the journey was inviting the worst possible fortune.

'I can try for another necklace,' he said, 'but I don't know. I don't know. This is extremely bad luck breaking.'

On his final visit to the Nandi Bears Club, Alan had laughed it off. Whether or not he was worried, it was impossible to tell.

'Cook says it doesn't bode well,' he said. 'Perhaps I'm going to sire a whole load of kids in England. Now that would be bad luck!'

While I had been reading about Alan Cooper's first trip across the Sahara in 1933, another article had caught my eye. It concerned a pilot called Captain W.N. Lancaster who was trying to break the London to Cape Town record set some time earlier by a Mrs Mollinson. The story which gradually unfolded over the next twelve days could have come straight out of *Monty Python's Flying Circus*.

Most of the articles appeared under the heading: CAPTAIN LANCASTER STILL MISSING.

It was reported on 16 April that, after landing at Oran, Lancaster stated he had obtained a permit from the British Air Ministry for the flight across French territory and had effected insurance against the expenses resulting from possible mishaps. Both documents seem to have been lost. The authorities at Oran, however, allowed Captain Lancaster to go on at his own risk.

On 18 April it was confirmed that the necessary insurance contract had not been made with the Trans-Saharan Company. No one knew he was lost. No one went to look for him.

Five days later, on 23 April, the details of the catastrophe were published. Having twice set off from Adrar in totally the wrong direction, by the time he eventually landed in Reggan, 93 miles to the south, he was both behind schedule and worn out. Undaunted, he rested while his aeroplane was being refuelled, and refused the food he was offered.

When he was ready to resume his flight there was no moon, and a strong north-westerly wind was blowing. M. Borel, the head of the Trans-Saharan Company at Reggan, warned Captain Lancaster that it was madness to take off. First, he would not be able to see the day-beacons on the Trans-Saharan motor track. Second, without any lighting in his instrument panel it would be impossible for him to steer a compass course.

Captain Lancaster dismissed the concerns of the Frenchman, claiming he could manage quite well with some matches. M. Borel gave him a pocket electric torch. According to the report, the captain then made a very bad take-off, and that was the last anyone had seen of him.

I wondered whether Alan Cooper had noticed this other 'Saharan' report. While not exactly an omen, it certainly testified to the blind stupidity of a certain type of Englishman, desperate to attain records. The fastest, the oldest, the highest: Cooper himself had been written about only because his car was the smallest thus far to cross the Sahara. I wondered how many other Englishmen had succumbed to this *Guinness Book of Records* mentality.

If there was a category for the most foolhardy, then surely Captain Lancaster would have found a place. Alan Cooper was to run him a close second.

Peter and Alan were woken the following morning by a servant bringing tea. At 4.30 there were still two hours to go before sunrise. It was cold, and Peter cupped the warm mug with his hands.

'Coming in for an early morning dip?' Alan asked.

'Erm. No, thanks, I don't think I will.' Unwilling to appear effete, Peter nevertheless hadn't the slightest intention of leaping into the freezing frog-filled water at that time of the day.

'Suit yourself,' Alan said as he dived in.

Having dressed, the two of them started to load up the car. Trying to get so much into so small a space was a feat in itself, and the packing had to be done with scientific precision. A couple of times, when it became clear that something vital would not fit, Alan announced that they would have to start all over again.

Peter's hands were numb and he was in that state of dozy half-wakefulness. It was still dark. The paving slabs around the pool were frosty. While stumbling to the car with two of the collapsible beds in his arms, he came perilously close to having the swim he had declined earlier.

'At least take your clothes off first,' Alan called over.

The women were woken around six o'clock and came out to inspect the car.

'Well done, you,' said Freda, obviously impressed by the intricate interlocking of luggage both in and on the car.

'Let's hope we don't need anything at the bottom,' Barbara commented.

From the other end of the path came the sound of Peter yelping in pain. Hopping round, first on one leg, then the other, he was swatting and brushing at his calves and shins.

Alan couldn't help laughing.

'It's not funny,' Peter yelled back.

'Oh, but it is,' Alan countered.

Drowsy still, Peter hadn't noticed the column of soldier ants cutting a swathe across the ground near the pool. Get from A to B, comes the swarm directive, and with inhuman single-mindedness that is precisely what they do. With millions of workers in the centre of the column, flanked by protective soldiers, they are the entomological equivalent of countless statues in former Communist states. And with the 'who is not with me is against me' programme firmly engrained, the ants attack anything that gets in their way. Peter had got in their way, and was now paying the penalty.

The bite from the mandibles of these ants is ferocious.

When they get a firm grip on the enemy's flesh, they are practically immovable. Africans have used ants for centuries as sutures. They hold the ant by the body, pinch the sides of a bad cut together and let the furious ant bite through the skin. The head is then twisted off. The clamped mandibles will stay in place until the wound has healed. The natural formic acid acts as an antiseptic.

'If you've quite finished, I think we ought to be setting off,' Alan said.

'Alan!' Barbara chided.

It was five to seven, Friday 15 April 1955, and they were ready for departure. The couple who were going to look after the farm, Alan's friend and all the servants, had come down to the car to see them off.

Barbara looked in through the window. 'You're sure we're all going to fit in,' she said.

'Snug as bugs,' Alan reassured her.

She was later to concede that he had been right. 'Actually,' she wrote, 'surprisingly enough, the inside of the car was really quite comfortable. Once in, one settled down and enjoyed it.'

They twisted their necks round to wave goodbye to the small farewell party as they skidded off down the embankment track. Everyone was happy. Everyone was grinning. Everyone, that is, except for the cook. He stood stock-still, dolefully surveying the car. After much endeavour, he had managed to come by a second *mchanga*, which he had duly presented. But he remained worried. The bad luck that his employer had already instigated could not now be nullified; at best the new charm might help to lessen the effects.

There is a children's game that involves collecting as many different items in a matchbox as possible. I must have been about eight the last time I played it and, though I thought I'd done quite well, I lost to a budding sadist called Janice Basin. Whereas I had listed *beetle* as one of my objects, Janice worked on the theory that anything she found could be more than the sum of its parts. Her list included, *beetle leg*, *beetle wing*, *beetle head*, *beetle antenna*, *beetle body*, et cetera. Janice won the game hands down.

Getting everybody and everything into the modest Morris seemed to be adopting the same principle as the matchbox game. When the doors were finally shut, this is what the car contained.

Inside, at the back

1. One huge, metal chop-box which contained all the food, cooking and eating utensils.
2. Four campbeds: two with concertina bases, one with a criss-cross arrangement underneath and a hard top, one totally collapsible one.
3. Barbara's two little grips.
4. Freda's somewhat larger leather grip. (When Alan had reduced the number of vehicles for the trip, he had persuaded Freda to send her three suitcases back to England by sea.)
5. A soda syphon always wrapped in Barbara's old army battledress (known as Duthy's duffel coat).
6. Freda's wireless. (Freda had spoken enthusiastically about picking up the BBC World Service as they journeyed through Africa. Unfortunately, it was broadcast on short wave, which her radio could not pick up.)
7. Freda's hats. (There were two – one a small, white straw hat known as the Paris model. She had fondly thought that it would be safer if she took it with her in the car. It belonged to a friend and she didn't want to risk its being damaged while being shipped back. The other was a large, flimsy sunhat with

61

embroidered flowers under the brim.)

8. Freda's clothes for when she arrived in England, all wrapped up in a calico bundle.
9. The bedding roll, containing Alan and Peter's six blankets and all four mosquito nets.
10. Peter's attaché case.
11. Barbara's kikapu, full of odds and ends including her knitting and hat.
12. Two small camp chairs.
13. Several 1- or 4-gallon tins which were used for petrol, oil or water.

On the car rack
1. The Kit Bag containing Freda's and Barbara's sleeping bags. (These, as well as the pillows, had been provided by Alan.)
2. Alan's suitcase.
3. Freda's suitcase.
4. Peter's suitcase.

Under the seat
1. Cine-films.
2. A bottle of whisky.
3. A large pack of Surf washing powder.

In the car
1. Barbara's handbag.
2. Barbara's cameras – one ciné, one manual.
3. The AA roadbook for Africa.
4. The Shell Company route for crossing the desert.
5. The handbook and various papers for the car.
6. Freda's handbag.
7. Freda's camera.
8. Freda's spongebag.
9. Everyone's dark glasses.
10. Various hats.

On the door handles
Two 1½-gallon chargals – canvas water containers – were hanging from the handles. (The theory is that as the water slowly seeps, through and evaporates, it keeps the contents cool and refreshing. For most of the trip, they were unable to maintain a fast enough speed for them to function efficiently.)

In addition, of course, were the four travellers. Freda Taylor, a feminine primary-school teacher from Chester; Barbara Duthy, a forty-year-old flying worm-expert who, through previous adventures, had already been dubbed 'the girl with a charmed life'; Alan Cooper, forty-seven years old and still trying to decide what to be when he grew up, a Jack of several trades, enterprises and ventures but as yet not master of his own restlessness; and Peter Barnes, the seventeen-year-old apprentice quantity surveyor who was about to set out on a trip with three people of his parents' generation. They could scarcely have been a more disparate foursome. If they had anything at all in common it was certainly well hidden.

Janice Basin might have managed to include several extra items on the inventory, but only, I would guess, by the means she had employed as a child. There would be many dangers *en route*, but dismemberment was one hazard the four travellers would not have to comfront.

SIX

THE TASTE OF PARAFFIN

IF he was to achieve the average of 200 miles per day he had intended, Alan couldn't allow any dilly-dallying. If they were any slower he would lose money – or rather, the trip would actually start to cost him. He put his foot down.

Hurtling along the track to the main road, Alan again lost control of the vehicle as he attempted to navigate a tight bend. The brakes locked and the car skidded ignominiously into the bank.

'Whoops,' he muttered, as they bounced back into the road. 'Nearly lost her there.'

'What do you mean, nearly?' Barbara demanded.

'Wonderful grip, these tyres,' Alan said, ignoring her.

'Well, perhaps better safe than sorry,' Freda added quietly.

Peter didn't say a word. He had noticed something more worrying. Unlike the others, he had done his homework for the trip, and in particular, he'd boned up on desert travel. All the guides stressed the grave danger of overloading the vehicle. 'It is the single greatest cause of failure,' he had noted down. The French authorities would not allow overloaded vehicles into the desert, so great was the risk of becoming immovably stuck. Nine inches clearance was the minimum needed.

And by the sound of the grass scraping along the bottom of the car, Peter estimated that the Morris was, at most, only four to five inches clear. But then Alan's done the trip before, he thought. He must know what he's doing.

If reckless speeding was one result of Alan's resolve to reach England as quickly and cheaply as possible, the other side of the coin was his reluctance to stop. The tension arising from the ceaseless pressure that Alan applied left all four of them frustrated and exhausted. Sightseeing was a waste of good driving time; a lie-in was an extravagance; meals were an indulgence to be postponed as long as possible. From their first breakfast on the road, the pattern of conflict was established.

'Just a little further.'

'But I'm hungry,' Barbara repeated. 'And thirsty. Isn't anyone else?'

'I could do with a little something,' Freda conceded. 'But I'm not desperate.'

'Look, there's a stream up ahead,' Barbara said. 'Why don't we stop there, and then we won't have to touch the water in the tin.'

'If we went on a bit further, we could have breakfast up in the hills,' Alan suggested. 'It's awfully gloomy in the trees here.'

'If we go on any further, it won't be breakfast. It'll be lunch. Or our evening meal. This trip isn't meant to be an army exercise, is it? Or is there something you haven't told us?'

'All right, all right,' Alan said curtly and pulled up at the side of the road. 'Now,' he said clapping his hands together, instantly jovial again, 'Peter, you go and fill one of the larger tins with water and I'll get some firewood together.'

'Why don't we use the primus?' Barbara asked. 'It's going to take ages to get a fire going. The wood's sodden.'

'It'll be OK,' he said. 'I've got some paraffin.'

Barbara looked at him closely.

'You have brought a primus stove?'

'Oh, we won't need one. All the resthouses have kitchens.'

'For times like now,' Barbara persisted.

'We'll be fine,' Alan said, unlocking the back doors.

Barbara turned away. She was furious. Not so much because of the primus stove. To an extent, Alan was right, they could make do without one – but he had promised her that he would bring one when clearly he had no intention whatever of doing so. He had lied to her. And that was something she found intolerable. If he's lied about the primus, she thought, what else has he left out?

The primus had clearly made a lasting impression. Mrs Simpson had mentioned it when we were watching the cine-film and I knew that, though trivial in itself, it epitomized for her the slapdash recklessness of Alan's behaviour throughout the trek.

Her fears were well founded. The list of items he had failed to bring was both long and significant. There were no tyre levers or foot pump, no sand-mats or ladders. He had omitted even the most meagre of spare parts: fanbelt, petrol pump, valves, spark plugs – all were soon to be highlighted by their absence. The set of tools would prove to be totally inadequate and the jack useless. Rather than the two spare tyres and six inner tubes that the French authorities insisted every car crossing the Sahara should carry, Alan had brought one of each. Moreover, the two 4-gallon tins he had promised to fit to the rear bumper had failed to materialize: instead of the minimum 40 gallons they were bound to carry, the party had the capacity for a maximum of 10.

Today, Alan would probably not have got away so

lightly with his deliberate deceptions. But this was colonial Africa, 1955. In that place and at that time it was not done for women and boys to criticize men.

He had been married briefly. Late on in the war, he had a whirlwind romance with a young American woman, whom he brought back to his Kenyan farm as his bride. The marriage was a total failure. They remained together at Kapsabet for only a matter of weeks.

'We used to throw things at one another,' he laughed, when the others had tried to pry into the more intimate details of what went wrong.

My guess would be that, coming from the United States, the woman had been far too self-willed for him. Her independent spirit, which at first had attracted him, proved far too unmanageable for life with Alan. It wasn't so much a simple matter of male domination, but rather his assumption that he had the right to make all the decisions without being accountable to anyone.

His wife had argued and fought and very soon left him. For the purposes of the trip, Freda, Peter and Barbara were far more inclined to give in to him.

I put my theory to Mrs Simpson, who nodded.

'I can remember bottling up my anger on several occasions – not that I was concerned about upsetting Alan, but I didn't want to spoil the atmosphere. It would have caused too much bad feeling. We had a very long journey ahead of us.'

'But he lied to you,' I persisted. From my brief acquaintance with Mrs Simpson I found it hard to visualize her acquiescing in silence to Cooper's whims. While not cantankerous, she certainly seemed a forthright and assertive woman.

'On the whole I'm easy to get along with, but when I'm tired I can be utterly bloody-minded – and I have a stinking temper when it's roused.' She smiled. 'Most of the time I was on my best behaviour.'

Alan had parked on a hill. As he opened the doors at the back of the car, there was a jolt as the contents shifted position slightly. An instant later, everything slid backwards. He tried to slam the doors shut in an effort to keep everything in place, but it was no good. Empty water containers were already clattering away down the road, followed by streaks of red and green as Barbara's balls of wool rolled and unravelled behind them. The bedding roll, camp chairs, calico bundle and assorted hats were adding to the heap of equipment on the ground behind the car.

'Give us a hand,' Alan called out, as he tried to prevent gravity forcing the enormous, metal chop-box down to where the rest of their equipment was lying.

A lorry came round the corner and stopped.

'Need any help?' the driver called over.

'No,' Alan shouted back rudely.

'But thank you for asking,' Freda smiled in her embarrassment.

'We're just picnicking,' Peter added, feeling that some sort of explanation was due.

'Funny way to have a picnic!' the driver commented.

The fire took a lot of paraffin, patience and puffing to get going.

'Phew!' Alan sighed as his blowing finally caused the smoking wood to catch. 'Now I know how Roger Bannister must have felt.' (Bannister had broken the 4-minute mile in the match between Oxford University and the Amateur Athletic Association on 6 May the previous year. He won the race in a record 3 minutes 59.4 seconds.)

A pot of water was balanced on the ring of rocks around the fire and Alan undid the clasps of the chop-box. When they'd been loading everything up earlier both Alan and Peter had noticed a curious crunching noise as Alan had pushed the lid down shut. Neither of them had given it much thought. They now found out what it had been. Of the two dozen hard boiled eggs they had brought with them, only three were still intact.

The eggs were gritty with stray fragments of shell, the biscuits shattered each time someone attempted to spread them with butter, and Freda put everyone off their pieces of chicken with her ill-timed: 'this isn't Ruby, is it?' – but no one complained. They were off at last. They were on their way, and everyone dutifully fibbed about how delicious food tasted when eaten in the open air.

'Right,' Alan said, and clapped his hands together. It was a gesture that would become increasingly irritating for the other three as their journey progressed. 'Let's get everything back in the car.'

Easier said than done. The slope which had caused everything to slide out now refused to let anything be replaced. Conceding defeat, Alan did a nifty 7-point turn and they started all over again. Meanwhile, the chop-box was obeying a law that Newton never got around to identifying – the law which states that even though logically a container is emptier, it is in fact fuller. No matter how they jiggled the contents around, the lid resolutely refused to click down into place.

'Hang on a sec,' Peter said, sliding his hand down inside the box to move a couple of jammed forks. 'This should do the . . . oh, NO!'

Peter had been holding the can of paraffin under his arm. The top hadn't been screwed on properly. As he leant forward to release the errant cutlery, the inevitable happened. It was like the party trick of asking the time of a person with a glass in their hand. The paraffin poured over the top layer of food and utensils, and disappeared out of sight.

Even though he righted the can almost immediately, so that the barest minimum landed in the box, the damage had been done. Paraffin is pretty pungent. You can taste the smell. And for the rest of the trip, the less than subtle hint of paraffin would accompany every meal they ate.

'What's happened then?' Alan asked.

'Spilt some paraffin in the choc-box,' Peter admitted.

'In the what?'

'The choc-box.'

'It's a chop-box,' Alan said, laughing. 'Not a box of chocolates.'

'What does it mean then?' Peter asked, glad that the spotlight had been taken off his cack-handed accident.

'I really don't know,' Alan admitted

'Perhaps it's because it's chock-a-block full,' Freda offered.

'No, that's a nautical term,' Barbara said. 'But I'm really not sure about chop-box.'

'It means we ought to be getting a move on,' Alan said. 'Chop-chop!'

The *OED*. lists *chop* as a West African colloquilism for food. It occurs in collaborations such as chop-day, chop-money and chop-room. A chop-box, therefore, is a food-box.

Peter, however, continued to refer to it as a choc-box throughout his diaries. Chop or choc, the one unequivocal feature of the box was the smell, which no amount of washing or scrubbing succeeded in removing. It tainted everything the box contained and remained a constant reminder of Peter's clumsiness.

An hour later they were back on the road. The Ugandan border was only 30 miles away and everyone was feeling good. Everyone except Freda. Fidgeting around on the back seat, she was looking unmistakably concerned. She would feel around the floor by her feet and check the seat where she and Barbara were sitting, then, still dissatisfied, she would crane her neck round and inspect the luggage at the back.

'What have you lost?' Barbara asked.

'Nothing,' Freda said, but continued her rummaging.

Barbara waited a polite couple of minutes before repeating her question.

'It's just . . . I don't know, has anyone seen the tin opener? I don't remember . . .'

Most of the food they were carrying was in tins. This was, according to both Peter and Barbara, a serious mistake. The unnecessary extra weight reduced the clearance between car and potential obstacles to a critical degree. The other problem with tins is that they are useless if they cannot be opened. The tin opener was essential.

Everyone began searching around as best they could. Even Alan, though he was still driving.

'This is hopeless,' Barbara said. 'Let's stop a minute so we can look properly.'

'It'll turn up,' Alan said.

'And if it doesn't?' Barbara said. 'We don't know what we're going to be able to buy once we leave Kenya, do we?'

'Do you think we've left it where we stopped?' Peter asked.

'I don't know,' said Barbara, 'but if we have, it'll be easier to go back for it now, while we still can.'

Bowing to Barbara's undeniable if irritating logic, Alan slammed on the brakes and jumped out of the driver's seat. He stomped round to the back of the car and unlocked the doors, this time remaining careful as he inched them open.

'Stop,' Peter said. 'It's here.'

71

'Where?' Alan shouted back irritably.

'You were sitting on it.'

As it nears Uganda, the road descends from the cool, forested hills, the temperature increases and trees give way to wide, flat areas of grassland.

'There we are,' Alan said as the tiny whitewashed huts came into view. 'The border.'

The arbitrary nature of borders is nowhere as obvious as in Africa. Many of those still in existence today were created at the 1885 Conference of Berlin, where representatives of the European nations sat down and drew lines on maps. They tried, of course, to use mountains, rivers and lakes to form natural frontiers; the problem being that exploration of Africa was then so limited no one was sure where anything was.

Nevertheless, the European concept of border controls was introduced, and at Busia, the Morris Traveller was inspected officially for the first time.

There had been a brief panic as they had pulled up at the guard post.

'Oh, I think I've forgotten my passport,' Peter announced suddenly.

He hadn't, but from then on all official documents were kept in the glove compartment. Alan climbed out of the car and handed in all four passports to be stamped. If their premises were shabby, the border guards themselves could not have looked smarter. Predominantly white, the spotless uniform was topped off with a red tasselled fez.

'And have you anything to declare?' the guard asked Alan.

'No,' he said. 'Not a sausage.'

The guard looked puzzled, but let them through without searching the vehicle. Had he checked under the seat, he would have found the whisky and reels of film they had omitted to mention. Heavy duty was payable on both.

They were soon speeding off into 'the Pearl of Africa', making up for some of the time lost at breakfast.

'Can she go 60?' said Freda.

'Can she go 60?' Alan repeated in mock disbelief, and pressed down hard on the accelerator, 60, 65, 70, 73 . . . 4 . . . The little car touched 75. 'Not bad for an eight horse-power engine, eh?'

Why were the others so dubious about his car's performance? It felt good now, racing along the perfectly straight, tarmacked roads of Uganda. He'd done it before, he'd do it again. No sweat.

SEVEN

UNWELCOME GUESTS

WHEREAS Kenya had been called the Kenya Colony, its western neighbour had been named the Uganda Protectorate. The distinction was important. The former was considered an area of land suitable for European colonization and farmers were encouraged to settle there.

In contrast, as the term Protectorate suggests, Uganda was 'protected' by the British – largely against the Germans who, at the turn of the century, were advancing in a north-westerly direction from their own colony of Tanganyika. Realizing the agricultural and mining potential of Uganda, the British set about building the infamous 'lunatic express' railway line between Uganda and Mombasa. The purpose was primarily to create a permanent line of communication with Uganda before the Germans could get there.

By 1955, the two countries had developed along very different lines. The 'colony' was becoming increasingly autonomous: the presence of so many whites ironically accelerating the process which would lead to independence. The 'protectorate', where few whites had ever settled, was more of an economic arrangement. The threat of German expansionism had disappeared abruptly in 1918 when, having lost the First World War, Germany was stripped of its African colonies. Britain, however, maintained its relationship with Uganda. The railway was now used to transport raw materials bound for Britain down to the coast, and to return with manufactured goods.

On the northern shores of Lake Victoria, Jinja consisted of one main street lined with single-storey shops. The travellers stopped only briefly before continuing on to the huge Owen Falls Dam. It had already been opened officially the previous year by Queen Elizabeth at the end of her Commonwealth tour, though the construction was still not complete. Eight hundred yards long and crossed by road, rail and a footpath, it was designed both to control the River Nile and to produce sufficient hydroelectric power to supply the rapidly developing area. Rather than export the rice, rubber and sugar, cotton, coffee and tea as raw materials, an increasing number of factories were being set up so that the produce could be processed at source.

With the lake on their left, they continued on to Kampala, the capital, and 'a very nice town too' as Peter wrote. Comparing it with Mombasa, the difference he noted was the price of petrol. It cost 2 shillings and 4 cents in Mombasa, becoming dearer inland; 3s. 6c. in Nairobi, 3s. 9c. in Nakuru. The seventeen-year-old was both fascinated and confused by the fact that in Kampala it was a mere 2s. 9c.

As it was still early, their original plan to spend the night in the capital was abandoned.

'What say we go on to Kamengo?' Alan suggested.

No one dissented.

As far as crops were concerned, Uganda could scarcely have been more productive. The situation with animal management, on the other hand, had become catastrophic. The introduction of herds of cattle to the rich grasslands around the lake had exaggerated the problem of sleeping sickness. With a massive increase in its food source, the number of tsetse fly had multiplied with disastrous effects. A hundred years earlier, the disease had been unknown in Uganda. Now the once populated islands scattered across the lake were all empty, devastated by the tiny flies which transmitted trypanosome parasites into their vertebrate hosts, putting them to sleep. There is still no guaranteed method of curing a person once sleeping sickness reaches an advanced stage.

'I didn't realize Uganda would be so gorgeous,' Freda said.

They had agreed to rotate their seating positions as much as possible, and Freda was now in the front with Alan.

'Superb, isn't it?' he nodded.

'So lush and green – and what are those bushes we keep passing? Look, there.'

'*Carissa edulis*,' Alan said.

Freda looked over at him with obvious admiration. He certainly was a wonderfully knowledgeable man.

'Hang on a sec,' he added, and pulled over to the side of the road.

He picked one head of the five-petalled, pink and white waxy flowers and presented it to Freda. She held it to her nose, inhaled deeply and smiled.

'Oh, that's lovely.'

She poked the stem through one of the upper buttonholes of her blouse.

'Quite lovely!' she would repeat at regular intervals as she dipped her head to breathe in the sweet perfume once again.

'And those there?' she asked, as they descended into a valley.

But Alan seemed to have tired of the Ugandan flora. He dismissed the tree as being 'a cork or some such' and went on instead to give their estimated time of arrival at the resthouse.

Cassia, erythrina, poinsettia ... In the back of the car, Barbara was mentally ticking off the shrubs and trees she recognized. She too had been impressed by Alan's display of erudition, but was already beginning to suspect that though his knowledge might be wide, it was also superficial. He should have known what the 'cork or some such' was.

'Must be nearing it now,' Alan said, as they reached Kamengo, some thirty-five miles after Kampala. According to the East African AA book, the first of the many government resthouses where they intended to sleep was situated somewhere in the vicinity.

'It says we need to get permission to stay there from the Sasso chief,' Peter read out.

'It's pronounced with a z,' Barbara said. 'Sa-zo.'

'It's not the way it's spelt,' Peter muttered. He was beginning to find Barbara a bit of a know-it-all. She was about the same age as his mother and, as he'd been so excited about the prospect of untying himself from that particular woman's apron strings, it was more than a little disconcerting to find himself sharing the back seat with someone who appeared equally overbearing.

'I think I'll stop and ask someone,' Alan said.

'What about her?' Freda suggested.

'Probably best to find a man.'

When they had stopped for lunch, they had got into a certain amount of trouble for trying to photograph the Buganda women in their elegant costumes. A single strip of richly decorated cloth was wound round the body and shoulders like a sari. But though they would all have liked a photographic record of their garb, the women's husbands, in their tattered Western clothes, had forbidden it aggressively.

Although the men had adopted the trappings of

colonialism they would attempt to keep their wives and daughters free from its pernicious influence. As a result, few of the women could speak English. Alan and Barbara's Swahili had proved itself to be of little use here so, for the purposes of getting directions, an English-speaking man seemed their best bet.

'Try him,' Alan said.

'Good evening,' Freda said, smiling brightly through the open car window. 'I don't suppose you'd be so good as to tell us where the local government resthouse might be?'

The man looked at her blankly.

'Resthouse, resthouse,' Alan called irritably from his side of the car.

'Ah, *rest*house,' the man replied and, with evident relief, he pointed out a small turning two hundred yards further on.

The narrow, earth track wound its way upwards into the hills. After a couple of miles they reached a clearing. There stood two buildings. One was a large country house which wouldn't have looked out of place in the Cotswolds; the other, a more modest rondavel with a grass roof. Permission to stay the night was obtained from the larger house and, with the help of the chief's staff, they soon had the car unloaded and most of their belongings transferred into the smaller one.

'This is all right, isn't it?' Alan said enthusiastically.

Freda looked round and sniffed. It was not exactly what she'd had in mind. Certainly, she had wanted to get to see more of the *real* Africa, but perhaps this was a little too ethnic. There was no furniture in the building, and although it had been divided up into rooms, neither doors nor windows had been fitted. Still, none of the others were complaining. It would do, she decided and lugged her case into the room she would share with Barbara.

From the beginning Alan had laid out the ground rules. He and Peter were to do the driving, Barbara and Freda the cooking and laundry.

When I interviewed them, both Barbara and Peter conceded that the division of labour had been unfair, if typical for the times. Without Alan's dominating presence, it is doubtful whether they would have slipped so neatly into their roles. After all, as a pilot and laboratory technician, Barbara was hardly the feminine archetype. And Peter's wife testified to the fact that he'd always been handy in the kitchen, his speciality being 'a mean curry'. In the notes written immediately after the trek, Barbara commented:

> Peter always made himself useful. Most of the hard work fell to him. Alan was quite good at finding important work elsewhere when the task of packing and unpacking the car was at hand. And especially when the time for putting up beds came along. Not that Alan didn't do quite a lot of hard work, but he did avoid the dull daily grind.

'Very nice,' said Alan, laying down his knife and fork. 'My compliments to the chef – or rather, chefs.'

Freda looked suitably flattered and began piling up the dirty dishes.

'I'll wash and you dry,' she said.

'I'm not a tea towel,' Barbara muttered. She was galled by Freda's delight in the scraps of praise she received from Alan. He was abusing the obvious admiration Freda had for him – and what was more, she seemed to enjoy it. Whenever Alan wanted anything done, Freda was there to do it. Analysing her feelings at a later date though, Barbara admitted that her annoyance stemmed not only from the stereotypical roles Alan and Freda had assumed. 'I, perhaps unreasonably, was a bit jealous that she got all the teasing, and not me.'

Sitting underneath the 'inspection' lamp which Alan had attached to the car battery, Peter was writing his diary.

Lamp giving off a good light, but how long will it last? Battery 12 volts, lamp 6 volts. No moon. Cold. Ate on the top of the choc-box . . . all in very good spirits.

'Of course,' Alan was saying, 'we all know what made Freda answer the advertisement, don't we?'

'Why was that?' Barbara asked.

Freda looked at him with slight apprehension. What was he about to say?

'She's after a sheikh,' he said, and roared with laughter. 'She's hoping a multi-millionaire sheikh is going to whisk her away on the back of his camel.'

The others were also laughing.

'But, that's not what I . . .' Freda began.

'Did you or did you not say to me that the whole reason you'd answered my advertisement was because of crossing the romantic Sahara?' he challenged her.

'Yes, but I meant . . . I mean, I didn't . . .'

'I rest my case,' Alan said and leant back, grinning.

It was to become a running joke for the entire journey. Freda didn't mind the teasing, though. A quiet and private woman, she found the gentle ridicule infinitely preferable to having to open herself up to her travelling companions. If they wanted their fun, so be it. What she couldn't tolerate, however, were the insects and when a huge beetle ran over the toe peeping out from her sandal, she screamed out loud.

'It's only a dudu,' Peter said. 'It won't do you any harm.'

Freda was not to be consoled. She had always had a

horror of insects. Beetles, bees, wasps, moths, ants, fleas and flies: she hated them all with a wet-palmed loathing. When she glanced around the room, she saw that the place was infested.

'Ugh,' she shuddered. 'I'm going to bed.'

'Hang on,' Alan said. 'I think there's something on your shoulder.'

'Where?' Freda gasped, and flapped wildly with her hands. 'Get it off, get it off me.'

Alan grinned. 'Just joking,' he said.

'Well, it wasn't particularly amusing,' she announced primly, and went off to check the inside of her sleeping bag for unwelcome creepy-crawlies.

Later, as Alan and Peter were setting up their own beds, the unmistakable fragrance of citronella drifted in from her room. Although there was a mosquito net over her bed, Freda had evidently decided that it was better to be safe than sorry.

'Good grief,' Alan said, screwing up his nose theatrically. 'I certainly don't envy Barbara sleeping in the same room as that. Let's hope they don't both suffocate.'

EIGHT

WRITTEN ON THE FACE

THE following day was Saturday – though, when travelling, one day is much like another and the allure of the weekend vanishes. By 7.30 they had already packed up and were back on the road. Less than an hour later, they were driving over the equator. It was marked by a thick white line across the road, at either end of which was a 5-foot upright concrete circle. The words UGANDA and EQUATOR had been painted at the top. At the base, a large S and N designated which hemisphere was which.

'Let's stop for photos,' said Peter.

'Good idea,' Barbara chipped in before Alan could start talking about deadlines and driving averages.

For the next few minutes there was a flurry of activity around the concrete circles as everyone posed for everyone else: leaning, crouching and standing with arms and legs outstretched like Leonardo's *Proportions of the Human Figure*. Barbara recorded it all on her ciné.

'Best camera in the world, the Box Brownie,' Peter announced as they set off once again.

The dogmatic arrogance of the seventeen-year-old irritated Barbara. She was not the type of person who could simply ignore a remark she disagreed with.

'Well, they're good and you can get some excellent

photos with them, but you have to have the right lighting,' she contended.

'I've taken some superb sunsets with this,' Peter maintained stubbornly.

'I'm sure you have. But you can get far better results with a proper camera – if you know how to use it,' she added.

'Well, we'll see who's taken the best pictures when we get back,' said Peter. He turned away sulkily.

It occurred to Barbara that she was being insensitive. She shouldn't forget how much younger he was than his three travelling companions. By slighting the one camera he had been able to afford, she was forcing him into a corner he was bound to defend fiercely.

'Anyway,' she said, 'I've got the cine-camera here, so you're very welcome to try out my Zeiss. It's a pre-war model, but the photographs it takes are crystal clear.'

'Thanks,' Peter mumbled.

'Oh no,' Barbara suddenly exclaimed.

'What is it?'

'I've just had a horrible thought. I don't think I took the lens cap off when I was filming.'

Peter laughed. 'See?' he said jubilantly. 'I said the Brownie was the best.'

Barbara had, in fact, removed the cap. I remember seeing the few seconds of film of Peter, Freda and Alan taking their place in the circle, one after the other, when I watched her film more than thirty years later. Due either to the condition of the projector, or the fluctuations of voltage, the film was running slow. The effect this produced was strange. Whereas the clockwork urgency of old silent films makes them comic in themselves, the slowness of movement in Barbara's ciné-film imbued the action with an exaggerated sense of dignity.

And the photographs Peter took on his Box Brownie? Well, of course they were not the best in the world.

Barbara's comments were correct. Good light was vital and, if the subject of the photograph was not to become an unrecognizable dot, a proximity was needed which superstitious Africans and timid wildlife would often not allow.

In his diary entries for that day – 16 April 1955 – Peter described the taking of several of the pictures I had already seen in his photograph album. A sense of displaced time overwhelmed me as I compared his hopes that the shots might come out with the actual prints, knowing what he himself would have to go through before he ever got to see them. It was the same feeling I'd had watching the cine-film at Mrs Simpson's; those four grinning people at the equator, blissfully unaware of the horrors awaiting them, yet moving artificially slowly on film, as if somehow reluctant to proceed to the desert.

If I have any criticisms of Peter's photographs, it is that there are not enough of the travellers themselves. This is inevitable. The priorities of a writer are quite different from those of a seventeen-year-old embarking on his first big trip. The diaries indicate Peter's own interests clearly.

Had big breakfast at Kiwala Hotel (although we arrived late). Terrific view. On lawn a Kavirondo Crested Crane. Got to within 5′ of crane to photograph it.

Later on in the day another entry refers to the massive long-horned Ankole cattle, native to the Ugandan plateau of the same name.

Brake suddenly because of Ankole cattle – end of tsetse fly belt. Horns – span of up to 5′ wide and 4′ long. Jumped out to photograph them.

Further on still, having passed fields full of curious

mushroom-shaped anthills, Peter details the methods the locals had of tricking this rich source of protein from their nests.

> Over some anthills were dome/pyramid shaped wooden structures. Covered with a blanket and then the natives beat the ground all round with stones. The ants think it's rain. The flying ants emerge, get trapped in the blanket and are fried or eaten raw.

When I looked at the album for the photographic record of the day's journey, it came as no surprise that the majority of the photos were reproductions of cranes, cattle and anthills. Peter seldom thought to capture on film the tedious yet essential daily chores. Their next stop was to be an exception.

They had passed through Bushenyi in the early afternoon, and begun the slow climb up into the scrubby elephant-country of the Kitwamba Hills. Having reached a height of 7,000 feet, they stopped to breathe in the 'wonderful, cold, fresh air', before descending 2,000 feet to the crater lake below.

The situation of the Rutoto resthouse was idyllic. Set among trees at the foothills of a grassy mountain, it looked out over the crater lake. This was one of the few places where the travellers did not pack up and leave at sunrise. It is the only stop where the day-to-day routine was recorded. The photographs are revealing.

There is one of the square whitewashed resthouse with its thatched roof and veranda. Freda, Alan and Barbara are staring towards the camera. Four black villagers sit near the Morris – wherever the party spent the night, they never lacked for locals who, for a little pocket money, would help them with the cooking, cleaning and packing up.

Another picture shows Freda washing some clothes.

She is perched above the basin on a low stool. The modesty which dictated that seated women's knees should remain clamped together has caused her legs to twist round at an awkward oblique angle. To Freda, discomfort is clearly preferable to any lapse in her standards of decency. Yet there is something coquettish about the flimsy embroidered sunhat she is wearing, and it is this clear contradiction between the prim schoolma'am and the carefree world-traveller image she wished to put over which offers the best clue to the woman she was. The camera can lie on occasions, but Peter's Box Brownie was a model of fidelity. The mouth it recorded was small and tight, and the lines extending from its corners could never have been those of a thirty-eight-year-old woman.

A third photograph shows Barbara smiling happily into the camera. Her hair is light brown and cut into a practical bob. The scars she sustained in the near fatal cycling accident when hurtling down Countisbury Hill are visible. She was eighteen at the time. In the photograph she is forty. I asked the seventy-four-year-old Mrs Simpson whether she felt that coming so close to death had intensified her zest for adventure. She could not say. Yet there is something in the naughty grin which suggests a lust for life that only the nearness of death might have awakened.

The photographs of Alan confirm what Barbara told me about his ability to avoid the 'daily grind'. While the others are working, Alan is scrutinizing the map for the next day's stretch. He is a stocky man, with dark hair, combed back, slightly receding. Even from so small a picture, it is clear that Alan oozed charm. His face is broad and friendly, the slightly small mouth more than compensated by large warm eyes. For me, the contrast between these two features sum up his character. I can imagine him fixing people with his gaze, charming them into accepting his dreams and sense of fun. And yet, confronted by faceless bureaucrats who would remain immune to the mesmerizing power of his eyes, his lips would tighten and he would retreat into himself. Alan was not a man to take kindly to any orders from a higher authority.

There is a German word for which I have never found an adequate translation. It is *konsequent*. Although it looks like our word 'consequent', the meaning is quite different. Dictionaries translate it as 'consistent', but the connotations it assumes when applied to a person are much wider. A person who is *konsequent* can be relied upon to see things through; to live out personal beliefs with 100 per cent dedication; to subjugate all decisions to this central imperative.

Alan Cooper was not *konsequent*. Rather the opposite. He'd had countless schemes and scams for making money, none of which paid off because he would lose interest too soon. If there was anything 'consistent' about him it was, as friends of his confirmed to me, that 'he loved life'. But life for him should be uncomplicated, spontaneous, pleasurable. In a word common enough in the 1950s, life should be gay.

It is one of the pictures of Peter which I find most revealing. It offers an insight which only a photograph could give. He is sitting outside, poised over his diary, unaware of the fact that one of the others has taken his camera to record him so. The combination of short-sleeved shirt, knee-length baggy shorts and regulation short back and sides fixes him solidly in the mid-fifties. He is slim, of medium height, with thick dark hair. But it was something else that caught my attention.

At first glance I thought he was wearing white socks. But he was barefoot: the pale feet contrasting strongly with the sunburnt skin they adjoined. As well as this block between his socks and shorts, there was also the triangle of skin at the top of his chest, the face and neck, and the arms emerging from the baggy short sleeves. These areas of skin became, for me, a metaphor for the boy who, bit by bit, was being exposed. Initially burnt, the skin then toughened up. Ultimately, however, through the very nature of the sun the skin would age.

Peter's mother had considered the trip might 'make a man of him'. Little by little, it was doing just that.

I would have liked to see more of these shots. A chance snap often adds a totally unexpected angle to a character. In particular, I would have welcomed more close-ups. The Brownie box camera was always better at mid-distance scenes. Barbara's Zeiss, of course, could have recorded the inner feelings of those four travellers better: the worries, the hopes, the dreamy preoccupations. But as Barbara herself pointed out, 'Peter and Freda both had box cameras, and though they periodically borrowed mine, they firmly refused to learn how to work it.'

The evening started pleasantly enough. While the women were getting some food ready, Alan and Peter visited the local game warden to enquire about nearby game parks. The warden was there with a friend and, having got the information he wanted, Alan invited the pair of them back to the resthouse for drinks.

'Toasties, anyone?' Barbara asked when everyone had a full glass in their hand.

'That would be very welcome,' the game warden said. 'But before we go any further, I'd like to propose a toast. To the good fortune of your expedition!'

'To good fortune,' everyone chorused.

'So tell me,' the warden's friend asked Alan. 'You do not feel that your car has insufficient clearance for the desert?'

'No,' said Alan curtly.

Excellent though the warden's English was, he didn't

notice the irritation creeping into Alan's voice as his cross-questioning continued. Freda certainly did, and she began to wriggle with embarrassment as Alan's face coloured; and when Barbara returned with a tray full of assorted toasties, Freda leapt up and began distributing them enthusiastically.

'Delicious,' she exclaimed as she bit into her own.

Their two visitors were not so convinced. They wrinkled their noses and sniffed suspiciously. Realizing that they could smell the spilt paraffin, Freda repeated her praise with increased vigour.

'Absolutely delicious!'

Peter began to snigger.

'Tell me,' Alan said, eager to shift the topic of conversation from both car and toasties, 'are there any fish in the lake?'

'Many kinds,' the game warden said. 'The black bass are particularly good to eat.'

Dusk had fallen, and the nightlife was beginning to stir. At first, it was limited to a couple of beetles and moths. Freda lit a cigarette and surrounded herself with a protective smoke screen. Anything that strayed too near was incinerated by the glowing tip.

Suddenly a dark form flapped in front of the inspection lamp, casting a huge shadow on the back wall.

'A bat,' Peter cried excitedly.

Freda screamed as it fluttered past her head. A moment later, it was joined by three more. And three more again. Clearly disorientated by the presence of people in the building they normally had to themselves, the bats' radar let them down. Perhaps Freda's continued high-pitched screeching jammed their signals. They collided with the walls, with the people, with each other and some, temporarily stunned, fell to the ground, where they scurried awkwardly across the floor like cloaked rats.

Alan and Peter cornered one and, taking care not to get bitten by the razor-sharp teeth, they picked it up for a closer look.

'Ugly little so-and-so, isn't it?' Alan said.

'Get rid of it!' Freda was shouting.

At that moment the inspection lamp blew – the 12-volt battery finally proving too much for the 6-volt bulb. The room was plunged into darkness. Alan let go of the bat. Inevitably it headed straight for Freda, before getting its bearings and disappearing out through a window.

'It's all right, it's all right,' Barbara was saying. 'I brought candles in. Just give me a moment.'

Before long the room was again lit up. One by one, the bats evacuated the building and the gamewarden and his friend followed them out.

'Peace!' Barbara sighed, happily. She spoke too soon.

The reason bats have such sharp irregular teeth is so that they can hold and crush insects. They eat beetles, moths, cockroaches . . . it soon became all too clear why the bats frequented the resthouse. From every crack and crevice, huge buzzing insects emerged.

Freda stayed put for as long as she could, but it all proved too much.

'I can't bear it,' she shuddered. 'I'm going to bed. Barbara, could you make sure that my mosquito net's tucked in all the way round.'

None of them slept well that night. With only the fine net separating them from the hordes outside, they lay on their campbeds listening to the constant whirring, scuttling and thudding as the massive armoured insects moved about the room. Even when they dozed off, the beating wings permeated their sleep and twisted dreams to nightmares.

'Thank God for that,' Freda whispered to herself as the sun finally rose the following morning.

NINE

MEMORIES ARE MADE OF THIS

A LAN went for a swim in the lake that morning. Having forgotten to pack his bathing costume, he had to go in naked: something he admitted he would not have done if he'd known the creatures he'd taken for tadpoles were in fact leeches. Black and rubbery, they would swell to a length of over four inches when gorged with blood. Mercifully, the only one to bite into him had merely attached itself to his ankle.

It wasn't only his trunks that Alan had omitted to bring. On several occasions he found he had left behind things that he could have done with. Barbara gave me one reason for this.

It appears Alan was becoming increasingly incensed by what he saw as biased accounts of the Kenyan situation in the British press. He felt that the liberal media was far too favourable in its coverage of the Mau Mau. He suspected that this was deliberate policy, and that the Government, via the media, was signalling its willingness to grant independence to the colony.

'They're just going to sell us down the river,' he would say. 'They couldn't give a tuppenny damn.'

To redress the balance, he had filled his case with a large pile of anti-Mau Mau pamphlets. These he intended to distribute to friends and relatives, to send to

91

the various papers; to read out at Speakers' Corner if need be. He was determined that the British public should know exactly what was going on.

Today this might sound extreme, yet Alan was not out of step with contemporary feeling among the European settlers in Kenya. Barbara, who would often come into conflict with Alan on the trek, had nothing against his views on the colony: 'he had very sound ideas about Africans and Kenya generally,' she wrote. Even Peter, who by 1963 was pro-Independence – 'I thought it was a good thing: I wanted to see it come' – was, in 1955, concerned by what he considered the ill-advised haste of the changes.

'The country simply wasn't ready,' he explained to me. 'We Europeans felt that no one at home really understood the situation. They just wanted to wash their hands of the colony and be done with it.'

In Britain, it was the *Daily Express* and the *Daily Mirror* which championed the two extremes of popular opinion. Beaverbrook's patriotic *Express* was unremittingly anti-Mau Mau or any other terrorist organization which threatened the stability of colonial strongholds, an attitude the *Mirror*'s Keith Waterhouse lambasted on 7 September in his weekly column, under the headline: THE NEWSPAPER WITH A BLIND EYE. Continuing with their *cause célèbre*, the *Mirror* editorial of 3 October launched a scathing attack on the white settlers themselves: 'Their narrow-mindedness belongs to the Dark Ages.'

Peter was unable to let pass what he saw as slanderous inaccuracies concerning his own community.

'It was all just so distorted,' he told me. 'I remember writing to the *Daily Mirror*. They did an article which I thought was very anti-Kenya and wrong – totally incorrect.'

With hindsight, the sensitivities of the white populations of Africa proved irrelevant in the accelerating drive towards independence. By 1963, a mere eight years after Alan, Barbara, Peter and Freda had set off to cross the continent in the Morris, all the countries they passed through had thrown off the shackles of colonialism. As the Duke of Edinburgh officially handed over the instruments of independence to Jomo Kenyatta on 12 December he joked that it was still not too late for him to change his mind.

But, of course, it was. In 1955, it had already been too late to halt the inevitable course of history.

'What was the water like this morning?' Barbara asked.

'Cold,' said Alan. 'Why? Thinking of going for a swim?'

'I thought I might.'

'Oh, I'll tell you what I did see,' Alan added, looking up from his letter. 'A canoe. Big dug-out thing. Why don't we try it out?'

Suddenly childishly enthusiastic, he chivvied the others into accompanying him back down to the edge of the lake.

'Are you game, Freda?'

She wasn't keen. The resthouse at night was bad enough – who knew what hideous creatures might be lurking below the surface of the water? But not wishing to appear a wet blanket in front of Alan she jumped up eagerly.

'Take me to her,' she said.

'Right,' said Alan, clapping his hands together. He led them all to the steep concealed path which snaked its way through tangled undergrowth right down to the shoreline. They emerged next to the canoe. Hollowed out of a tree trunk, it was about two feet wide, but well over twenty feet long. Disproportionately narrow for its length, balancing it would not be easy, and the rounded keel would make the task harder still.

They scooped out the water from the bottom and, with Alan holding it still, Peter climbed in and made his way to the far end. The canoe swayed. Plucking up courage, Freda came next. She gripped hold of Alan's arm as she lowered herself, and proceeded to totter along the boat on her totally inappropriate 1½-inch heels.

'Good grief,' Alan yelled, 'can't you balance a bit? Use your arms!'

Some people can get their balance in a boat, some cannot. Freda belonged to the second category. The flapping motion she had obediently started up merely exaggerated the pitching and rolling of the little craft. Barbara was laughing loudly on the bank. Conscious that, if he laughed too, the boat would move even more, Peter bit into his lower lip.

'Oooooh!' Freda yelped. There were no seats and the bottom of the canoe was far lower than she had anticipated.

Alan released his grip on the end and prepared to step in. At that moment Freda began to wriggle. The canoe lurched.

'What the devil's the matter now?' Alan shouted.

'I'm trying to get comfortable,' Freda replied.

'Well, hurry up.'

'I can't, I . . .'

The wriggling continued.

'What are you *waiting* for?' Alan demanded.

'I can't move,' Freda panted. 'I'm stuck!'

Peter couldn't hold himself any longer. He erupted into howls of laughter. There were tears streaming down Barbara's face as she tried in vain to capture the ludicrous scene with her movie camera. Even Alan was grinning.

'Did I tell you about the leeches I saw this morning?' he asked unkindly.

It had the desired effect. Freda jerked herself upwards

94

and settled back down in a marginally wider part of the hull. Alan then pushed the boat away from the bank and leapt in. The canoe rocked ominously, but soon righted itself. They were afloat.

Barbara began filming.

'Action!' she shouted. 'Let's see a bit of movement.'

Peter and Alan grabbed their paddles and began to propel themselves away from the bank.

'What shall I do?' Freda asked.

'You're already doing it,' Alan said.

'What?'

'You're keeping the boat stable.'

'Ballast,' said Peter.

'Go and wash your mouth out!' Alan called back.

'I'm getting ever so wet here,' the ballast in the middle announced miserably.

Every time the paddle cut through the water, more came pouring in. They were only about ten yards out by now, but the canoe was already considerably lower than when they had set off. Suddenly it became all too clear that they were sinking.

'Abandon ship,' Peter yelled as the boat capsized.

He and Alan managed to push themselves out. Freda merely rolled over with the boat, making no effort to free herself. She was stuck again.

The bats, the plague of insects, the dug-out canoe: each of the little incidents was helping to bring together the four people who, apart from the fact that they were all returning to England, had nothing whatsoever in common.

In a letter to her friend Mavis, back in Kenya, Barbara described the fun that the group was having. With a single sentence she summed up the general atmosphere at this point in the trek.

'Things are going jolly well.'

* * *

Having dried off and eaten a light lunch, it was time to move on again. The next resting place was the Hunting Lodge in Princess Elizabeth Park which the game warden had told them about the night before. They were on the point of leaving when Peter suddenly dashed off with one of the chargals.

'I'll just fill this up,' he called back.

'But it's full,' said Alan.

Barbara had watched Peter lay the canvas bag down on the ground as he'd put his case on the roof. The water had come gushing out of the top. She remained silent. Presumably it was the pressure of being with three people much older than himself that was making him so clumsy: it would only make him worse if they drew attention to it.

'There we are,' he panted and hung the water container on the door handle.

He leapt into the back of the car and slumped back heavily on the seat. There was a crack.

'My knitting needles!' said Barbara. 'Why on earth can't you look,' she snapped, ignoring her own advice.

'Sorry,' said Peter, pulling the kikapu out from under him. 'Only one of them's broken. Have you got any spares?'

'One,' said Barbara.

Peter cheered up.

'I know I'm clumsy,' he said, as Alan was driving away from the crater lake, and proceeded to outline a recent week of particular cack-handedness. The semi-boasting tone which crept into his voice as he detailed the best china he had smashed, the wireless he had shorted and the two road accidents he had caused was clearly a cover-up for the embarrassment he was feeling.

'And to think I've let you drive this car,' Alan chipped in.

'I was less experienced then,' Peter explained. 'I'm fine now. Honestly.'

The route took them over the Kasinga Channel – a narrow strip of water joining the lakes George and Edward – and turned on to a small road near Katme. The Hunting Lodge lay at the far end. It consisted of twenty luxury bungalows, each with two double bedrooms, bathroom, kitchen, lounge and verandah. The contrast between this lodge and the previous night's bat-infested hovel could hardly have been more marked.

They dumped their luggage on their beds and went straight off to find a guide for the afternoon's game-park drive.

Peter noted the animals they saw and photographed: buffalo, elephant, waterbuck, warthog, hippo, as well as innumerable species of birdlife. The photographs are disappointing. It is simply impossible without a zoom lens.

The album made me smile. Not only had Peter labelled the mounted prints: 'Buck near Hunting Lodge' and 'Elephant', but he had also drawn arrows on the photographs to show exactly where the elusive animals were standing.

The best shots are of hippo, taken on a narrow isthmus at the far end of the reserve. He must have got extremely close to them, something I would not have done. Apparently more people in Africa are killed by hippo each year than by any other animal: they become especially aggressive to anything or anybody coming between their dawn grazing pastures and the water. This is no doubt due to the fact that, if they do not immerse themselves in water once the sun has come up, their skin rapidly dries out and cracks.

Throughout the 1970s, the hippos had far more to fear from humans than the threat of sunburn. Idi Amin's troops used them as targets in artillery practice.

In the restaurant that evening the four travellers were rowdy. Hot baths, clean clothes and a large familiar meal of roast beef and Yorkshire pudding had raised their spirits to near euphoria.

'That's the first time I've ever eaten artichokes,' Peter said.

'And what did you think?' Alan asked.

'Delicious!'

'It's odd to think that everything we do we once did for a first time,' Barbara mused.

Alan looked at her and nodded: 'What's your earliest memory?' he asked.

'My earliest?' she repeated. 'Hard to say. Some of the memories are mixed up with what I've found out since. I mean I know that Mummy and Father travelled a lot and it was difficult for them to get cow's milk when I was a baby, so they took a goat round with them.'

'A goat?' Freda said, and laughed.

'It couldn't have done me any harm,' Barbara said. 'I was born underweight, but I soon thrived.'

'You couldn't have actually *remembered* that,' Alan said.

'No,' Barbara conceded. 'Well, I was born in India – before partition. I can vaguely remember my brother as a baby, and he was born when I was two. But then again, I know that even some of those memories are from photographs.

'Oh, I know what I do remember. There were riots, and Mummy had to take us up to the hills by railway. The compartment we were in was completely surrounded by armed guards. To protect us. Mummy was the only British woman on the whole train.'

'What about you?' Peter asked Alan.

'Me? Having fun mainly. There were seven of us and it was a constant case of "us versus them" at home. My poor parents,' he added and chuckled. 'I remember staying on the coast with my aunt. Every day, whatever the weather, she'd send us all down to the beach with this funny old woman whom she employed. Well, even at that tender age I was on the lookout for ways to make an easy buck, and Miss Donaldson – I think that was her name – seemed a pushover.

'I became the world's first toddler with a prostate problem. Writhing about I was, desperate to spend a penny the whole time. Altogether I managed to wangle tenpence out of her. She must have told my aunt though, and Auntie smelled a rat. I was made to empty my pockets. And so ended my first venture into the world of high finance.'

Freda, who had been smiling throughout the story, laughed appreciatively.

'You must have been an adorable little boy,' she said.

'Oh, I was, I was,' Alan grinned. 'Peter, what about you?'

'Well,' he started seriously. 'I was only six months old when my parents left British Guyana. My first memories are of Zanzibar. I remember I had an African ayah who used to look after me. And later – I suppose I must have been about five or six – I used to go and play with the Sultan's children. I kept being given baby gazelles as presents.'

'Gazelles,' Freda said. 'How sweet.'

'Not really,' Peter admitted, looking down at the table. 'You see, they all died. My mother insisted on the floors being polished and gazelles have got, you know, delicate, stick-like legs. They kept breaking them, and then, well, had to be . . . disposed of.'

'Not sure the RSPCA. would have approved,' Alan commented. 'Freda? How about you? What's your earliest memory?'

Freda looked embarrassed.

'My . . . I . . . Oh, good heavens,' she faltered. 'India,

British Guyana, Zanzibar – you've all got such exotic memories. I'm afraid I simply can't compete.'

'Go on,' Peter encouraged her.

'I can hardly remember what happened last week,' she said, trying to laugh it off, 'let alone when I was a girl.'

Seeing how flustered she was, Alan came to her rescue.

'This time tomorrow,' he said, 'we'll be in the Belgian Congo.'

Peter, who hadn't really been interested in Freda's past anyway, seized on the new topic immediately. He wanted to know how many miles they would cover, who could speak French, how far the border was. But Barbara continued to look at Freda. She couldn't help wondering precisely what it was she hadn't wanted to reveal.

TEN

GUILT AND INNOCENCE

IT was neither concern that she might bore the others nor a failing memory that had caused Freda to become so evasive. What compelled her to hold her tongue was the fear that she might give away her secret. When the others had pressed her to reveal some snippet of her childhood, she could feel herself becoming increasingly ruffled.

The reason for her guilty panic was simple. Freda had lied about her age.

When I received a copy of her death certificate I could see why the incident had so unnerved her. She hadn't lopped a modest one or two years off her age. No, Muriel Freda Taylor had decided that she could pass herself off as a woman seventeen years younger than she really was.

The certificate is illuminating. In the column reserved for age, 38 was crossed out and replaced with 55. Adjacent to this are her details:

Spinster, Teacher
Born at Darwen, Lancashire, on
December 5th, 1916.

The year has also been amended. She was born in

1899. An explanation of these alterations had been included down the right side of the paper. The original certificate had been filled out with the information from her passport. At that time it wasn't always necessary to produce a birth certificate in order to obtain one – a driving licence or a tax form would suffice. She must have already established the fictional year of her birth some time earlier.

Later, when confirmation of her real age was received, the original death certificate was amended. I remember Mrs Simpson's words when we had first watched the cine-film.

'She told us she was thirty-eight,' she said. 'And that's what it had in her passport. But if she was thirty-eight then I'm a . . . oh, I don't know. It would have made her younger than me, and she quite obviously wasn't.'

I had the proof now that Mrs Simpson's suspicions were well founded. I thought I had solved the mystery.

Subsequently, however, I began to have second thoughts. I heard from two people who had known her personally, and neither could believe that she had been so old. The first letter I received came from Mrs P.L. Woodward, the retired headmistress of Capenhurst School, where Freda was employed as a primary-school teacher.

The age (55) surprises me. She certainly did not look over 50. To me she looked more like about 45. With regard her passport, do you think figures could have been blurred through exposure and heat?

I next heard from one of Freda's former pupils. Christine Ellwood. 'Also her age – you quote as 55. I know time plays tricks – but I feel she was much younger!'

It was enough to have me racing back to St Catherine's House. I checked in the volume for October to December in 1899. There was no record of a Muriel Freda Taylor. I was now in a quandary. Which information should I believe? Plodding laboriously through each of the volumes would have been a nightmare. I decided to take my problem to reception.

'Try 1900,' the woman at the desk suggested. 'People often used to register their babies late.'

I did as she said, and there was the name I was looking for. When a copy of the birth certificate came through I finally had conclusive evidence. 'Born in Darwen, Lancashire, on 5 December, 1899; registered on 31 January, 1900. Muriel Freda Taylor, daughter of John Taylor (a master pawnbroker) and Elizabeth Ann Taylor (formerly Dawson).'

Mrs Simpson laughed when I told her what I had discovered.

'I knew it!' she said. Even at the time, when jotting down impressions of her travelling companions, she had written of Freda. 'A very small neat person who oddly enough looked a good deal more than the 38 years shown on her passport.'

Peter's reaction was different. Unlike Alan and Barbara, he hadn't questioned that she was as young as she said.

'I don't suppose I even thought of it. To a seventeen-year-old, the difference between thirty-eight and fifty-five – I suppose they are both just old,' he said, and laughed. 'And that's that. I mean anything over thirty is old to a young person, isn't it?'

The following day was to prove a day of disillusionment for Peter. The Mountains of the Moon, bread-fruit and pygmies: all three would fail to come up to his childhood expectations.

Ever since they had arrived in the area, Peter had wanted to have a clear view of the Ruwenzori – or

Mountains of the Moon, as they are more commonly known. The name, which conjures up such a bleak, alien wilderness, had enchanted him at an early age and now he wanted to see them for himself. But it was not to be. From the gamewarden's house during the safari, and now on their drive to the border, the mountains remained shrouded in thick mist.

Ruwenzori and Mountains of the Moon weren't the only names given to the range. In January 1876, Henry Morton Stanley caught sight of the 5,120-metre peak in the distance. At a loss to know what to call it, he finally decided to name it after the American journalist and editor of the *New York Herald* who had commissioned him to search for Dr Livingstone. Accordingly, in the late nineteenth century, it was known as Mount Gordon Bennett.

At the border Peter soon forgot about the mountains. There was too much to look forward to. Belgium rather than Britain had colonized this part of Africa, and so it seemed all the more exotic to the boy. People spoke French and drove on the wrong side of the road. The food, the architecture, even the time of day would be different. There was something else more exciting still: he would get to see pygmies for the first time.

When he was a boy, his mother had told him about the curious forest dwellers with their poison darts, which they wouldn't hesitate to shoot at any visitors who failed to bring them a present of salt. I asked Evelyn Barnes if she remembered telling her son the stories of the pygmies.

'Oh yes,' she said. 'It was quite embarrassing on one occasion. I suppose Peter must have been about seven or eight, and I'd been telling him about the pygmy customs. Anyway, he disappeared to get something and about half an hour later I heard raised voices outside. What on earth's going on? I thought. I went out and there was Peter. He looked up at me and said, "I found one, Mummy." Well, the poor chap was a dwarf, not a pygmy at all. Somehow, though, Peter had persuaded him to come back to the house to meet me.'

Unlike politics and laws, vegetation does not change the moment a national border is crossed. Before coming to the Ituri Forest where the pygmies (Bambuti) lived, a wide flat plain had to be crossed. It was very hot and sticky in the car and as usual it was Alan who took it upon himself to keep morale up.

'Of course,' he said. 'I've often been here before.'

His aunt had visited him in Kenya several times and he had organized numerous excursions into the Belgian Congo. As the wealthy proprietor of an exclusive millinery business, the woman was used to her comfort. The trips Alan arranged were therefore considerably more luxurious than the present trek.

'We'd stay in hotels and I always brought at least one African with us to help out,' he explained. 'Unadventurous though – not at all like this.'

'It sounds marvellous,' Freda muttered wistfully.

After the Semiliki River, the slow upward incline of the Beni Escarpment began. Despite the weight it was carrying, the 8 h.p. engine of the Morris managed the ascent without difficulty.

Beni was, for its time, relatively large. The main street was made of reddish earth and lined on either side with Dhom palms. A photograph Peter took shows the thick hairy trunks, topped off with feather-duster fronds, in two regimented rows disappearing into the distance. It was the tropical equivalent of the lines of poplars planted with equal mathematical precision along the roads of Belgium and France.

As they drove through the centre, children emerged from the 'keyhole' doors of their houses and raced towards the car. In their hands were ivory carvings.

Processions of elephants, trunk to tail, had been fashioned out of complete tusks, bookends and letter openers; pillboxes and combs, and statues of naked pygmies looking woefully anaemic in the pale ivory. Even in 1955, this local trade was illegal. But the items were incomparably cheap: three of the four travellers were tempted.

'Do let's have a look,' Freda said. 'They're gorgeous.'

'I think I'd really rather press on a bit further,' Alan said. 'We're behind schedule as it is.'

The others remained quiet, but from Peter's diary it is clear that Barbara was not the only one who objected to the constant pressure to cover as many miles as possible.

> Unfortunately we never stopped as Mr Cooper informed us that we would see very many later on and could stop then. As it happened we never did see any others. He was always in a terrific hurry to get on.

Shortly after Beni, the scenery changed dramatically. They were plunged into the deep-green sumptuous excess of the tropical rainforest. Massive iroko and sapele trees, with broad-leaved parasitic succulents – familiar to us as spindly indoor plants – rooting themselves higher and higher up the trunk in their attempt to reach the elusive canopy. The entire forest resembled the innards of a vast and complex living machine, with every woody component wired together by mossy lianas.

'It's stunning,' said Peter.

'And all the fruit!' Freda said. 'Certainly no danger of starving to death here.'

The forest offered its human inhabitants a wide selection of produce. Bananas, mangoes, pawpaws, oranges, limes, pineapples, yams: an abundance of fruit and vegetables was there for the taking.

'Look,' Alan said, pointing to a tall tree with large, knobbly growths halfway up. 'A bread-fruit tree.'

'Where?' Peter asked excitedly. His childhood reading had been full of islands: *Treasure Island*, *Robinson Crusoe*, *Mutiny on the Bounty* – distant South Sea paradises where people had wonderful adventures and thrived on a diet of ever-at-hand bread-fruit. The word itself was enough to evoke memories of precisely how he'd felt as a boy. If it really was bread-fruit, he would have to try it.

'We've got to stop,' he insisted. 'I've always wanted to know what it tastes like.'

Alan grinned. 'All right, all right,' he said, and he pulled over to the side of the road.

Using the panga, Peter slashed through the dense undergrowth towards the tree. He shinned up the trunk and hacked off two of the bread-fruits. They were similar in shape and colour to large custard-apples. Back at the car, Peter cut into the soft, white flesh and divided it up into portions.

It tasted vile.

Like 'sour dough', Peter wrote in his diary. Perhaps this comparison of tastes should have led them to see the mistake they were making. Just as you bake dough to make bread, so the bread-fruit should also be either baked or roasted. Personally, I like them cut into regular rectangles and deep-fried in oil. They make an excellent substitute for chips.

They didn't cook them: they simply spat out the sour pulp and drove off. Behind them, the two bread-fruits lay discarded by the side of the road. No one seeing them could have guessed the disappointment they represented to the boy who had just seen another of his childhood dreams shattered.

As they travelled on through the forest a new game started up. Spot the pygmy. Freda, in particular, was so excited about seeing the people she taught her young pupils all about that she started seeing them everywhere. From a distance, of course, everyone is a potential pygmy and it was only as the car neared the person in question that the singularly average proportions were confirmed. The atmosphere of eager self-delusion in the car was mirrored in Peter's album. One of the photographs is labelled somewhat enigmatically: 'Tall pygmy women'.

Finally, however, they did come to a real Bambuti village. The dwellings were round domed huts made of sticks and leaves. As soon as they heard the car, all the villagers poured out on to the road. The women wore grass skirts. The men – as was so often the case in Africa – had abandoned traditional costume and were dressed in ragged Western clothes.

Even though Freda was fully aware that pygmies reach a maximum height of 3 feet 9 inches, being confronted with fully grown adults who barely reached her shoulders was a totally different experience. Not that she wished to be patronizing. Yet, as she distributed cigarettes, she was overcome with a wave of guilt for encouraging children to smoke.

Small they undoubtedly were, blow-pipes they certainly had, but as for the salt ... This aspect of the stories Peter had heard as a boy was clearly untrue. None of them asked for any. None of them threatened to become violent because they hadn't been given any. And when – thinking they might be shy – Peter offered some, they refused with a confused grin.

The travellers reached their day's destination as the sun was setting. Mambasa was one of the few towns where they stayed that had no government resthouse, and they were forced to check in to an expensive hotel called the Vichy Congo.

In the restaurant Peter sat down to his first French

dinner. Bottles of wine stood in the middle of the table, and at each place was a pile of plates; the dirty, uppermost one to be removed at the end of each course.

'The French have such a civilized attitude to food, I always think,' Freda commented.

Peter was thinking about the Mountains of the Moon and the bread-fruit. When he'd set off from Kenya, he had felt he was already an adult, but being forced to reassess much of what he'd learnt as a child was making him realize just how young he still was. Reaching over for the salt, he remembered the pygmies' lack of interest in the stuff.

'Hey!' said Alan, breaking into Peter's thoughts. 'Try it first.'

'What?'

'Your food. It's considered very bad manners in France to put salt on your food without tasting it first.'

'But I always need more salt,' he said sulkily.

'Anyway,' said Barbara, coming to his aid, 'the Congo's Belgian, not French.'

ELEVEN

TELEVISION ON WHEELS

THE map that the four travellers used to cross the Belgian Congo looked quite different from those of today. In 1970 Joseph Mobutu introduced his 'authenticity' campaign which effectively removed all the colonial names given to cities and towns. Overnight, Stanleyville, Elizabethville, and Leopoldville became Kisangani, Lubumbashi and Kinshasa. Paulis became Isiro. The Belgian Congo itself re-entered the international stage as Zaire. In 1997, following the toppling of Mobuto's regime, the country was renamed once more, becoming the Democratic Republic of the Congo.

In a letter to Baron Solvyns in 1877, King Leopold of Belgium wrote: 'I mean to miss no chance to get my share of this magnificent African cake.' Other European leaders took heed and the so-called 'scramble for Africa' was on.

As well as being the first, King Leopold was perhaps also the worst. The brutal enslavement of the tribal populations living in what he considered his own private estate became increasingly embarrassing to the Belgian Government. In 1908 the king was forced to relinquish his claims to the Congo. It had finally become a Belgian colony.

Nothing was done during that half-century of colonial

rule to prepare the people for independence. Indeed the Belgians had never intended to pull out at all but, in the late-1950s, a combination of events in neighbouring countries and subsequent internal upheavals caused an abrupt switch in Belgian policy towards her colony. At the beginning of 1960 African politicians were informed that free elections and independence were to be granted. They had six months to prepare. The subsequent civil war and United Nations presence in the newly independent country were inevitable.

In 1955, when the Morris crossed the Belgian Congo, political parties were still banned. Furthermore, unlike the colonies of France and Great Britain, the European settlers had no say in the politics of the country.

What then was the atmosphere of the country Alan, Peter, Barbara and Freda encountered? The diaries and letters the travellers wrote depicted a poor, simple land with a breathtaking tropical rainforest and an impenetrable bureaucracy. The actual people were more often than not omitted.

I asked Peter about this.

'We didn't associate with them very much. I mean, you got to a village and you asked the chief where the resthouse was, and he'd point to it. And you'd go over there and get a couple of people to help you out for the night. Otherwise they kept away. Because these were colonial days and the white man was considered aloof and remote – and of course a bit mad – and left like that. We didn't really associate with them like one does now, after Independence. You just gave an order and expected it to be obeyed.'

'So how did you feel? Superior?'

'No, I don't think we felt superior. We were on a journey, we had a destination, we had a timetable, and after driving all day you simply wanted to get to the place where you could put out your beds, have a wash, a meal and go to sleep. You really didn't want to do any more than that. Of course, there was no entertainment or anything in the villages. And Alan was always wanting to press on, he didn't want any delays. No, I don't think we felt anything in particular. How they viewed us, I don't know. Just as people passing through as others had, I suppose.'

The confidence that the Belgians had in the immutability of their colony is perhaps best summed up by the event Peter describes in his diary.

While preparing to leave, the Belgian flag was raised to the accompaniment of bugles, and everyone (including ourselves) stood to attention. This brief ceremony is held every morning at 6 a.m.

The timelessness of a daily ritual is hypnotic. The spurious tradition of the past it draws on inevitably mesmerizes those concerned into believing nothing can ever change. It happened like this today, because it happened like this yesterday, the day before and the day before that, therefore it follows that the same pattern will be repeated tomorrow and tomorrow and tomorrow.

There were strong winds during the night and a considerable number of trees were brought down. The travellers had gone only 20 miles through thick forest when they were brought to a halt by the result of the storm.

'Blast,' Alan said, simultaneously braking and glancing at his watch.

'This could take hours,' said Barbara.

They got out and inspected the situation. A massive tree had come crashing down, stripping neighbouring trees of their branches as it did so. Uprooted and horizontal, it was now lying across the road. There was no possible way through. They were stuck.

'Now what?' Peter asked.

Alan shrugged his shoulders. 'Anyone for chess?'

'Just a minute, I think I can hear something,' Freda said.

It was the unmistakable low-gear rumble of an approaching lorry. A few minutes later it appeared on the other side of the fallen tree and a gang of black workmen leapt out. The Belgian in charge saw the group of stranded Europeans and came through a gap between the branches for a word. Alan's French must have been good enough to convey the urgency of their predicament.

The trunk of the tree was some eight feet above the ground, supported underneath by its own thin branches. The Belgian got his men to cut through these – carefully selecting ones which would not cause the entire trunk to collapse – and created, in effect, a tunnel through the tree.

Gingerly Alan let out the clutch and slowly depressed the accelerator. Although the baggage on the roof-rack scraped ominously along a sawn-off stump of wood, the Morris slipped through easily.

'Merci, mille fois,' Peter called back, keen to start using his schoolboy French a little.

The Belgian and the gang of workmen waved back. Alan checked his watch again.

'Just over an hour.'

'Well, it could have been worse,' Barbara said philosophically.

'It needn't have happened at all,' Alan countered.

They drove on in silence.

Gradually the forest began to thin out and a narrow gauge railway crossed the zigzagging road. At times the strip of cleared land between the trees was so narrow that the railway and the road were one and the same.

'I think the 11.48 Paulis Express should be due about now,' Alan said, and burst out laughing.

'Don't say things like that,' said Freda. 'It's tempting fate.'

Alan merely laughed all the louder.

The railway line continued on to the town of Paulis itself, named after General Paulis (1885–1923). The same type of history book that teaches us Nelson fought Napoleon at Trafalgar – as if describing a couple of thugs scrapping – and that Julius Caesar came, saw and conquered, ostensibly all on his own, also teaches us that General Paulis was the man who built the railway. So be it.

Peter described the town as beautiful, 'with bougainvillaea growing everywhere.' They each did a little shopping – a bulb for the inspection lamp was found, Freda bought some white paint, and stocks of general supplies were replenished. Two hours later they arrived at the deserted government resthouse.

It was the typical mud and thatch whitewashed affair but, unlike the buildings in which they had stayed in Uganda, it was closed to the outside not by a door and windows, but by wide straw roller-blinds. The effect was very cosy, though all four of them felt distinctly vulnerable when the forest animals began to growl and roar in the night.

Peter awoke the following morning unrefreshed. 'Bad night's sleep,' he wrote. 'Wild animals loud and *near*!'

Everything I have read about treks and expeditions stresses that if morale is to be maintained, meals must be well planned. They should not be simply nourishing or filling, but varied and palatable. Alan made many mistakes in his preparations for the trip but food was perhaps the one area he got right. In his diaries, Peter

114

would often record precisely what they ate – asparagus, mulligatawny soup, strawberries: at one place Alan even prepared a light snack of caviar on toast. Even the lingering smell of paraffin couldn't spoil the pleasure they got from those long-awaited mealtimes.

That evening, 19 April 1955, they had mock turtle soup, chicken, spinach and rice; then bananas and coffee. Soup, rice and coffee they had taken with them; the spinach and bananas had been bought in Paulis. They had come by the chickens in a more roundabout way.

The first had been obtained the previous day. During a stop in one of the pygmy villages, Alan decided that he'd quite like to have meat for dinner. It occurred to him that the locals might be willing to sell one of their birds.

'They're awfully scraggy,' Barbara said, looking at the pitiful creatures scratching around in the dust.

'I'll make sure I get a young one,' he assured her and asked whether any were for sale.

A noisy discussion broke out. It looked, from the outside, as if the villagers were about to come to blows. As abruptly as the squabbling and shouting had started, however, it came to an end: an old woman had a chicken she was prepared to sell. Both were pointed out and an amicable bargain was struck, the only drawback being that the travellers would have to catch the bird themselves.

Alan handed over the money and he and Peter started after the bird. Clearly bemused, the villagers stood round, cheering on their efforts as the valiant creature put up a brave fight to maintain its freedom. Two against one proved too much, however, and Alan finally managed to get it cornered. Peter went for the panga.

The reaction of the villagers then took a curious turn. Perhaps they thought Alan had wanted the bird as a pet. Perhaps this was the one vegetarian Bambuti tribe in the entire forest. Whatever the reason, although the onlookers had been laughing and chattering throughout the episode, when Alan sliced through the chicken's neck, a howl of anguish went up from the crowd.

Every man, woman and child turned tail and ran.

'Odd,' Alan muttered.

He wrapped up the chicken and placed it in the back of the car. The villagers remained out of sight.

'Coo-ee,' Freda called, but to no effect.

'May as well press on,' Alan said.

It was a curious ending to what had seemed a friendly encounter. As they drove away the village might have been a ghost town.

Chicken number two had also been killed by Alan, though this second death had resulted from an accident. They had been driving fast along a road when the bird ran out in front of them. There was neither time enough to stop nor room enough to swerve.

With a broken leg and wing, the chicken was clearly in pain. Alan wrung its neck and slung it in the back with the other one. At that moment an old woman approached him and began gesticulating angrily. Assuming that she must be the owner of the dead bird, Alan gave her a 10-franc note. The woman glared at him defiantly.

'Do you think she wants more money?' Freda asked.

'Well, she's not getting it,' Alan said. 'Not for that bag of bones.'

The old woman stretched out one hand and lightly brushed her fingers against Alan's arm. He burst out laughing and bid her a hasty farewell.

'What was all that about?' Barbara asked as they were driving off.

'I don't think she saw the chicken at all,' Alan said, still chuckling to himself. 'She thought I was trying to pay her . . . for her services.'

Barbara and Freda drew, plucked and cooked the chickens. One would definitely have been insufficient for dinner. Quantity was one thing, quality was another. Both birds tasted of stringy cardboard.

'I expect the mock turtle soup tasted good, though,' Peter laughed when I reminded him of the episode.

I found Peter's diaries invaluable. His attention to detail helped me build up a clear picture of the places they visited and, to a limited extent, the people they met there. And yet there was something missing. I couldn't put my finger on it until I saw Barbara's cine-film for the second time, then I realized what it was.

The daily entries noted the noteworthy; described what was worth describing. Even if the events or people or places were not positive, they had certainly stood out. What Peter did not mention was something far more basic to the journey but considered not worth recording. It was the tedium of travel. It was the miles of character-less khaki, beige and green which lay between the photo opportunities. It was the monotonous average of 200 miles a day.

The way Mrs Simpson and her late husband, Sandy, had spliced the film together ensured that this aspect of the trek was captured perfectly. Of course, like the Box Brownies and the diaries, the cine had been used to record individual incidents. Barbara, however, had gone further. Anxious to capture the entire trip and not just edited highlights, she had left the camera running while they were in the car, notching up the miles.

'It was such an important part of the journey', she explained, 'that I couldn't simply miss it out. Even though often it wasn't particularly pleasant.'

At the beginning of his first diary Peter lists all the towns they would pass through. In the cine-film she shot through the windscreen, Barbara shows the spaces in between. Mile after dusty mile of slowly changing landscape blurring past the windows – dry plains to grassy hills and dense forest, and back to plains again. It is this sense of movement that the diaries could not include.

In a book I read some years ago it was suggested that, because car windows frame the landscape, to the occupants inside travel becomes mere TV on wheels. The passengers are in a hermetically sealed compartment which precludes any contact with 'the real world' outside. I asked Peter if he had felt this way on their trek.

'No, I don't think so,' he said. 'I think we felt very much a part of this earth, because this earth was quite savage: there were rough rivers to cross and the forest was very close. On some of the tracks you're brushing the vegetation on each side of the road with the car, like a tiny insect going through thick grass.'

Once again, the cine-film confirmed this. It captured the branches and lianas slashing at the windscreen, the spiny suckers and coiled tendrils whipping in through open windows, scratching the passengers.

'Oh no, I think we felt very much a part of it,' he added.

By the time they reached their next stop they had covered 1,257 miles since leaving Alan's farm. It was day six. Alan was keeping to his schedule but the strain was showing in the travellers' faces, and the constant tiredness was making them tense.

When they arrived, the entire village descended on them. Ostensibly they were there to help, but in their enthusiasm they were to prove more of a nuisance. Everything was transported from the car to the rest-house. Everything. Even the spare tyre. And when the car was empty, the villagers stood round the building peering in through the windows.

The four travellers became increasingly embarrassed.

Alan backed into Barbara with a campbed in his arms. Barbara dropped the plates she was carrying and all the villagers laughed as they crashed to the floor. They turned to glare, but the grins were replaced by instant solemnity. Peter went out for a pee, but returned a couple of minutes later.

'They just followed me,' he said angrily.

'You shouldn't be so shy,' Alan laughed.

At dusk the villagers retired, but the four of them were still not alone. To her horror, Freda discovered that this latest resthouse was also bat-infested. It had already become an in-joke that she was incapable of keeping to her own dictum of 'a place for everything and everything in its place'. The rooms she occupied were always a mess – but how could she be expected to keep a place tidy when there were bats flapping round her head and cockroaches scuttling over the floor? It made her sick. Alan should have told her the conditions she'd be expected to sleep in.

She bit her lip and went outside. She had decided to paint the names of the countries they were to visit on one of the back doors of the Morris. Now seemed as good a time as any. With painstaking slowness she began:

Kenya to England
   via

It was uncomfortable crouching for so long. She called out for someone to bring her a stool. One of the Africans they had taken on for the evening heard but didn't understand. He went to fetch Peter. Barbara had heard Freda's original request, and she told Peter, but he ignored her and went to see what Freda wanted for himself. Feeling a little foolish, and annoyed because she was doing something else, Barbara followed the others outside. She handed the stool to Freda and said,

119

'I wish people would listen.'

'Why should they?' Peter snapped. '*You* never listen to anyone.'

It was a small incident, but one that upset Barbara. She wrote at the time: 'I was very taken aback and rather hurt.' As usual, it was Alan who calmed them all down. Always the life-and-soul, he took it upon himself, as leader, to keep spirits high. The irony was, of course, that the cumulative effect of his pressure to forge ahead was what had caused the mounting exhaustion and tension.

Freda continued with her lettering by torchlight. The moon disappeared behind the clouds and the air was filled with countless thousand fireflies. She didn't mind these: they kept their distance and were pretty.

When she was finished, she called the others out to admire her handiwork.

'It looks great,' said Peter.

'And neat of course,' Alan added. 'Typical school-teacher?'

Kenya to England

via

Uganda, Belgian Congo,

French Equatorial Africa,

Nigeria, Sahara Desert,

Spain and France.

The more typical wording on the back of a car intent on crossing the globe is 'Destination (be it Sydney or Timbuktu) or Bust'. This at least allows for the possibility of failure. It is the absolute certainty of success conveyed by Freda's message which, given what lay before them, is so poignant.

TWELVE

GETTING TO KNOW YOU

COMMUNICATION was a problem throughout the trip.
The four travellers were now in the centre of the
Belgian Congo and apart from the universally known
'Jambo' their Swahili was useless. Practically no one they
now encountered spoke English, and even when
they were muddling along in French, knowledge of the
language was no guarantee of comprehension.

They got up very early the following morning. It was
Thursday, 21 April. The plan was to make it all the way
to Monga before nightfall. Thankfully, with the
exception of one man, the villagers were still asleep
and the beds, nets and cases were all packed away without the many helping hands that had caused such chaos
the previous evening. The one exception made no
attempt to talk to them. He simply stood there, ten yards
from the car, watching.

'What do you think he wants?' Peter asked.

'I've no idea,' said Barbara. 'And I'm far too tired to
find out.'

Freda trudged out to the car with her heavy case. She
was humming. 'Oh, what a beautiful morning' – a sure
sign that she'd had a bad night.

'He's a lot smarter than the others,' Peter continued.

This was certainly true. The man was dressed in a

white shirt, a jacket and a neatly pressed pair of trousers. On his feet he was wearing black leather shoes which, though down at the heels, couldn't have been more highly polished. A medium-sized leather case stood next to him.

'Alan'll sort it out,' Barbara said. 'His French is far better than ours.' On cue, a voice from behind her boomed out cheerfully.

'Bonjour. Puis-je vous aider?'

The man smiled and advanced, hand outstretched.

'I'd like to travel with you,' he explained.

'We're going a long way.'

'So much the better.'

'Thousands of miles.'

The man merely nodded.

'To a country where everything is very different,' Alan added.

'It is not a problem. I am a Catholic.'

'Do you know where we're going?'

'It's not important,' the man persisted, with a broad friendly grin on his face.

'England.'

'Ing-gland,' the man repeated slowly. There was no hint of recognition in his voice. 'And you will take me to Inggland?' he said.

'We can't,' Alan explained. 'The car is full.'

'My bag is very small.'

'The bag isn't the problem,' Alan said.

'I am very small,' the man said, rounding his shoulders.

'There's nowhere for you to sit.'

'I can go on the top.'

'Sorry,' Alan said finally, and he shook hands with the man again. 'Not possible.'

As they drove away they left the solitary figure standing where he was, waving after them. The case was still next to his feet. His shoes were getting dusty.

'He didn't understand a word I said.'

'But you seemed to be saying such a lot,' Freda said.

'That's not what I meant,' said Alan.

Buta was 50 miles on. Although not large, the town was important in 1955 as a railway terminus and army depot. It was however neither interesting nor attractive for the passing traveller, and after a leisurely breakfast they set off again.

Peter took over the driving, with Barbara sitting next to him at the front, and while Alan and Freda fell asleep in the back, the two of them got talking. As the miles passed, Barbara began to see she had been wrong to take everything Peter said at face value. His aggression stemmed from insecurity. His lack of respect for her was surely due to his attempts to assert his own personality in a group so much older than himself; the rudeness nothing more than cynical adolescent humour that he hadn't yet mastered. The more Peter tried to communicate with Barbara on what he assumed was an adult level, the more she bridled against his insolence. This only served to sharpen his thrust. It was a vicious circle.

On the bus from Nairobi to Lumbwa, Peter had told her that he lived for his work. He would be bored without it. Barbara had thought how sad it was for a seventeen-year-old to have so little interest in life. This affected air of arrogant world-weariness, she discovered, was quite simply untrue.

He talked animatedly about his love of music, of the piano exams he had passed, and the accordion he would play at parties. He spoke knowledgeably about the cultivation of garden flowers and vegetables. He told her about his attempts at scientific poultry management, how the feed had to be carefully balanced, how detailed records and accounts were kept, and how the chickens themselves were bred selectively. One day, he told her, he would like his own farm.

As their understanding of one another slowly changed, so did the landscape outside. The dense fertile rainforest gradually gave way to a wide expanse of giant bamboo. The shade of colour shifted through emerald green to a deep dark turquoise. The thick smooth stems of the outsized grass speared the gloomy light, and high above the road the tips of the bamboo touched. It was like driving along inside a gargantuan upturned boat.

'It's the most wizard sight I've ever seen,' Peter enthused.

The previous day, Barbara would have felt obliged to challenge so bald a statement. She felt she knew him a bit better now, and smiled.

'It is rather spectacular,' she agreed.

'Should we wake the others?' Peter asked.

'Oh no. Don't disturb them,' Barbara said. 'Freda hardly slept at all last night.'

It wasn't only consideration that influenced her. Due to the poor quality of the petrol and a drop in altitude of some 6,000 feet since leaving Alan's farm, the car had begun to pink. Whenever Peter drove, it was accompanied by a constant stream of dos and don'ts from Alan as to how to prevent the car from making any noises. The further he drove, the more irritable Alan would become. Far better if he slept in the back after handing the wheel over to the boy.

They arrived in Bondo, a small town with a disproportionately large Catholic church, in the late afternoon. It lay on the far side of the wide crocodile-infested Uele river. Despite the fact that Alan and Freda had slept soundly throughout the noisy jolting drive across the bamboo glade, as they arrived at the river's edge and Peter braked the pair of them woke up.

124

'What time is it?' Freda asked drowsily.

'Almost three,' said Barbara.

'Three!' exclaimed Alan. 'We'll have to go flat out if we're to get to Monga before dark. I think I'll take over the driving, if that's all right with you, Peter.'

'I can drive fast.'

'I'm sure you can,' Alan said, 'but if anyone's going to have a crash I'd rather it was me.'

'If it's all the same to you,' Barbara put in, 'I'd rather neither of you did.'

The ferry was a strange construction which looked like a large floating section of metal bridge, and was propelled by a motorboat attached to the side.

They stopped in Bondo only long enough to refuel. If the road to Monga had been direct, there would have been no urgency. But there was still another river to cross – the Bili – and if they arrived there after dusk, the ferrymen would already have left. This would mean spending the night on the riverbank. Alan put his foot down. A sudden cloudburst had turned the earth road into a slippery mud track and it proved impossible for him to sustain any great speed. When they finally arrived at the ferry stage, the place was deserted.

'Damn,' Alan muttered.

'Now what?' asked Barbara.

'Doesn't look too promising, does it?' Alan conceded as he sounded the horn. The blast of sound echoed up and down the river before being swallowed up by silence. It was that eerie hour of quiet wedged between the noisy day and the noisier night. Alan tried the horn a second time. Again the silence overwhelmed their attempts to summon help.

But someone had noticed them. As they all stood disconsolately round the Morris, a young man came running up to them. He and the other ferry workers had been having their evening meal about a mile along the road; they'd seen the headlights of the passing car.

'They're just finishing their dinner,' the man explained, 'and then they will be here.'

'No hurry,' said Alan. Now he knew they wouldn't be sleeping outside, he could afford to be magnanimous.

This second ferry, more primitive than the metal construction they'd used earlier, consisted of fifteen dug-out canoes, each 100 feet long and 3 feet wide. Having been laid out on the ground, with a small gap between each one, heavy planks had been nailed into place across the top, yoking the dug-outs together and forming a platform on top for the passengers and vehicles. The ends of the dug-outs were left uncovered. This is where the ferrymen who paddled them across would sit. Once the platform had been enclosed with a set of bamboo safety railings the ferry was complete, and was launched into the river. William Heath Robinson would have been hard pressed to better the contraption.

The other men arrived. There were twenty-four or so in all, and while Alan drove the car carefully up the ramp on to the ferry, the paddlers took their positions.

'Ay-oooh,' the leader called out, and the men on the platform pushed away from the bank with long poles. Once the ferry had swung round so that the bows of the dug-outs were pointing towards the opposite bank, the men started paddling.

The rhythm of the strokes became established, the men began chanting. On the platform, the beat was taken up by others who clapped and danced and kept time on tom-toms of hollowed logs. The rhythms proved infectious. Peter, Barbara and Alan clapped and danced with the rest and, as the light began to fail, Freda picked up a drumstick and hammered away at a log-drum. A cheer went up, and the leader of the men began a song which the others would interrupt at the end of each line, with a recurring refrain.

Solo:	'These people are going to England by car!'
Chorus:	'Wish them luck!'
Solo:	'Their car is small but strongly built!'
Chorus:	'Wish them luck!'
Solo:	'We hope they will succeed
	And return the same way they have come!'
Chorus:	'Wish them luck!
	Wish them luck!'

Over and over, louder and louder, the song echoed across the broad slowly flowing river, and as they reached the opposite bank, the final 'wish them luck' built up to a roaring crescendo. Then, as if each person had been following a conductor whose invisible baton suddenly fell, the clapping, banging, singing and dancing abruptly ceased. There was stillness.

A cheer of approval went up, and everyone congratulated everyone else on a crossing well done. It was only later that the four travellers discovered the meaning of the words they had been singing. And yet, for those moments on the ferry when the rhymes and rhythms had come together, all those niggling problems of communication which beset them throughout the trek, all the misunderstandings, cross-purposes and wrong-ends-of-the-stick, simply disappeared.

THIRTEEN

DAY OF REST

'IT has happened again,' Peter wrote despairingly in his diary. Despite his front of bravado, he hated the reputation he had developed for forgetfulness and clumsiness. And yet, no matter how hard he tried to concentrate, there seemed to be no cure. 'It' continued to plague him throughout the trek.

They had arrived at the Monga resthouse late. Everyone was tired and scratchy and wanted to go to bed. When they went to unpack, Peter realized with a sickening jolt that the rear-door keys were missing.

'Well, who had them last?'

'I did,' Peter admitted miserably.

'I don't believe it,' Barbara muttered. The journey was proving to be exhausting enough without all the extra little problems Peter insisted on contributing.

'I think I must have left them in that shop in Bondo,' he said. 'When we got the petrol.'

'Right,' said Alan heartily, 'we'll have to unload it all through the front then. Peter, jump inside and pass the bags forward.'

When they had first set off, it was undoubtedly Peter whose behaviour was the most careless. If anything was ever dropped, forgotten or mislaid, he was inevitably the one responsible. As the trip had progressed, however,

128

his reputation had become less justified. Although he had snapped Barbara's knitting needles, forgotten to pack the inspection lamp, broken a couple of glasses, burnt the handle of the carving knife and now lost the keys, the others had been catching up.

Barbara couldn't find the lens cap to her cine-camera, had left a blouse behind and had dropped three plates. Freda had mislaid a pair of jeans, broken two pairs of sandals and was developing her own reputation for knocking over other people's drinks. If Alan's record was marginally better, it was primarily because he continued to busy himself elsewhere whenever the washing, cooking, loading or unloading was taking place.

The reason for this spate of losses and breakages was simple: exhaustion. Getting up at 5 a.m. and packing in the dark, travelling for an average of fourteen hours and then unpacking, also in the dark – this tough daily schedule was guaranteed to lead to accidents. By the time they arrived at the Monga resthouse, everyone was so drained that they reached a consensus: the following day should be one of rest. Even Alan did not disagree.

The resthouse was situated on a wide stretch of the Bili river. Immediately below them were white churning rapids where two channels of the same river reunited and plunged down over a jagged jumble of massive boulders. The deafening roar woke the four travellers early, but as the fine spray had made everything cold and damp, they all remained gratefully tucked in until the warming sun rose. It would be their only lie-in.

Once finally up, there was a lot to get done. It was a day of rest only insofar as they were not travelling. Peter went down to the river to rinse out some of his clothes. Not that they were dirty. He had already washed them at the Rutoto resthouse, but as the resthouses were never reached until after dark, there had been no opportunity for the clothes to dry out, and after five days they were beginning to smell distinctly brackish. Peter sprinkled the trousers, shirt and socks with a liberal dose of Surf and began pounding them against a flat rock.

'Aaargh!'

The scream seemed to come from two directions at the same time as Peter was walking back towards the house. He stopped and looked around.

Behind him was the latrine hut. Constructed (for obvious reasons) a hundred yards from the sleeping quarters, it consisted of a hole in the ground, modestly concealed by a roofed circle of matting. It was dark, smelly and, due to the recent rain, extremely slippery.

'Are you all right?' Peter called out.

The answers 'no' and 'yes' floated back simultaneously. There had been two screams, not one.

The 'no' had come from the latrine, and a second later Freda emerged, looking pale and dishevelled. There was mud down her skirt and she was wearing only one sandal.

'I'll never get used to the things,' she muttered to Peter as she stomped lopsidedly past him on the one remaining heel.

Trying to balance toilet paper and torch in one hand, while holding up your skirt with the other, was no easy matter. Particularly when crouching. And yet Freda had managed. She was about to congratulate herself on a job well done when, attempting to stand up, her knee had given way and she had crashed back down again, landing on her bottom in the squelchy mud. Her shoe, which had come off, hovered for a couple of tantalizingly long, long seconds before sliding ingloriously down into the dark hole.

There was, in contrast, no hole in the kitchen; not even in the roof where there should have been one. Accordingly, there was no escape for or from the acrid smoke from the fire over which they cooked. The damp wood made things particularly unpleasant, and as Barbara fumbled blindly for the eggs, eyes streaming, she cursed Alan all over again for failing to bring the primus.

'What is it?' Peter asked as Barbara appeared.

'Oh, nothing,' she said. 'It was just a bit of a shock.'

Peter and Alan went in to inspect. There in the pan beside the half-done fried eggs were two bedraggled dead chicks.

'Mmm, fried chicken,' said Alan.

Lunch was a far more palatable affair. Raffia and bamboo fish traps extended out into the river below the rapids. These were inspected morning and evening by the local fishermen who would paddle past in canoes. They'd had a good catch that morning and Alan had bought several fish. Despite being bony, they tasted delicious.

After their meal, Peter began playing with the lock on the back of the Morris. No one wanted a repeat performance of the palaver they'd had getting the luggage out of the car. He unscrewed the entire mechanism and tried to disconnect the locking device from the inside.

'Try to remember to put the screwdriver back when you've finished,' Alan said, and winked. 'I'm going to see if the place next door has got an iron.'

The lock did not prove difficult to dismantle, and when Peter screwed it back into place, the doors opened and shut once again. There was only one problem: it could no longer be locked.

'Not that there's much worth taking,' Barbara said.

Alan returned a while later grinning happily. The neighbouring building belonged to the Belgian district consul, and his wife had been happy to allow Alan to borrow both iron and ironer.

'Only in Africa,' Freda marvelled. 'Only in Africa.'

Freda was wrong. Be it the religion, the judicial

system, eating with cutlery or smoothing away wrinkles with a block of hot metal, Europeans had imposed their own idea of what it meant to be civilized wherever they had settled. There had, it is true, been a shift of emphasis in the type of colonialization. Those who had claimed the Americas and Australia for themselves had wanted the land, new territory for their expanding populations. In contrast, it was primarily the raw materials of Asia and Africa which attracted the latter-day colonialists. Relatively few Europeans settled in these countries permanently. The telephone, the electric light, the railway, the machine gun, the internal combustion engine – all were at the disposal of the new colonialists. The scope these new machines offered meant fewer Europeans were needed to hold the indigenous population in thrall. The saving in European man-power was enhanced by the policy of divide and rule, whereby certain groups were 'trained up' to manage the population as a whole. The results of this strategy often unpredictable.

Peter and Barbara had decided to go to the local post office. They had some letters to send off and also wanted to buy sets of the local stamps for their collections. Since they were leaving the Belgian Congo the following day, this would be their last opportunity.

A makeshift hut with a corrugated iron roof bore the words 'Bureau de Poste' above the door.

'This must be it,' Barbara said.

Inside were several Africans, stripped to the waist, and a Belgian, sweating uncomfortably inside a crumpled suit. All of them were hammering away on typewriters. The noise was deafening. The Belgian looked up and raised a quizzical eyebrow.

'Nous voulons acheter des timbres de poste,' Peter bellowed in laboured schoolboy French.

'Certainly,' the Belgian replied, and he led them out on to the veranda.

A portly official was sitting at an overflowing desk, dealing with a line of people there to pay a local tax. The Belgian spoke to him briefly and Peter and Barbara immediately found themselves at the head of the queue.

'Yes,' he said.

'I'd like the stamps,' Peter explained.

'Which stamps?'

'To send letters.'

'Aah,' he said, and asked them both to sit down while he sent someone for them.

There were no seats. Barbara took him at his word and perched herself on the edge of his table. It wobbled ominously.

'Not there, not there!' he shouted.

The people in the queue sniggered.

Five minutes passed. Ten minutes. The man at the desk had been busying himself with official documents, ticking this, deleting that. He glanced at his watch. Twelve minutes. The crowd was beginning to mutter and he knew that his authority was being compromised.

'Leo!' he bellowed.

The youth came running back with a handful of stamps. Unfortunately, he had not quite grasped the request. The stamps were used ones he'd torn off any envelopes he had come across.

'Idiot!' the man shouted as he stormed off to fetch them himself. He returned a minute later, somewhat subdued and empty-handed.

'What about the drawer there?' Barbara suggested.

A smile of supreme happiness spread over his broad face as he pulled out the wad of stamps. He laid them down on the table and looked up.

'What did you want?'

'Two stamps for Kenya,' Barbara said.

'Kenya?' he repeated, his face looking blank.

'A British colony,' Peter offered, 'in East Africa.'

'British?'

Peter attempted to draw a map of Africa showing the relative positions of Belgian Congo and Kenya. The man at the desk misinterpreted it as a map of the river Bili and shrugged his shoulders. Not wishing to lose face, though, he suggested a figure of 140 francs per letter.

'A hundred and forty! You must be joking,' Barbara said. She went off to find the Belgian.

He returned with her and explained the cost of postage to Kenya and England – yes, there was such a place. Just north of Belgium itself.

When they then asked for three sets of stamps, bearing one of each denomination, the official finally lost his temper. The idea of stamp *collections* was something he had never before encountered.

'You make joke,' he repeated.

By this time, both Peter and Barbara had been there long enough to persevere that little bit longer. In the long run it would be worth it. The entire ludicrous scenario would come back to them when they were putting the stamps into their albums.

Inevitably, when it came to paying, the amount that Peter and Barbara calculated did not tally with the figures of the post-office man. Faced with increasing jocularity from the crowd, however, the latter decided to compromise.

'Thanks,' Peter said, licked the stamp for Kenya and affixed it.

Immediately, it peeled itself off the envelope and fluttered down to the floorboards. The hot, humid weather had dissolved the paste on the back and none of the stamps would stay in place. Peter's French was not up to explaining what must have happened. He held up the stamp and the letter and mimed the problem.

The man took a deep breath. 'Leo,' he called.

A few minutes later Leo returned with a handful of

berries. These the man split open and smeared over the back of the stamps. It did the trick. Without raising his head again, he quickly franked the envelopes and pushed them back across the table to Peter and Barbara.

'Post box outside,' he said.

'Thank you,' said Peter. 'Goodbye.'

'Or should that be *au revoir*,' Barbara muttered.

As they were posting the letters, two more of the stamps fell off. Barbara looked at Peter and burst out laughing. She picked them up and posted them as well.

'They can sort it out,' she said.

It was like old-fashioned methods of teaching arithmetic, where young children would parrot their times tables but had no concept of what numbers actually were. They could chant 'four sixes are twenty-four' by rote, but give them four groups of half a dozen apples and they would have to count them all.

The imposition of abstract systems and conventions on the colonies proved similarly unintelligible to those who were expected to implement them. Employees would go through the motions of what they knew was expected of them without grasping the concept behind their actions. Both the complexities of the postal service and the triviality of uncreased clothes were doomed to remain bizarre European eccentricities.

This was entirely the fault of the European powers who failed to educate their subjects. They demanded obedience, not understanding. In 1955 there was only one *lycée* throughout the French-speaking countries of Africa.

It is probably unnecessary to add that none of the letters reached its destination. And when Peter and Barbara arrived back at the resthouse, they found that although their clothes were all totally devoid of wrinkles, two shirts, one handkerchief and a skirt had been irreparably scorched.

FOURTEEN

IN NEED OF CHRISTIAN CHARITY

RELATIVELY refreshed and looking forward to crossing into another country, the four travellers were up, packed and ready to leave by 7.15 the following morning. The border between the Belgian Congo and French Equatorial Africa was only 50 miles to the north-west, and Alan intended to get into the French colony before stopping for breakfast. It was Saturday, 23 April.

'Hey look,' Peter shouted. 'Lunch!'

A flock of guinea fowl were pecking for seeds in the middle of the road. Alan took up the challenge and headed straight for them. Unperturbed they hopped up the banks. Alan drove after them, causing the luggage in the back to bounce around and the birds to squawk indignantly and scuttle off awkwardly into the undergrowth.

'Next time,' Alan said.

A couple of hours later, they came to the Bomu river which formed the natural boundary between the Belgian and French colonies. A sign next to the ferry warned that a maximum of 4 to 5 tons could be safely transported across the river.

'Do you think we'll be all right?' Freda asked nervously.

Alan looked at the teacher in disbelief. It didn't b
well for the poor pupils of Chester.

The river was wide but shallow, and the ferrymε
used long poles to push them across. Keeping a strict
rhythm going was important and once again Freda took
to the drumsticks. She kept it up for the entire width of
the river, and by the time they drove off the ferry on
to the land, they were in another country.

Nowhere is the illogicality of the colonialists' arbitrary
borders more in evidence than in this area of Africa. The
Belgians and French divided up the Kongo people, so
that even today they live in two countries – Congo and
the Democratic Republic of Congo – while in the French
area tribes of widely differing cultures were lumped
together in a convenient administrative area on the
grounds that they were all 'equatorial'. Today, in
partial recognition of those tribal origins, French
Equatorial Africa comprises four separate countries: the
Central Africa Republic, Congo, Gabon and Chad.

For the four travellers, all these differences were
irrelevant. The only changes they would notice were
those which reflected the two European neighbours. As
Peter wrote in his diary: 'We were leaving Belgium and
entering France.'

The first place they came to was Bangassou, the large
sleepy town near the border. Pressing on, they stopped
at the spectacular Kotto Falls for photographs. The spray
carried on the wind was so thick that Alan had been
forced to use the windscreen wipers on their approach.
While standing, looking down over the magnificent
cascade of water, a vivid rainbow formed an arc across
the stony drop as the sun suddenly broke through the
clouds.

Whereas the roads had been good from the border to
the falls, they deteriorated abruptly soon afterwards. 'A
disgrace to the French,' Peter wrote in an untidy scrawl

as they bumped and lurched over the worst corrugations they had encountered so far on the trek. It was not only these ruts that slowed them down; deep ditches caused by lorries getting stuck in the rainy season remained unfilled while washaways from the swollen streams had removed entire sections of the road. For long stretches, their average speed was forced down to single figures.

'I suppose we've just got to be grateful the rains haven't started,' Alan said. 'Even caterpillar tracks get bogged down then.'

'Talking of caterpillars,' Freda said, 'has anyone else noticed the number of butterflies around here?'

They hadn't, but now they did. The farther into the country they drove, the more butterflies there were. Predominantly white and yellow, they flapped and fluttered from flower to flower at the roadside. Hundreds of them were gathered at puddles, their wings quivering, ready to launch themselves off at the approach of a vehicle.

'Beautiful,' Freda said, as they came flitting past the car like feathers and tumbled over and over in the slipstream.

But as the old cliché observes, you can have too much of a good thing.

'Unbelievable!' Alan said, switching on the wipers again, this time to clear away the butterflies which had mistaken the Morris for a giant flower. Even if the road had been better, the thick fog of shimmering wings would have prevented him from driving any faster.

The forest gradually thinned out and they found themselves passing through a scrubby khaki-coloured landscape. There was a new hazard. High winds and heavy rains had uprooted innumerable thorn bushes and these now littered the roads. Their three-inch thorns, radiating out from the twigs in all directions, had been baked rock hard in the kiln-like heat. These could puncture the Morris's standard tyres as easily as a hot knife cuts through butter.

Alan bounced on over the rutted surface of the road, skidding and swerving to avoid the treacherous thorns.

'Well,' he said, 'I think we should count ourselves lucky if we can average five miles an hour through this lot.'

'So what's our new E.T.A. in London?' Peter asked.

'Oh, I should say October,' he said. '1963.'

There was no alternative but to continue. As they were all to say at different times during the day, it could only get better.

It did and it didn't. The number of butterflies and thorn-bushes decreased but, if anything, the road surface grew worse. The constant jarring loosened the roof-rack. Every time the car jolted, the clamps shifted and Alan and Peter would have to leap out of the car to tighten them up again. With his arm stretching through the open window, Peter tried to hold the rack in place, but it was hopeless. As the car juddered over the jagged corrugations, the rack was shaken off more and more frequently.

What made the driving especially difficult was the unpredictability of the road. Sometimes it would improve and, after taking it cautiously for a while, Alan would try to regain some of the lost time.

'It doesn't seem too bad here, does it?' Peter would say as the car reached thirty-five or so. Almost inevitably, at that moment, a deep gully would open up in front of them, Alan would brake abruptly, and the luggage would come crashing over on to Barbara and Freda in the back.

The first time, everyone had laughed, but when it happened again, and again, and again, the joke began to wear thin. Alan refused to stop unless it was necessary to navigate an exceptionally deep hole, and the bags kept slumping forward on to Barbara's and Freda's shoulders. In the humid heat of 105 degrees Fahrenheit, tempers were beginning to fray.

'This is ridiculous,' Barbara snapped irritably as, for the umpteenth time, she attempted to push the bags away from the back of her head.

'Oh, stop complaining,' Alan barked back.

'Well, do you have to keep slamming on the brakes like that?'

'No, I could go soaring off into the air if you'd prefer,' he said sarcastically. 'I'm awfully sorry, but the French seem to have forgotten to signpost their holes.'

'Then just drive a little slower.'

'If I go any slower the corrugations'll be worse, and then we'll use twice the amount of petrol.'

Barbara fell silent.

What Alan said was, as always, only half true, but Barbara wasn't in a position to argue. In the desert the corrugated or washboard surfaces are on average three to six inches deep, and the best way to get over them is to drive as fast as possible. Although it can be fairly painful reaching the optimum speed, if 45–50 miles per hour can be maintained, the vehicle skims over the tops of the ridges and the ride is remarkably smooth. What Alan failed to mention was that, for this to be possible, the road has to be broad and the corrugations regular. The road to Bambari was far from either. The pits and gullies and soft sandy patches made any attempt to drive fast foolhardy. The point was driven home to them when a particularly violent jolt tore the luggage-rack right off the roof. Bouncing on to the bonnet, it landed on the ground immediately in front of the car. It was as much as Alan could do to prevent himself running over the scattered suitcases. From the back of the car, there came a muffled squawk as the beds, bedding and tins came hurtling down on the two women.

'As tight as you can,' Alan instructed Peter, as they replaced the roof rack.

By the time they had finished, the clamps were so tight that the roof was almost bowing upwards. Alan didn't say anything else in the car, but Barbara felt vindicated: he kept the speed down to 25 miles per hour. They arrived at Bambari at 6.40, shortly after dusk.

Hot, tired, dusty, dirty, aching, irritable, hungry, thirsty, fed up – every single negative adjective dissolved the moment the travellers were ushered into the resthouse by the toto they had asked for directions. He gave Alan the key and left.

'Now this is what I *call* a resthouse,' Alan said, throwing himself on to the bed.

'It's wonderful,' said Freda breathlessly as, for the first time, their accommodation matched her preconceptions of how it would be.

It was a large modern bungalow with heavily curtained windows and polished parquet flooring. The kitchen was equipped with a fridge, cooker, washing-up unit, radio and well-stocked cupboards. The huge double beds were made up and the long polished table in the dining room had been laid for dinner.

'Very nice, very nice indeed,' Alan said as he completed his inspection of the rooms. He picked up a bottle of red wine from the sideboard. 'Typical French hospitality.'

It seemed too good to be true. It was.

Already there was some kind of a commotion going on outside. A moment later, a loud pummelling began at the door. Alan shrugged and opened it.

'Can I help . . .' he started to say, but the policemen had already pushed past him and were all talking at once.

Peter, Freda and Barbara watched in silence as Alan began to colour. It was the first time they had seen him look embarrassed. If only they could understand exactly what the policemen were saying, though the general import of the tirade was clear enough. This was not the resthouse.

'It belongs to the local French bigwig,' Alan explained. 'He uses the place when he's on safari – and apparently he's expected any minute.'

They all traipsed out. Freda was the last to leave. She wanted one final look at the dream villa she now knew she would never sleep in. At least, not on this trip. A policeman was already down on one knee scrubbing away at the mud they had carried in on their shoes.

To compound the difficulties for that night, they discovered that the resthouse itself had closed down. An expensive hotel had been opened and the rooms cost way beyond what they were prepared to pay – or rather, what Alan was prepared to pay. The £525 which the three passengers had initially paid was now in travellers' cheques in Alan's name. If he was to get back to England for nothing, it was in his interests to find the cheapest accommodation possible.

It was now half past seven and after the worst day's driving they had experienced so far, they found themselves without anywhere to sleep. Alan sensed the others were becoming restive.

'There's an American Mission in Bambari,' he said, taking control. 'We'll try there.'

'Why should they put us up?' Barbara asked.

'Because they're Christians,' Alan answered sharply, and that was clearly an end to the conversation.

If he'd expected they would be welcomed with open arms, the curt 'no' he received from the missionaries soon persuaded him otherwise.

Reminiscing on the incident, Mrs Simpson commented

on how rude Alan had been. While far from perfect himself, he expected anyone who professed to 'believe' to be holier than holy. The fact that they had presumed to suggest that their funds were primarily for poor blacks rather than adventuring Europeans filled him with a vicious contempt.

'Call yourselves Christians,' he said, looking around at the three well-appointed bungalows.

'Yes, we do,' they answered simply.

His antagonism towards the missionaries went far deeper than the inconvenience they were now causing him. They represented everything he disliked about organized institutions. From the French authorities he had avoided before his first crossing of the Sahara to the British 'raj' he antagonized at the Kisumu Tennis Tournament, Alan loathed the strictures imposed on him by bureaucrats. To him, missionaries were nothing more than religious clerks, bribing hungry people to accept their own narrow interpretation of the spiritual.

Their refusal to offer beds for the night made Alan all the more stubborn. Barbara and Freda were shuffling around awkwardly, but Alan was damned if he'd let these Yankee hypocrites close the door in his face. His sheer bloody-mindedness finally paid off, and the obvious lack of Christian charity in their offer made Alan feel even better.

'You can sleep in the church,' one of them said, 'when the service has finished. There's a kitchen just in front.'

'Thank you,' Alan said, and turned.

'Yes, thanks very much,' Freda added. She hadn't liked the edge that had crept into Alan's voice.

'Leave everything as you find it,' one of the missionaries added as a parting shot.

'And there I was planning on burning the whole place down,' Alan muttered under his breath.

The service was still in progress when they arrived at

the church and the sound of 500 black Africans singing Christian hymns to the tune of 'She'll Be Coming Round the Mountains When She Comes' echoed through the air. There was a prayer, another hymn – this time based loosely on 'Swanee River' – a final blessing and at about half past eight the flock finally began to disperse.

'They certainly look happy,' Freda said to Alan. He merely snorted.

Wherever they stopped, the travellers faced the daunting business of putting up the mosquito nets, three of which were the large rectangular type that needed to be attached to the ceiling from each of their top corners. Finding suitable points in the resthouses had proved difficult: in the open-style church it was looking impossible.

'I, for one, am not going to sacrifice myself to the mozzies,' said Alan.

'What do you suggest then?' Barbara asked.

Alan looked round. He eyed the pulpit and pews mischievously. 'They haven't left us a great deal of choice, have they?' he said.

'Oh, we can't,' Freda said.

'Why not?' Alan asked with mock innocence. 'As long as we put everything back afterwards.'

It was decided. The cavernous, pillared church was soon echoing with the screech of heavy benches being pulled over the wooden floor. One by one, Peter and Alan placed pew upon pew to form stacks at the head and foot of each of the campbeds. Unsteady they might have been, but they did the trick. The mosquito-net tags were tied neatly to the uppermost points of the makeshift leaning towers. The only remaining problem was Barbara's bell-shaped net, and Peter solved this by suspending it from a rope which he attached to two of the pillars.

'Wonderful,' Alan said, standing back and admiring their handiwork.

After a hurried meal of bread, Irish stew, pawpaws and coffee (all laced with the lingering whiff of paraffin), they retired to their beds. Getting in was no easy matter. The pews rocked ominously every time the nets were touched, and owing to the fact that they sagged in the middle, it was impossible *not* to touch them. Slowly and carefully, they inched their way under the blankets.

'Night,' they called to one another before turning over.

A moment later Barbara was sitting up. 'I can smell burning,' she said.

The single candle that Alan had decided to leave alight was under the preacher's table. The wood above was beginning to smoulder.

'I didn't realize you really meant to burn the church down,' Peter said.

'Isn't someone going to blow it out then?' Alan asked.

'You're nearest,' came the chorused reply.

Alan winched himself up on to his elbow, lifted the corner of the net carefully and blew. The flame danced around, but remained burning.

'Damn!' he muttered, and leant further forward. Still the candle would not go out.

Lowering his hand to the ground to support his body, he pushed himself as near to the candle as possible and blew hard. The flame flickered. The tower wobbled and creaked. Suddenly the candle gave up the struggle and the entire church was plunged into darkness. At the same time the pews slipped and came crashing down.

For a second there was silence. Then began the muffled sounds of Alan struggling with the blankets, the net and the heavy pews. He cursed and grunted as he wrenched at the tangled mass in his increasingly bad-tempered attempts to free himself. The others stifled their laughter, nervous that any movement might cause an avalanche of their own church furniture.

'Very funny, isn't it?' Alan shouted as he finally pulled himself clear. Deciding to abandon the idea of the net entirely, he lay down, unprotected, on top of the bed.

'Thank you all so much for your help,' he added sarcastically. 'And goodnight.'

FIFTEEN

RECALLING THE DANCING GIRLS

T IRED, bruised and bitten, Alan was in a bad mood the following day. He decreed that they were not using the so-called main road again. There was a minor road also going to Fort Crampel and, as less traffic used it, the driving conditions were bound to be better. What was more, it was a short cut. The decision had been made.

The road was not better. Peter wrote in his diary: 'Worse road so far! Max, 20 mph. Road disappeared several times and we nearly got lost.'

There was one advantage to this less popular route. They saw things they would not otherwise have seen. Apart from the red bananas, giant cane rats, fruit being carried in calabashes, and grain pounded in hollowed logs (which Peter noted down), they also witnessed a Wedding Ceremony Dance.

Although it wasn't the first group of dancing girls they had passed, it was the first time they had stopped the car and taken photographs. Naked to the waist, the girls wore short grass skirts, and beads, bangles and necklaces which jangled as they jigged about. The men stood around watching. Once the dance was over, the serious business of haggling began.

From the photographs I saw, it was clear that some of the girls were no older than ten or eleven. I asked Peter if this wasn't a little young to be paraded as a bride.

'They didn't actually become wives at that point,' he explained. 'They were each betrothed to one man and would go to him once they had reached maturity.'

Following recent rain, the road had become a quagmire. It was so wet that there were ducks swimming in the puddles in the middle of the road. Ironically, the weight of the car, which would cause such problems on the soft sand, was working to their advantage here: the tyres gripped the slippery mud firmly. Apart from having to stop at regular intervals to wash the windscreen, there were few problems.

They had a hurried lunch in Fort Crampel and continued on to Kabo. The road remained atrocious. Suddenly a huge unseen ridge sent the Morris flying through the air. When it landed again, the roof rack buckled and one of the four rubber suckers slipped off. Even with the help of a passing lorry-load of workmen, the sucker remained missing. Alan substituted a piece of cardboard, but it was unsatisfactory and their average speed was slashed by the number of times they had to stop to adjust the roof rack. They arrived in Kabo in sullen silence, and the sight of yet another dirty, infested resthouse did nothing to improve anyone's mood.

It had been a bad day, and yet was it that much worse than any of their other gruelling journeys through the hot and sticky tropical countryside? I doubt it. The main difference on that particular day was in Alan. His dominance in the group cannot be overestimated. When in a good mood – as he usually was – he would jolly everyone along with jokes, games, and comic badinage with the people they met. But after the previous night's lack of sleep he had woken feeling dreadful. It was his oppressive rancour which poisoned the atmosphere and made everything seem that much worse than it really was.

With his characteristic understatement, Peter summed up the mood that evening: 'morale a little low'.

The following morning Alan woke refreshed. He was first up and, singing loudly, brought tea to the other three in bed.

'*Land of hope* . . . Madame, votre thé, . . . *and glory* . . . et pour vous, Madame Tayleur, . . . *Mother of the free* . . . et Monsieur, thé au lait . . .'

Feeling responsible, if not guilty, for the previous evening's gloom, Alan was attempting to rally the troops. It did the trick. The weather, which had been hot and sticky the day before, was now pleasantly warm; the cramped, dirty resthouse seemed cosy and informal. And the thought of another day cooped up inside the Morris became the keen anticipation of all the new sights, smells and sounds they would experience between here and their next stop at Koumra.

Back on the main road, the mud rapidly dried under the hot sun. It was bumpy, but by midday the danger of being bogged down had passed. Kabo, Mbo, Bonda: Peter ticked the villages off his list as, one after the other, they disappeared behind them. At Moyo they were flagged down.

'What's all this about, then?' Alan asked, easing his foot off the accelerator.

'Lucky mongoose,' a thin youth called in through the window. 'You buy?'

'Is the price lucky?' Alan asked.

'Very very,' came the reply. 'One for twenty. Two for thirty and packet of cigarettes.'

'A bargain indeed,' Alan said and, despite the increasingly anguished noises Freda was emitting, he opted to buy the pair.

'You look after, for good luck,' the youth said as he

handed Alan the two bamboo constructions – half cage, half basket.

'I shall, I shall,' he assured him, putting them in the back.

'I just hope they don't escape,' said Freda, glancing round nervously at the agile little animals leaping around their baskets. 'Peter, you wouldn't mind changing places, would you?'

With Barbara and Peter sitting on the back seat, trying to stroke the animals through the bars without getting nipped, and Freda in the front, as far away from the vermin as she could get, Alan set off again.

'I've always liked mongeese,' said Peter.

'Mongooses,' Barbara corrected him.

'But it's goose – geese,' he argued.

'I know that,' she said, 'but the plural of mongoose is mongooses.'

'You're sure it's not mongice?' Alan called back. 'Like mouse – mice.'

'No,' said Barbara, laughing. 'It's like moose, not mouse. One moose, two mooses.'

'Ah, now there I will have to disagree,' Alan said. 'I know for a fact that the plural of moose is meece!'

They arrived in Fort Archambault at midday. As in any French town, the shops were shut and would remain so until three o'clock. Walking along the shady main avenue, lined with plane trees and giant poinsettias, they could have been in the south of France. The cafés and restaurants all had forecourts where people would sit to eat a long leisurely lunch under massive sunshades. Red- and white-striped awnings kept elaborate window displays cool.

The very *Frenchness* of this distant African outpost was a necessary outcome of the French form of colonization, quite different from the British variety. The latter would settle in a country but remain separate from the indigenous population. They would govern from their small pockets of expat security, knowing that until independence came they would control the entire country. In contrast, those living in areas that France colonized automatically became a part of *la plus grande France*. The concept of independence was seldom even entertained. You can resign from a club, but not from a family.

For this reason the overall effect of colonization by the French was often far more pervasive. Their culture permeated the everyday life of ordinary citizens – wine, Camembert, language, pastis and boules – while, in contrast, British influence seldom extended beyond the exclusive clubs they established in the cooler highlands of those countries they occupied.

The food, the wine, the language, all of these Alan could appreciate. The one aspect of French life he could not tolerate was the interminable lunch break. Less than an hour had passed before he was anxiously shepherding the others on to the road again.

'Long way to go yet,' he said, clapping his hands together.

It was with obvious reluctance that the others finished their tangerine juice and traipsed back to the car.

As they continued north-westwards the temperature rose and the view changed. Leaving the fetid emerald rainforests behind them, they drove into scrubby savannah: 'typical lion country', Peter wrote. They hadn't seen any wild animals since leaving Uganda and game-spotting became that Monday afternoon's way of passing the time.

By the time they arrived in Koumra, Freda had won with her sighting of a single, nondescript buck. What they had seen, however, were more dancing children.

The first group were boys, aged between twelve and seventeen. The dance was part of the complicated circumcision ceremony which marked the shift from adolescence to adulthood. The ritual was performed only ten times a year, according to the moons. On those particular nights – the third after the New Moon – the boys would dance and sing from the afternoon through to the following morning. Due to the infrequency of the ceremony, it was one seldom captured on film.

'Let's stop,' Peter said.

'I am,' Alan replied.

As soon as the boys noticed the cameras they started shouting and gesticulating. Despite their lack of either English or French, it was quite clear what they were saying. Freda backed away nervously.

'Ignore them,' said Alan, and raised the camera to his eye. Peter and Barbara followed suit.

Instantly, the boys stopped shouting and instead formed a silent circle around the car and the four travellers. The sight of those hostile, sullen faces proved too much, even for Alan; the four of them conceded defeat and withdrew.

Peter had managed to get three photos. It took me a while to work out what I was actually looking at.

Apart from the loincloths and bangles, each of the youths was wearing an intricate headdress. Made of raffia and grass, it consisted of three parts. At the top, a crest of spiky grass stood up like a lion's mane. Below this a thick bundle of raffia, fashioned into a crude hat, completely concealed their faces. From the back and sides of this hat long strands formed a swaying curtain of grass.

It was not only their costume that marked them out; the ritual also defined the posture they should assume. Each of the boys carried a 12-inch stick, which they used to lean on as their shuffle-dance continued. Due to the shortness of the sticks, the boys were forced to bend double, and the long grass down their backs reached to below the knees.

As the travellers drove away, Peter turned round for a final glimpse of the dancing boys. The lasting image he was left with was strange. 'All together in a line, they looked like a huge hairy animal supported on loads of spindly legs.'

They arrived at Koumra before dark and found that the resthouse was much cleaner and more comfortable than usual. A better end to a better day.

After dinner, Alan asked if anyone had noticed anything as they had driven in to town. Peter had of course. He'd already entered it in his diary: 'many small huts had drawings on their whitewashed mud huts'.

'The last time I came this way they did that,' Alan said as he pulled an old photograph out of his wallet.

'The Morris,' Peter exclaimed as he saw it.

'The old one,' Alan said, nodding.

Apart from the fact that the wheels had been attached to the ends rather than the sides of the vehicle, the drawing on the side of the hut was a fairly faithful reproduction of the car Alan had used to cross Africa in 1933.

'So was it very different twenty-two years ago?' Peter asked.

'The crossing? Not really. Of course, it was just Walshy and me then, so we didn't go in for all this comfort.'

'Comfort?' Freda exclaimed. 'Where?'

Alan laughed.

'We had very little with us at all. Some clothes and a couple of blankets. No camping equipment, but then we did have a few people we could stay with on the way.'

'Who was that?'

'Oh, friends of the family. Friends of friends. The good thing about it was that the two of us could do long spells of driving – cover vast distances – and then be able to relax for a couple of days and get everything washed and cleaned.'

'And how was the Sahara?' Freda asked.

'Very well, thanks,' Alan replied with a grin.

Freda blushed.

'The Sahara,' Alan said, thinking back. 'Hot and sandy. We crossed the main part in one of those bursts of driving. It was the end of February, I think, and damned cold at night. So we took it in turns to sleep and just kept on moving.'

'But no problems?' Freda persisted.

'Not really, no,' he said. 'But we went a different way then. Much farther to the west, through Gao and Reggan. It's all right, but a bit boring – just mile after mile of hard, flat sand. The route we're taking this time should be much more impressive.'

Freda leant back, content. She had always wanted to see the starry night sky of the Sahara, and there was something so reassuringly bluff about the way Alan spoke: she felt utterly safe in his hands.

'Of course, the best place we visited was Timbuktu. Amazing. Markets, bazaars, caravans of camels – absolutely enchanting. It's a shame we can't spare the time to visit it this time.'

Peter was still scrutinizing the photograph. He was looking puzzled.

'I thought there were only two of you in the car,' he said finally.

'That's right.'

'But they've drawn three people,' he said.

Alan burst out laughing.

'That was Kingston,' he said.

'Kingston?'

'Our chimpanzee. I'd quite forgotten.'

'You crossed the Sahara in a Morris Minor with a chimpanzee!' Peter repeated incredulously.

154

'I wonder what happened to him?' Alan said. 'I think Walshy might have sold him in Paris. I'm not sure. I know we weren't allowed to take him all the way to England.'

'Was he in a cage?' Freda asked.

'No, we just let him play around in the back of the car,' Alan said. 'Absolute rascal though. He'd undo the water containers and empty them, knock over the candles, break things, lose things, drop things out of the window.

'Yes, I knew I'd miss Kingston on this trip,' he said, his face set in an expression of mock seriousness. 'That's why I decided to bring Peter along,' he added, and roared with laughter all over again.

The following morning, Peter's diary started off with an entry about more dancers and, I had to admit, I was getting a bit confused with all their encounters with dancing children.

A brief recap showed that they had stopped to watch and photograph traditional dances on eight separate occasions. Each had been different. Each had been characterized by specific costumes, instruments, music and movements according to whether the inspiration behind the dance had been circumcision, fertility, harvest, climate or the buying of wives. For the four travellers, the only feature they shared in common was the fact that they all seemed to turn nasty.

On one occasion, the old woman in charge of a group of dancing girls had become livid. She was insulted either by the insufficient amount Alan had given her, or by the fact that he had offered her money at all – whatever the case, she chased after the car shaking her fist at them furiously. On this particular Tuesday morning, the dancing boys had threatened their houseboy that if the travellers didn't cough up generously enough, he would be in trouble. It had ended up with the four of them leaping into the Morris and making a hasty getaway.

Without specifying, I asked Peter what he remembered about the dancing boys or girls.

'We arrived at this very primitive and remote village in a clearing in the middle of the forest,' he began. 'Quite a large village – a lot of people.

'Well, every now and then they go through their ceremonies. I don't know whether it's every six months, or every year, but anyway, they have a ceremony where they marry off all the young maidens. I don't remember whether it was that evening or the next morning, but at one time or another the maidens were all being paraded.

'I'm not sure whether it was for us or not. But assuming the maidens were all being paraded for us – well, basically they were of any age from about thirteen years to about seventeen years, as far as I could see. Completely naked, except for a small loincloth – down below – and, of course, quite a lot of beads. And they were put on show; about ten or fifteen of them. The idea was that eligible men would come along and possibly take their pick and pay the bride-price – and that would be that.

'The villagers seemed to understand we were going to England and they thought it would be a good idea if we were to take one of them. She'd go off with us, and look after us, and be trained as a maid. And eventually, she'd make her fortune in the UK, come back and make them all rich.

'So, there was a bit of pressure put on us to take one of them with us. And we kept saying that there was no room – but they wouldn't accept that. The men were arguing with us.

'We went to bed in this pretty primitive government resthouse, and in the morning the arguments got a little fiercer. The women were on parade again and we took a few photographs and things seemed to get out of hand!

'There were a lot of men – I mean a couple of hundred, and they started shouting and saying, "You've got to take her" and things to that effect. And quite a lot of them were armed with bows and arrows . . . and spears.

'Alan Cooper said he didn't like it. He told us to get in the car while he pretended to bargain. I sat revving the engine, ready. All of a sudden, Alan dashed across and leapt into the passenger seat and we sped off; with a crowd of very angry villagers – and actually very angry girls – chasing us.

'They actually went for us. And we were very glad to get out of what could have been a very ugly situation.'

I liked the way Peter told the story. It was engaging and evoked the menace far better than the written account. It was also completely inaccurate.

Returning to his diary, I discovered that he had merged several of the separate incidents together. Clearly, it was not the first time Peter had recounted the tale, and with each successive telling extraneous details had been omitted, until the current honed-down version had arisen. In the end it had become an immutable after-dinner anecdote.

As part of this definitive account had been borrowed from an incident with dancing *boys*, I asked Peter if he remembered seeing any at all. He paused for a long while.

'Yes, I do . . . a circumcision rite, I think it was.'

I nodded.

Human memory is notoriously selective. I found with both Peter and Barbara that they remembered what they remembered, but despite prompting, almost nothing more. That is, through their repeated recounting of the event over the years, certain aspects of the trek had become fixed – some accurately, some less so. Furthermore, the more I pressed them for confirmation of small factual details I found in their diaries and letters, the more I discovered that what they had remembered was at the expense of all they had forgotten.

Without the written accounts they made at the time, I could never have pieced together the entire episode accurately. On the other hand, without the anecdotal fictions Peter and Barbara have both created, the story would never have come to life.

SIXTEEN

A CHAPTER OF ACCIDENTS

IF Alan's breaking of the *mchanga* that he'd been given by his cook signified ill-fortune, if the coincidence of the hapless Captain Lancaster's time of death was a warning omen, then the disappearance of one of the mongooses should have concerned the four travellers. There is no point having lucky mascots if they are not looked after.

'Well, who left the top open?' Alan asked.

No one owned up.

'It didn't even have a name,' said Peter. He slipped Alan's gloves on as protection against nipping and picked up the remaining mongoose. 'It's not going to happen again. You,' he announced to the squirming bundle of fur, 'are Rikki.'

'After Kipling?' Freda asked.

Peter nodded.

'Did you know the best-selling saucy seaside postcard is about Kipling?' Alan said. 'Man to attractive woman: "Do you like Kipling?"; woman to man: "I don't know, I've never kipled." Ta-da! Lazangennermen, I thangyou!'

Alan could always be depended on to brighten the atmosphere and raise morale, but with superstitions – if indeed they counted for anything – he was powerless.

That Tuesday was punctuated by a succession of accidents and mishaps.

They left Koumra at 8.30 and headed for Bongor, a town near the Cameroons border. It was a relatively modest 202-mile drive and, despite the loss of their mascot, they set off in good spirits. In his diary, Peter noted seeing a turkey buzzard (or ground hornbill), 'with its colossal, long black beak' – the charlatan whose night-call people mistake for lions. A while later they stopped to observe a hoopoe, a rare black, white and beige bird with its distinctive crest. Without a word of dissent, Alan even pulled up for Barbara to collect some seeds from a yellow dahlia-like plant she didn't recognize and wanted to grow back in Kenya.

'The road seems a lot better than yesterday,' Peter commented.

'Not too bad at all,' Alan agreed, 'even though it is sandier.'

A moment later a tell-tale jolt and swerve announced their first puncture. They were ten miles short of Mourongoulaye. Having covered some 2,300 miles since leaving Alan's farm without needing to change a wheel, they hadn't done badly. All the same, it was a nuisance. Any technical problem undermines the feeling of invulnerability a car gives its occupants, and this particular breakdown was to reinforce Barbara's and Peter's fears that they were ill-equipped for the desert. Even those few tools that Alan had brought proved inadequate.

'This is hopeless, Peter said, as the jack sank deeper into the soft sand.

'We'll put it on a base,' Alan said.

'What kind of base?' Barbara asked.

'Oh, we'll improvise.'

She knew she ought to bite her tongue and keep quiet, but she simply couldn't. It was so typically irresponsible of the man. 'We shouldn't need to improvise,' she said. 'What use to us is a jack which we can't use on sand? What were you planning on improvising with in the Sahara?'

Alan picked up a couple of broad pieces of wood and placed them underneath. This time, as Peter cranked up the car, the jack remained rigidly in place.

'You worry too much,' Alan said to Barbara quietly.

When the car was fully raised, he removed the hub-cap and began loosening the bolts. The third one was tight, and as he wrenched the spanner to the left the jack slipped and the car sank back into the sand. It was only the mudguard that prevented the axle being buried.

Barbara folded her arms and walked away a couple of paces. If she were ever as careless with her aeroplane . . .

'Right, let's try again,' Alan said, as he slid the jack into position.

The wheel did finally get changed, but it took the best part of two hours before they were ready to set off once more. Peter and Alan were hot and sweaty. Barbara was angry and sweaty. Freda was none of these. A pattern had been established at this minor breakdown which was to be repeated throughout the rest of the trek. Whenever anything happened, Freda would remain curiously detached. If asked, she would help out, but otherwise she would retreat into herself and wait patiently until the crisis had passed.

By lunchtime the temperature was over 110 degrees. The road had been following the river Logone for some time and as they continued driving, all four of them looked longingly to their left at the cool, clear, deliciously inviting water.

'Let's stop and eat next to the river,' Freda said.

'I've got a better idea,' Alan said, 'let's stop and eat *in* the river.'

And that is precisely what they did. There is a

photograph in the album to prove it. Taken by Barbara, it shows Peter, Alan and Freda sitting fully dressed in the shallows, eating from plates. In case anyone might wonder what they are doing, Peter had annotated the photo: 'We lunch in the river because of the heat in Fr. Eq. Africa.'

What the album does not show is the fact that, immediately after lunch, all four of them were to get hotter and stickier than they had been all day. While they were cooling down, the car was sinking into the soft riverbank. They had to unpack everything from the back, push the car up on to the firmer gravel and then hump all the luggage over to where it was parked 200 yards away.

'That was exhausting,' said Peter, as they finally closed the back doors. 'It is so hot.'

'We must remember not to drive on to sand like that again,' Barbara said.

'Oh, we will, we will,' said Peter. 'I, for one, don't intend to let pushing the car become a habit.'

Usually, once they were motoring, the breeze they created would keep them cool. This afternoon was different. They found themselves driving along a grass-fire for mile after mile after mile. Sometimes it was a sheet of white flame that roared up into the air, licking menacingly at the passing Morris and bumping up the temperature in the car viciously. At other times, the flames subsided and the grass smouldered. Then thick pungent smoke would drift across the road, forcing them to keep the windows closed. Flames or smoke – it made no difference. Either way, they were bound to remain hot, sweaty and uncomfortable.

Shortly before their destination, Alan noticed a settlement off the road to their left. It was the ancient town of Kim. Built on a yellow treeless plain, it was a bizarre collection of tall round mud houses with conical matted roofs, all enclosed by a thick dark wall. Windowless, cramped, with gaping black doorways, the buildings shimmered in the sun like a cluster of jostling blind beggars.

'It's eerie,' said Freda.

'I don't like it,' said Peter. 'It's all . . . I don't know, sort of squashed up and . . .'

'Claustrophobic,' Alan offered, looking at the buildings.

The bang that followed – the worst so far – occurred where the Kim road met their own. In the wet season, heavy rain had turned the small track into a river, eroding the surface and gouging a deep trough out of the main road it crossed. As the Morris fell into the gully and bounced out the other side, all four occupants and every single object were thrown about. Luckily, the loud crashing noise was not caused by any important part of the car breaking but by the chop-box thumping back down. The shock of the accident, coupled with the relief that it hadn't been too serious, brought a ripple of nervous laughter. In the back, Peter and Freda pushed the bits of stray luggage behind them.

'Ooh, quite shook me up,' said Freda.

Alan turned and looked at her. 'I knew there was a northern lass lurking somewhere beneath that schoolma'am exterior,' he said, and laughed as Freda turned pink.

The dips and holes in the road increased, and the average speed dropped. A distant blur of dust gradually revealed itself as an approaching Connaught diesel bus.

'Good afternoon,' the driver called over.

'Afternoon,' Alan replied. 'You're English.'

'You too. Where are you heading?'

News was swapped and it transpired that the party of three – two men and a woman – had just crossed the Sahara along the route Alan was planning to take. They said that the desert had been 'fair going', but pointed out that their bus was suited to the tough conditions, whereas the Morris . . .

Everyone was quiet as they drove off. Alan was incensed that someone should have the audacity to lecture him about the desert – HIM! – hadn't he crossed it before? Hadn't he been the first man to drive across with a mere 8 h.p. engine?

Peter and Barbara considered the day's incidents: getting a puncture, being stuck in the sand, crashing down into gully: how much worse it would all have been in the middle of the desert. At this time of year the Sahara would be as hot as the grassfire had been – and not just for a short stretch, but for the entire 2,324 miles between Kano and Algiers. Peter automatically turned round and stroked their mascot. Rikki was already becoming as tame and playful as a kitten.

'Soon be able to let him out of the basket,' he said.

Freda shuddered.

Driving into Bongor, they saw their first dancing *men*. Naked, apart from skimpy black loincloths, they each had a white cloth flapping at the back and glowing in the dusk like a rabbit's scut. As the travellers passed by they turned back to look at the dancers' grotesquely painted faces: skulls, wild dogs, devils' masks.

'They must have known we were coming,' Alan commented, as he always did when they arrived at a new place where something out of the ordinary was taking place.

They stopped for aperitifs at a café where Europeans were drinking on the veranda. The establishment was run by a French woman and her daughter who explained that the men still filing past would be dancing at the local carnival later that night. There was something disconcerting about the sight of them all dressed up for saturnalian festivities, simply ambling along the street. It was like seeing a clown on a bus, or the cast of a pantomime having a pre-show pint.

'I wonder what's on the menu,' Freda said. 'I adore French food.'

'None of that,' Alan said. 'I've already decided that Peter and I will prepare tonight's little feast. We'll show you *cordon bleu*.'

On reaching the resthouse, Alan and Peter disappeared into the dirty kitchen, and an hour later the two women, who had been trying to instil some order to their luggage, were summoned to the table.

'If only I knew the French for all the courses,' Alan teased. 'It's the only way to impress Mademoiselle Tayleur.'

'I love potted shrimps in any language,' Freda assured him as she dug into her starter.

The main course consisted of lobster, asparagus and new potatoes, and although everyone was full, a dessert of pears and cream completed the banquet. The whole lot was accompanied by generous glasses of red wine from the gallon flagon they'd bought along the way.

'Fit for a king,' Alan said and patted his stomach lovingly.

'I'll do the washing up,' Freda said, collecting up the plates.

'No, no, no, I wouldn't hear of it. Anyway,' he added and laughed, 'it won't take us a minute to throw all those tins away!'

It was quiet when the men returned to the main room. Barbara was sitting on a chair, bent over the latest instalment of the letter she was writing to her friend Mavis. Freda was sitting on a blanket on the floor, legs folded to one side, evidently lost in her own thoughts. She was smoking and, as she exhaled, she made a circle of her lips and puffed little smoke rings into the air which she then speared with the glowing tip of her cigarette.

Occasionally she would notice something out of the corner of her eye and brush at it absent-mindedly. It was this gesture that Alan immediately seized on. He motioned to Peter to keep still and the pair of them stood watching. Unaware of her audience, Freda continued to smoke, continued to blow rings, continued to flap her hands at the obstinate little insect in the middle of the blanket.

Peter began to snigger.

'Ssshh!' Alan hissed, trying his best to stop himself from laughing.

Barbara looked up and Peter pointed to the blanket. She saw what was happening immediately and had to smother her own giggles.

It was when Freda finally lost the patience with the bug and slammed her shoe down on it that the other three lost all self-control and howled with laughter. Shocked by the sudden outburst of noise, Freda looked round at the three faces convulsed with amusement.

She smiled. 'What is it?'

None of them could answer. Alan mimed the splattering of the insect. Peter tried an explanation, but collapsed laughing again, clutching his aching sides. In the end it was Barbara who leant forward and picked up the shoe. With tears running down her face and unable to speak, she merely pointed.

'She's seeing them everywhere,' Alan spluttered. 'Insects galore, and all out to get Freda.'

Freda looked down. The cockroach she had attempted to crush wasn't a cockroach at all. She'd been shooing away at and finally attacked a small hole in the blanket.

'It wasn't that funny,' she sniffed.

'Oh, but it was,' came the reply. 'It was.'

Peter was the first up the following morning. Sleeping on the veranda had been cooler during the night, but as the sun had risen the burning dazzle had woken him. It was well over 100 degrees by seven o'clock.

By eight, the other three were also up and dressed. Even if they had wanted a lie-in, the heat made it quite impossible. Alan drove down to the local garage to have the punctured tyre mended. Freda and Barbara washed out some clothes. Peter sat and played with Rikki, wondering whether their mascot would bring them better luck today.

They intended to get to Maiduguri by nightfall. It was a 228-mile trip and would take them out of French Equatorial Africa, through the Cameroons, and into Britain's most significant West African colony: Nigeria.

Alan returned, hot and irritated.

'The garage can't do the tyre,' he said. 'No ruddy tools.'

Peter put Rikki back in his basket. He didn't like the idea of travelling without a spare tyre. But if the garage was without the necessary equipment, they had no option. If only Alan had given as much thought to the toolbox as he obviously had to the 'choc-box'.

They set off at 10.30, and crossed the border into the Cameroons – a long, thin country, or collection of countries – before midday. The route they were following would take them across a narrow strip in the north. Their time in the Cameroons was to be so brief that Freda hadn't even included it in the list of countries she had painted on the back of the Morris. Fate, however, was to allot a significance to the place quite disproportionate to the time they would spend there.

As Peter wrote in his diary: 'this was the country where disaster struck'.

SEVENTEEN

OUT OF LUCK

IT has been said that present-day Cameroun is the most artificial country in Africa. It comprises over 130 different ethnic groups – a lack of homogeneity which was both exacerbated and exploited by the European colonialists.

The country was discovered and named by the Portuguese in 1472. Legend has it that those first sailors to land were so surprised by the size, quantity and quality of the giant prawns they encountered off the coast that they proclaimed loudly and excitedly: 'camarõs, camarõs.' The Cameroons were born.

Apart from the coastal area which was plundered by slave traders, the rest of the country remained untouched until the arrival of the Germans in the late nineteenth century. They wrested the land from the influence of Nigeria (then called Sokoto) and established plantations of palm oil, cocoa and banana.

The League of Nations took the country away from the Germans in 1919 and divided it between the French, who received 80 per cent of it, and the British, who acquired two smaller, separated regions. In 1961 there was a referendum in the two British areas. The southern region rejoined with the newly independent French-speaking majority. The north decided to become a part of its western neighbour, Nigeria. By 1955, when the travellers passed through, the country already resembled what it would officially become after independence.

The dips and hollows which had made driving in French Equatorial Africa so hazardous were even worse in the Cameroons. Rather than the occasional eroded gully, Alan now had to contend with driving across wide dry river beds. These wadis, or oueds, were treacherous.

'If they were totally dried out, they'd be OK,' Alan explained, 'but sometimes you find yourself in a wet area and the car just sinks. You can't afford to lose concentration for a second.'

'Isn't the wet sand darker?' Peter asked.

'Yes, it is, but a thin, dry crust forms over those bits, so you can't always see them. Oops, here we go again,' he said, as they reached the steep bank of the third wadi in as many miles.

They slid down the incline and sped across the sandy bottom as fast as the pitted surface would allow. At the far side, the wheels spun powerlessly for a couple of nerve-jangling seconds, before gripping and pulling the car up the steep bank. The whole process was painfully slow. In his diary, Peter wrote, 'so far in the last two hours we have only managed to cover 15 miles.'

'Good practice for the Sahara, anyway,' Alan sighed. His average speed was being shot to pieces by the appalling roads.

Maroua was the only town of any size in the north of the Cameroons. They passed street stalls selling bags of leather, snake and crocodile skin. Freda wanted to stop, but Alan was insistent.

'We've lost too much time already.'

She did not argue. The roads were always better on the outskirts of towns and Alan was able to put his foot down. When the accident happened they were driving along at a comfortable and relatively smooth 40 miles an hour. There was no warning. No one saw the rock. No one shouted. The surprise element of the incident is best summed up by Peter's diary entry: 'large rock bounced up'.

The grinding crunch and squeal of stone on metal was unmistakable. Everyone fell silent, wondering what damage might have been done to the car. Alan lifted his foot off the accelerator slightly, but did not stop.

'Seems all right,' he said, after a while.

'Don't you think we should have a look?' Barbara said.

'It's probably just dented the exhaust a bit,' Alan said, and continued.

This was the worst possible decision he could have made and, though they didn't yet realize, it signified the beginning of all their troubles. When the green light on the dashboard began to flash a couple of miles further on, they discovered that it wasn't the exhaust pipe that the rock had damaged; it was the sump. A hole had been ripped into the bottom and all the oil had drained out.

'This is disastrous,' said Barbara, as they all stood around the car. A thin broken line of the last dregs of oil was traced into the sand behind them.

Barbara was seething, and inwardly cursed the arrogant stupidity of the man. Not that she blamed him for hitting the rock – that could have happened to anyone – but to refuse to stop and check for damage was unforgivable. What was more, she was angry with herself for not insisting. Barbara was an independent, self-reliant woman, accustomed to being in control; it was proving difficult on the trek to strike that balance between compliance and defiance.

'Idiot!' she muttered, and walked away from the crippled car. Otherwise she would say something worse, something she might later regret.

'What do we do now?' Peter was asking.

'Bung up the hole first,' Alan said, rummaging through the back. 'This should do the trick,' he added, pulling out a tube of Bostik.

'Are you sure?'

'Sure I'm sure,' he said and slithered under the car.

The others sat down on the bank and waited. There was no traffic. In fact, when they thought over the day, they realized they hadn't seen a single vehicle since leaving the resthouse. Alan plugged the hole as best he could, but they wouldn't be able to find out whether it leaked or not until they refilled the sump with oil, and they didn't have any.

Quarter of an hour passed. Half an hour. Everyone was becoming increasingly restless.

'Peter, do you fancy walking back to Maroua for some?' Alan asked. 'It's not that far. Otherwise we could be sitting here all day.'

Peter nodded. He was the type of person who hated inactivity. If there was a problem, he would always prefer to try and solve it, rather than simply sit around waiting for something to happen.

A large lorry driven by an English-speaking Nigerian pulled up beside them as he was about to set off.

'You need help?'

Alan explained.

'You're in luck,' the driver said, and he let them have a spare gallon of oil he was carrying.

Thank-yous completed, they went their separate ways. The driver had suggested that he accompany them back to Maroua, where they could get the car mended properly. But, for various reasons, they decided against it. For one thing, they were unlikely to find spares for the English Morris in a French colony. It was also considerably more expensive. All the same, the main reason for continuing was the psychological harm it would do to morale, having to retrace their steps at this stage.

With the engine knocking ominously, they carried on. It was a nightmare journey. The rocky terrain they were passing through reflected the sun back on to the car, blinding its occupants and intensifying the heat. In addition, the number of wadis increased. Everyone held their breath each time they crossed another stretch of the treacherous wet sand.

It was dark by the time they got to the border with Nigeria. The soldiers laughed at their complaints about the roads and assured them that they would soon improve. No one was sorry to see the back of the Cameroons.

The roads in Nigeria were better, but it was by now far too late to reach Maiduguri. The knocking in the engine had grown worse, slowing them down and putting them all on edge.

'There's a resthouse at Bama,' Peter said, checking down the AA list. 'It's about ten miles from here.'

To everyone's relief, Alan made no attempt to convince them they should press on further.

'Let's hope they have a shower,' was all he said.

'It'll be all right when we get to Maiduguri,' Alan had promised, and it was these words Peter repeated to himself over and over again as he drifted off to sleep.

As had become usual, the two men had put up their beds on the veranda. It was cooler, fresher there, with a light breeze blowing. When later the wind got up, it sent the hurricane lamp banging into the mud walls. The dull thud, regular as a metronome, permeated Peter's dreams as the ominous knocking of the damaged engine. Even asleep, it was Alan's words which calmed him down: 'It'll be all right in Maiduguri; it'll be all right.'

If their first hour there was anything to go by, Alan's

172

prediction would be correct. Maiduguri was all right. They arrived at lunchtime, following a nerve-racking 40-mile drive during which the engine had knocked continuously.

'Do you know the way to the resthouse?' Alan asked a third person as they drove along the main street.

As on his previous two attempts, the question prompted an immediate crowd to assemble. Everyone there would shout, gesticulate, point this way, that way, until a consensus was finally reached. The person would turn back to Alan and sheepishly admit that he didn't know.

'Hey, what about him?' Peter said.

Alan leapt out of the car and ran over to where a European was getting into a Buick. A Union Jack fluttering patriotically on the bonnet suggested that the man was important: it transpired that he was the local British Resident – an appointed civil servant directly answerable to the Secretary of State for the Colonies in London. Not only did the man take them to the resthouse, he also invited them to become temporary members at the local club.

'Make your stay a little more tolerable,' he said, and guffawed loudly.

'We don't intend being here more than a couple of days,' Alan said.

'You never can tell,' the Resident replied. 'Never can tell.'

The resthouse was the best they had stayed in so far. It was of the catering type typical of Nigeria: each person paid one pound, for which they received food and accommodation. For Peter, there was something far more welcome than either the bath, the vegetable garden or the servant - 'at last, a roof fan!'

While the others were unpacking, Alan drove the car down to the garage. Brian Walker, originally from Derby, soon diagnosed the problem.

'You've run the big end,' he explained. 'The bearing shells have gone – they'll have to be replaced. Do you want to hear the good news or the bad?'

'The good news,' Alan said.

'Only number three cylinder is really damaged. The others are OK.'

'And the bad news?'

'We haven't got the parts here. Have to wire Kano and get them to send them down on the plane.'

'When's the next one due?'

'Not until Sunday, I'm afraid.'

Three more days. Alan could feel his forehead prickling with apprehension as he realized how critical the timing of the trip was becoming. The desert road was closed to vehicles from the 15 May, due to the intolerable heat. Sunday was the first. If they were delayed much more, they would have to abandon any hope of crossing the Sahara. But that was the worst-possible scenario that Alan wouldn't even let himself consider.

'Sunday,' he repeated. 'Wire away!'

Alan's acceptance of the situation was merely a cover. He was becoming more and more concerned about the problem of actually getting into the Sahara. Aware that, in an attempt to cut the cost of rescuing stranded vehicles, the French had recently tightened up their controls on whom to allow into the desert, Alan couldn't help thinking about the Morris. An obviously damaged big end was something he could do without. While the other three wandered round the market, went out for afternoon drinks, swam and played badminton at the club; while the others unwound, Alan went to bed with a fever.

For the first time, the travellers got to talk to people. Locals, expats, travellers like themselves: Peter's picture of Africa, previously so sketchy, began to acquire some colour, some shadow. He had drinks with the local

Resident, the Chief Justice and their wives; he
berated by a communist journalist; he chatted about th
differences between Derby and Maiduguri with Brian
Walker. The conversations ran the gamut of rational to
racist.

'You see, the thing is,' Walker said, 'independence is
inevitable. All we can ensure now is that it runs as
smoothly as possible'.

'Inevitable?' Peter said, thinking back to the chaos at
home in Kenya, where nothing seemed inevitable.

'Inevitable,' Walker repeated. 'The future is all a
matter of history,' he said.

The Nationalists were already on the move, he
explained. It had begun with the infamous Crossroads
Incident in the Gold Coast on 28 February 1948, where a
nervous British Inspector lost his head, grabbed a rifle
from one of his men and fired on a peaceful demonstration. Comparatively little blood was spilt, but it was
the first real sign that the British Colonialists were losing
their grip.

Nigeria was more of a problem. The West African geo-
graphical giant encompassed a diversity of cultures
which, in the twentieth century, had split itself roughly
into two. The north was predominantly Muslim, the
south was a mixture of Muslim and Christian. Although
this southern area was smaller, it was far more
advanced. In terms of how colonization had affected
them, the two regions also differed. In the north, the
British ruled by proxy with the compliance of the local
chiefs and kings, whereas in the south, British officials
had been forced into more direct contact with the people
they governed. The ironic result was that those in the
south were gradually becoming accustomed to a less
autocratic, more democratic form of government than
the north.

'So how?' Brian Walker said, 'how do you unite those

? Their needs, their experience, their
— they're so different.'

er end of the scale were the diehards. Those
e words of Cecil Rhodes imprinted on their
memory:

> I contend that we are the finest race in the world and that
> the more of the world we inhabit the better it is for the
> human race. Just fancy those parts that are at present
> inhabited by the most despicable specimens of human
> beings: what an alteration there would be if they were
> brought under Anglo-Saxon influence.

Finding an all-purpose definition for racism is
difficult. Rhodes' unequivocal words offer no problem,
neither do the various groups who have assumed a
similar dictum: the Nazi Party, the British Movement,
the Afrikaaner Weerstandsbeweging. But when there are
no badges, no uniforms, no flags, does this mean racism
is therefore also absent?

I met an old lady in Nairobi and we had tea together
in the Norfolk Hotel while I was waiting for Peter one
afternoon. She was a delightful person with white hair
and the weathered brown skin that only a lifetime in an
equatorial climate can bring. Evidently lonely - 'one has
so little opportunity to talk these days' – she reminisced
about her childhood, her late husband, her house on the
coast.

'Now,' she said, 'I am all alone.'

'You haven't got any servants?' I said naively.

'Oh yes,' she said. 'Wonderful band – though don't tell
them I told you,' she added in a conspiratorial stage
whisper.

'They've been with you a long time?'

'Years! Simply years. I've had Betsy for, oh, must be
getting on for . . . And she's such a clever woman.'

'Yes?' I said, wondering vaguely whether she had a degree or a career.

'Yes, she irons beautifully.'

By Saturday night they were all eager to press on. The desert was by now under 700 miles away, and Peter and Freda in particular were excited by the prospect of their first glimpse of rolling sand-dunes. Already, that morning, they had woken to find a curious haze in the sky which kept the heat of the sun at bay. Brian Walker had told them it was a sandstorm and the realization of how near the desert was made them all the keener to get there.

Alan was less tense than before. His temperature had returned to normal and he was waiting for the arrival of the aeroplane, due the following morning, with far more grace. They all went out for a drink to toast the successful crossing of the Sahara and returned feeling optimistic.

As Barbara and Freda were packing their bags, they heard an agonized squeal. It sounded like a baby, like a kitten – it was the mongoose.

'Rikki!' Peter said, cradling the animal gently.

Tame enough now to be allowed to run loose in their rooms, the inquisitive mongoose snooped round everything. It would jump into their bags, emerge from the bedding roll, scale the mosquito nets and wrestle with any object left lying around. Having been assured that mongooses were the best possible defence against snakes, even Freda had grown used to the kittenish antics of the playful animal.

Lying semi-paralysed in Peter's hands, it didn't look as if it would ever walk again. It had been standing in the doorway when a gust of wind had slammed the door shut. Rikki's hindquarters had been crushed.

'Should we put it out of its misery?' Peter asked.

'Leave it for a couple of days,' Barbara said. 'It doesn't seem to be in any pain, and it might gradually recover.'

Nobody mentioned it, but everyone was aware that their remaining lucky mascot had been injured. The further they travelled, the more superstitious they were becoming. What if the plane didn't come the following morning?

Alan went to bed early. He was still thinking about the state of the car: it needed a complete overhaul and that was simply impossible where they now were.

It'll be all right when we get to Kano, he thought.

EIGHTEEN

HANGING ON BY A THREAD

'I THINK the children are brighter here,' Freda said.

'Brighter than what?'

'Those children in Monga,' Freda said, 'don't you remember?'

Barbara certainly did remember. Wherever they had stayed, Freda the schoolma'am had taken it upon herself to determine the IQ of the children she encountered. When they surrounded her, clamouring for attention, she would employ specific techniques to grade them. While this was at least conceivable in the English-speaking areas, Freda would not let her methods be obstructed by mere language difficulties. Armed with a phrase book, she would take the children aside and pose the key questions. Her accent was atrocious and even when the children managed to decipher her tortuous French, she could not understand their replies. Nevertheless, she had come to the conclusion that the urchins of Monga were of particularly low intelligence.

'Definitely, much brighter.'

Barbara smiled. As the journey had progressed she had grown to like the Englishwoman. In her own quiet way, she was really quite eccentric. She had talked about her trips to Switzerland, to Rhodesia, to South Africa. On paper she appeared well travelled, but at no time had either adventure or uncertainty been included in her itinerary. It was the Thomas Cook package-type of holiday – the upmarket 1950s equivalent of two weeks in Tossa del Mar. She had been cosseted, cared for, kept in splendid isolation from her surroundings.

'This trip isn't at all what I imagined from Alan's advertisement,' she had confessed the previous evening. 'I've never camped before in my life.'

Freda was a very modest woman. Barbara remembered how one evening at the Mwenga Rest Camp, while she was rinsing out some clothes in the sink, she had suggested that Freda use the bath if she wanted. The prim lips had tightened, she had blushed, horrified at the thought and said that no, she could never do that. As Barbara noted, 'life must have been most difficult for her as we always shared a room'.

Yet despite the changes Alan had made to his original plans, Freda had decided to go ahead with the trek. It showed a willingness to experience life unusual in a thirty-eight-year-old brought up as she must have been, much less in the woman of fifty-five she actually was. Mrs Simpson confirmed that they would all have been more understanding of her idiosyncrasies had they known her real age.

As it was, throughout the trip, Freda was never in the best of health. She had sprained her ankle on Alan's farm before setting off and it had been bandaged up for the first ten days. The constant strain of early mornings and long days had led to her being almost permanently exhausted. By the time they reached Maiduguri, she had dysentery.

'I did warn them,' Mrs Simpson told me. 'It was on the ferry just before the Cameroons. Alan was thirsty, so he filled his bottle from the river. Madness! And Freda . . . I don't know if "crush" is the right word, but certainly she never wanted to appear a wet blanket in front of Alan, so she drank some of the water too. And of course they both paid the price. By and large, though, she enjoyed the trip,' she added. 'She'd come along largely for the glamour of crossing the desert, and she was eager as any of us to get the car fixed and continue. I remember how agitated she became when the aeroplane arrived on the Sunday without the spare parts we needed.'

'I just can't wait to lie out under the full moon in the Sahara,' she had said. 'Of course, there are so many more in the desert than elsewhere.'

'Well, perhaps you notice them more clearly, but there are the same number,' Barbara had replied.

'Oh no,' Freda had persisted. 'There are more full moons in the desert. It's a well-known fact.'

Barbara looked at her bemused. Never a hundred per cent sure to what extent Freda was being serious, she kept her thoughts to herself.

Once it was clear that the aeroplane had not brought the essential spare parts, Alan lost his temper completely. His face, initially white with impotent rage, turned red as anger found expression. He railed against the bloody roads, the bloody garage, the bloody imbeciles who worked there . . .

'Now what do we do?' he shouted furiously.

Brian Walker let him complete his tirade before making a suggestion.

'Of course, it won't be permanent,' he said, 'but it ought to get you to Kano.'

'I really haven't any other option,' Alan replied calmly. 'And please don't think I'm not extremely grateful to you.'

Walker's plan was to re-flash the two worn bearings with white metal, and then fit them back. With a bit of luck, the improvised engine should hold out until they reached a garage where they could get the car properly serviced. He was prepared to give up his Sunday to get the work started.

* * *

The Maiduguri market, which had already impressed the four travellers, was at its most gloriously hectic on Monday. Apart from the usual local traders, men and women would come in from distant villages, doubling the number of stalls. There was an area reserved for bread and sweet cakes, another for meat, another for fish – easy to locate by the tangy odour and the squeal of cat fights – and yet another for vegetables. Rather than use tables, most of the farmers kept their produce in sacks, which they would roll down with each successive sale, to ensure the continued appearance of overflowing abundance. Grains and pulses, small maroon onions and waxy red chillies, carrots, okra and yams: each were scooped from the hessian bags, weighed out on a hand-held spring-balance, and tipped into open shopping baskets. From preliminary haggling to payment in cash, the entire transaction took no more than seconds to complete.

Some stalls were out in the open, some enclosed by papyrus matting which protected more delicate wares from the windborne sand. You could buy almost anything – horse tackle and camel saddles, crocheted skullcaps and tasselled fezes, intricately patterned carpets and rugs, ivory bangles sold direct from a laden arm, embroidered cloths bearing Islamic inscriptions, combs, pipes, brooches, bells . . .

'And it was strange knowing that it had nothing to do with tourism,' Peter said. 'Nowadays half the produce in the markets is specially made for Europeans and Americans to take home with them as souvenirs. There was no tourism in Maiduguri then – apart from us.'

'Did you buy anything?' I asked him.

He pointed to a knife on the mantlepiece. It was an iron dagger in a snakeskin sheath.

'Took a lot of bargaining, that,' he said. 'Of course, you

could knock them down to a fraction of their original price and they'd still be making a tidy profit.'

There were other services. White-robed scribes, sitting on the ground in the shade of trees, wrote out legends and prayers in Arabic on specially carved handled tablets of wood. A young girl was kneeling in front of an old woman who was oiling, beading and plaiting her long hair; nearby, a man on a rickety stool was having his head shaved. At the well, the donkeys and camels which had carried the villagers and their merchandise into town were being watered.

Everywhere there was activity. Everywhere was the curious odour of dust and sour milk. Everywhere people were going about their business the way they had for centuries.

By three o'clock the car had been tested and declared 'satisfactory', if not a hundred per cent. Brian Walker warned them that it ought to be run in for fifty miles or so, and after that they would just have to hope that the pro tem measure would hold out.

They were off again and the desert, which had began to look increasingly far off, was now a mere stone's throw away. Alan took the first fifty miles slowly. A mile further and he began to accelerate. Everyone fell silent, either in expectation or dread. Peter was the first to speak.

'Seems fine,' he said.

'It does indeed.' Alan agreed as he put his foot down on the accelerator. He broke into a rendition of 'No Regrets', banging his chest for the authentic Piaf warble.

The others joined in, building up to a raucous cacophony of quavering Gallic phonemes. When the knocking started again no one heard it, and for a few seconds after that, it was ignored. No one could believe that the engine had gone again already. It simply wasn't fair.

Alan eased his foot from the pedal. The singing stopped. And they limped on to Potiskum, arriving there at dusk.

'Well, we made it,' Alan said cheerfully. 'Tomorrow Kano, and then we'll get her properly sorted out.'

The road the following day proved worse than expected. Although some parts were tarmac, long stretches of the unmetalled roads had dried out altogether in the pre-monsoon heat, leaving wide areas of soft sand. Only by driving in the compacted lorry tracks did Alan manage to avoid getting stuck.

The landscape began to take on the appearance of desert. Spirits were temporarily lifted when Barbara spotted their first date palms; when Peter pointed to their first camel caravans. Although the engine was still knocking, it didn't seem to be getting any worse. With the gradual increase in the number of villages, they knew they were approaching Kano itself and Alan called for 'Three Cheers for the Morris'. At six o'clock they drove through the crumbling walls of the city.

Maritime terminology does not stop at the camel being 'the ship of the desert'. Kano has been called a port on the southern shore of the Sahara. The allusion is revealing.

The desert was seen as something not only wild, but also impossible to tame. All the eleventh-century founders had been able to do was to build a wall round their city in an attempt to keep the waves of sand from swallowing it up. Caravans setting off across the desert on trading expeditions were like fleets of ships leaving Plymouth or Portsmouth, their riders as intrepid as the sailors who would also disappear over shimmering horizons into the unknown.

In 1955, the wall of the old city was falling down. The trucks which now crossed the sand so smoothly and unproblematically had deprived the desert of a degree of its notoriety. The feeling that the desert was lapping at the walls of the city, waiting to wash it away, had receded. A modern commercial centre had sprung up alongside the old quarter. Well placed geographically, Kano benefited from the new methods of transporting goods, and the life-blood of trade was pumping stronger than ever before.

The station resthouse was roughly furnished, but there was a bath with hot and cold running water, and Alan decided it would do. The fact that it was free was a welcome bonus.

It was dusk by the time they had unpacked. Ali, the houseboy, suggested a restaurant they might try. It was select (with prices to match) but after the long hot trying day, everyone felt like being pampered.

'I like it here,' Freda said firmly.

'So do I,' said Barbara, and the two women sat down. The red wine went straight to their heads. They became loud; they told jokes, they relived the ups and downs of the previous two and a half weeks – everyone agreed it seemed much longer – and Alan burst into another refrain of 'No Regrets'.

'Come on,' he said, 'let's see what the great metropolis of Kano has to offer.'

The labyrinth of tiny sandy streets was baffling. They were soon lost. Only a few of the buildings were two-storeyed, the rest shabby squat constructions with stalls, or 'dukas', clinging on to the walls like barnacles. Most of these dukas were shut, sealed off for the night with sheets of corrugated iron. One, however, was still doing business. A solitary oil lamp was hung outside the counter-window, casting a deep yellow halo around the tiny shack. Freda stopped for some cigarettes.

They passed a small, peeling cinema. The garish posters announced that *Johnny Dark* was showing.

'Look,' Alan said, 'three and nine a single, five bob for a double. We'll be two pairs, eh? What do you say, Freda?' he asked as he linked his arm through hers.

'It's already started,' Peter said.

'Oh well, in that case . . .'

Alan drove off. The wine, which had made them rowdy, was now making them drowsy. The streets continued to look identical to one another.

'I give up,' Alan suddenly declared. He slammed the brakes on, switched off the engine and began snoring loudly. Mildly hysterical, the others prodded him back into action and they were soon belting along again. Alan seemed to be working on the principle that the faster he drove, the faster they would get unlost.

It was during the cool evenings that the local population prepared their meals, cooking and eating in the narrow streets of the bazaar where there was at least the chance of a refreshing breeze. Careering round a corner, Alan found himself heading straight for a group of such people. They leapt up from their benches and jumped back. Alan managed to skid to a halt without hitting anyone or anything, but damage had nevertheless been done. Bottles had been upturned, pots and plates sent flying, one small child who had poured a bowlful of soup all down her front was howling with shock and indignation.

'Whoops!' Alan said, and ground the gears into reverse. The wheels spun and, as the angry men and women disappeared in a cloud of dust, the four travellers backed hastily away from what could have become a nasty situation.

They slept well that night, and while Alan took the car to the local garage the following morning, the others went round the stores, stocking up on provisions. By day Kano was quite different from the city they had got so lost in the previous night. They were able to orientate themselves by the tall white mosque, with its four sparkling minarets standing out against the cloudless blue sky.

Everything about the old buildings had been designed to minimize the searing heat of the sun. Thick walls of deep red-brown baked clay were decorated with painted swirls of cobalt blue and olive green. Doors and windows were mere apertures, tiny outside, larger inside, so that air but no dazzling sunlight could penetrate the cool rooms. Outside stairs led up to flat roofs surrounded by low parapets, punctuated every few feet with rounded protrusions which stood up, in Peter's words, 'like rabbits' ears'.

Test-driving the car round the backstreets of Kano, Alan and Peter passed massive pyramids of groundnuts.

'Seems all right, doesn't she?' Alan said.

'I don't think I'm going to say yes after what happened last time,' Peter said sheepishly.

'Better make sure you don't even think it, then,' Alan said with a grin.

As they headed back to the resthouse for the others they noticed a Land Rover, covered in flags, pennants and stickers announcing the fact that its driver was also about to cross the Sahara. Peter waved and Alan slowed down.

'Bonjour,' the man said.

'Hello.'

'Ah, English. And you also going north, across the desert. Perhaps we could travel together.'

Alan reacted badly, though far from untypically. Even Peter was surprised by the vehemence of his refusal and wrote in his diary: 'Mr C. rejected his offer rudely.'

Had nothing gone wrong in the desert, the Frenchman would probably never have given the incident another thought. As it was, their chance encounter was subsequently reported in the press. Under the headline,

I WARNED HIM, the *Daily Express* of 11 June 1955 reported their interview with the young Frenchman when he reached Algiers.

Said 29-year-old Antoine Laugel: 'I saw the Morris at Kano, in Nigeria, and asked Mr Cooper to join me in the desert crossing. He was rather short with me and told me he wanted to go alone.

'He said: "I know what I'm up to – I was the first driver to cross the Sahara in a light car in 1929 (sic)." So I dropped the idea.'

... 'If only we had gone together this would never have happened,' he said.

One hundred miles after Kano, the Morris drew up to the barrier which signalled the end of British Nigeria. They were about to enter the desertlands of French West Africa. It was the fifth day of the fifth month, nineteen fifty-five. They had covered 3,239 miles. It was their twenty-first day on the road.

PART THREE

THE DESERT

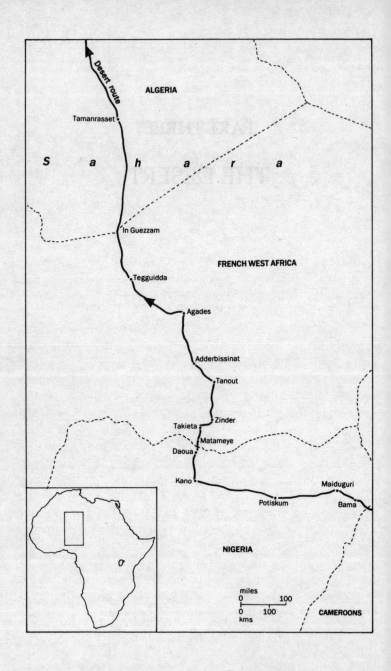

NINETEEN

INTO THE UNKNOWN

THE two constables in the border shack insisted on taking the details of the four travellers' passports. It would be highly irregular if anyone else were to interfere. Painstakingly slowly the first one copied Peter's name. MASTER PETER ROBERT BRUCE he wrote, and then stopped.

'But the surname,' Peter protested.

The policeman shrugged. The word at the end was smaller: it couldn't be as important. And, despite Freda's objections, MISS MURIEL FREDA followed.

'It doesn't matter,' Alan interrupted. 'Just leave them to get on with it and let's get back on the road.'

The land became increasingly barren. Scrubby thorn bushes and withered grass dotted the stony ground. Outcrops of rock cast rapidly lengthening shadows as the deep-orange sun sank down towards the horizon. No one was more aware of the hastening dusk than Barbara. The idea of setting up camp for the first time in the dark did not appeal to her. She shifted around in her seat, wishing one of the others would say something. Finally, she announced:

'I really think we ought to be stopping soon.'

'It'll be light enough to see for a while yet,' Alan said.

Barbara held her tongue, but she did wish they'd listen to the voice of experience.

Alan pulled up next to a small shrivelled wood and parked the car between conveniently sited thorn trees. With two beds on either side of the car, they were able to attach the mosquito nets to the roof rack at one end, and the stubby branches at the other. Freda and Barbara amassed a huge heap of sticks and started a fire. They discovered that the dry camel dung burnt well and gave off a remarkable amount of heat – and there was certainly plenty of it. Sausages were grilled over the hot embers.

'We'll probably get a caravan trundling over the beds later,' Peter said.

'Perhaps it'll be led by Freda's sheikh,' Alan said.

'Oh, you,' Freda murmured, smiling despite herself. She turned away and began busying herself with her lighted cigarette, exterminating the invading hordes of insects.

'It's all right,' Alan laughed, 'can't see if you're blushing or not in this light.'

Barbara shivered. 'I think it's going to be a cold night.'

Alan said, 'The nomads here say that the Sahara is a cold place where there's a hot sun!'

'I don't think anything could stop me sleeping tonight,' Freda said, yawning.

With no reason for them to stay up, the four travellers turned in before eight. Peter lay awake, listening to the multitude of unfamiliar sounds of the night. It was spooky. The almost-full moon cast weird steel-blue shadows through the twisted trees. Something howled. Something yelped. Something grunted.

Isn't this lion country? Peter wondered. He sat up and stared into the bright darkness. There was nothing there, but lying back down again, he couldn't rid himself of the feeling he was being watched.

'Alan,' he whispered, 'do you think there are any lions about?'

Peter, Alan and Freda at Rutoto Rest House, Uganda

A chicken for supper, but they had to kill it first

End of a day's journeying

Alan with the pygmies in the Congo

Clearing a roadblock by lopping off branches

Freda takes up drumming to urge the ferry on

Barbara and Alan and the onlookers wait while Peter checks tyre pressures in French Equatorial Africa

Waiting at the ferry for another vehicle

The mosque at Agades

Into the Sahara – too hot to travel

A party of Tuaregs

The last water supply at In Abangaret

Stuck in the sand for 5 hours 15 miles north of In Abangaret

Stuck again – Alan sets off on foot for help

The three remaining still try for In Guezzum

Rescuers from the French Foreign Legion

A hospital bed, 100°F in the shade

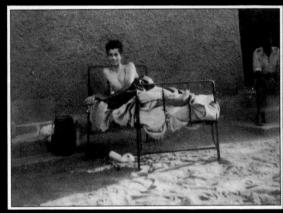

When the rain came, on returning to Kano

If there were, Alan clearly didn't care. His deep rhythmic breathing continued undisturbed.

Having slept better than anyone else, Alan was the first up the following day. He got the fire going and made tea, even though it was still dark. When the others stirred, the bitter cold ensured that they dressed quicker that morning than at any other time since leaving Alan's farm.

'I thought we could try and make it to Zinder for breakfast,' Alan said.

They had driven for three hours before they saw the French fort ahead of them. Square and solid, the fortress was nevertheless dwarfed by the jumbled mass of huge boulders from which it rose. It was not the only place where the might of the French military was undermined by the topography of the areas they controlled: Algeria, Chad, Vietnam – it was as much the hostility of the land as that of the people which brought about the end of direct French rule.

They pulled up at a hotel next to a small airstrip a couple of miles out of town.

'Do you think they'll still be serving breakfast?' Freda asked. 'It's ten o'clock.'

'We can but try,' said Alan.

Breakfast was indeed still being served, not because the proprietors were especially amenable but due to the fact that in crossing the border they had gone back another hour. It was now 9 a.m. Greenwich Mean Time.

'It's an odd thought,' Barbara mused, 'that while crossing the desert the time on our watches is going to be exactly the same as in . . . in, well, Beaconsfield,' she said, looking at Alan.

'Or Capenhurst,' Freda added. 'It all seems so very far away.'

'Like breakfast,' Alan said, impatiently checking his watch.

When it did arrive, Peter's diary entry summed up the general response: 'After 1 hour's wait had continental breakfast – coffee and bread. 30/- each! Exorbitant.'

The car was further weighed down by the time they set off again. The officers at the police post had informed them that they needed sufficient petrol to get them to Agadès, some 250 miles on. As the tank took only 6.5 gallons, they'd had to fill the two 4-gallon jerry-cans Alan had bought in Kano.

The extra pounds and ounces reduced the clearance still further. Increasingly, as they drove over the dips, gullies and corrugations of the road, they could feel the baked mud grazing the underside of the car. An additional hazard was the appearance of sand-filled, oblong hollows in the road. Apparently they were caused by camels cleaning themselves by rolling round and round in the earth, like a sparrow having a dustbath.

By lunchtime it was so hot that no one felt hungry. The travellers stopped briefly next to a rickety shelter and nibbled biscuits and mangoes. No one spoke. The unremitting intensity of the heat was surprising them all. It was like that initial blast when the oven door is opened, but the whole time.

Without stopping at Tanout, they continued until dusk. Once again, Peter's diary records the conflict about where and when to set up camp. 'Argument as to when to stop – Barbara wanted to before dusk, Alan wanted to go on. Mr C. got rather annoyed when Barbara persisted.'

The moon was full on this, their second night of camping out. After appearing above the horizon as a massive orange ball, it wobbled higher, solidifying and brightening as it rose, and by the time they were ready to eat their meal – celery soup, luncheon roll and bread – it was bright enough to see without the inspection lamp.

'There don't seem to be any mozzies here,' Alan commented.

'Too dry,' Barbara said.

There were, nonetheless, ants and spiders. The ants skitted everywhere, and although they didn't bite, no one liked the feeling of them running up their legs, over their hands, across their faces. They changed their mind about not bothering with the mosquito nets. Tying the strings from bush to bumper they found that the spiders had got there before them, suspending sticky filaments through the air which, as they walked through them, clung to their noses, their eyelashes, their ears, their hair. Freda stifled a scream: she was convinced that every thread she broke would herald the sudden arrival of an avenging arachnid the size of a saucer.

Peter was uneasy in his campbed again. He looked round in horror as the shadowy vegetation assumed the form of wild beasts. He had noticed rhino droppings earlier, and now the thorn bush to his left had been transformed into a huge male with a rapier horn, pawing the ground, ready to charge. To the right, a spindly acacia became a giraffe which would bow its head slightly as the wind blew past.

It's not a giraffe. It can't be, Peter told himself. And even if it is, they never harm anyone.

Despite this logical reassurance, Peter scarcely slept at all. It is difficult to remain rational when you are exhausted. The bright moon woke him at regular intervals throughout the night, and every time he was brought back to consciousness, he looked up to see whether the giraffe had moved.

It is impossible to describe the atmosphere in the car when the knocking sound returned. All four of them retreated into their own thoughts. Peter began to wonder seriously whether the entire venture wasn't jinxed. Rikki

195

the mongoose had partially recovered, but as he limped around, dragging his rear legs behind him, he served as a reminder of what had happened to their mascot. It seemed as if their luck too had been semi-paralysed.

There was nothing mystical or paranormal about the problems with the car. When, near Maroua, Alan had allowed the sump to run dry, it hadn't been only number-three cylinder which had gone: the crankshaft itself had been seriously damaged. All their subsequent problems were inevitable. And though he complained bitterly about the garage mechanics, the quality of the parts, the vindictive games that fate was playing with them, Alan had no one to blame but himself.

'Well, we can't go back to Kano,' he said finally. 'It's a round trip of 700 miles now, and even if they do fix it properly, the desert'll be closed off by the time we get back.'

'But what if they can't do it in Agadès?' Barbara asked.

'It shouldn't be a problem,' Alan said. 'We've got a spare set of bearings.'

The knocking became louder and wisps of smoke coiled their way from the engine. The more Alan thought about it, the more convinced he became that it would be better to get the repairs done sooner rather than later. The others disagreed. Outside, the wind was howling, and pale sand-snakes were hissing across the stony ground.

'Apart from anything else,' Peter said, 'how are we going to get under the car?'

This potential difficulty was solved a couple of miles on. The road had been deeply rutted by heavy lorries, and this had created a high ridge at the centre. Coming to a section where the side of the road rose up steeply, Alan manoeuvred the car so that the left wheels were on the ridge while the right ones were up the bank. The resulting space underneath ought to be enough for him to work under the car.

Everyone climbed out. The blast of heat knocked them backwards as they stepped into the full force of the midday sun. The car was unpacked so that Alan could get to the toolbox, and Barbara and Freda stood around the heap of belongings, making sure that the savage wind didn't whisk something away.

'Let me use your towel,' Alan said to Peter, and he laid it down under the car.

There was almost two feet clearance and Alan slithered upside down into the gap.

'At least I'm in shadow here,' he called up. 'If you could just switch the wind off for a minute.'

First, he allowed the sump to drain. The next step was the cover, and he took a spanner to release the nuts. The first was too big and Peter passed him another. It was no better and slipped round uselessly. The third was too small. There were no others. Alan re-emerged and squinted into the dazzling sunlight.

'Here,' he said, handing Peter his oil-soaked towel. 'It'll have to be Agadès.'

Desert and semi-desert alternated as they continued northwards. There were no trees now, just tufts of yellow grass. For miles it would be flat and featureless and then, in the distance, curious rocks would become visible through the haze. The constant fire and ice of the desert days and nights had shattered the rock like a hammer cracking nut-brittle. Slab on slab remained, as if gigantic alien toddlers had been disturbed midway through building replicas of the Mayan pyramids.

The travellers stopped to take photographs near a well. With the engine to consider, Alan was for the first time more inclined to be generous with the breaks he allowed.

'What on earth do the animals feed on?' Freda asked, as they stood watching the goats, mules, long-horned cattle and camels clustered round the well.

'Not much, by the look of them,' Peter said.

'Not a steak in sight,' Alan laughed. 'Nothing but herds of scrag end.'

That those bony creatures near the well were barely clinging on to life was testified to by those that hadn't made it. Huge, ungainly vultures hopped round the fresh carcasses, flapping their wings, jostling for position, ripping into the warm innards of the desert's latest victims. Within minutes, the bones were picked as clean as the bleached skeletons littering the sand.

The desert sun brands those unaccustomed to its heat with a dreary patience. It is impossible to hurry. It is impossible to compete. The animals stood in line, waiting their turn to drink the brackish water that two women in black were pouring into the troughs. As each cow or mule finished, it would stagger away, leaving a place free for the next in the queue. Only the camels broke the pattern – impatient, irritable, untroubled by the sun, they pushed in greedily, only to be sent to the back of the line by the angry goatherds.

It wasn't only the domesticated animals that were troubled by the intense heat. As she moved round, filming the emaciated beasts and heavily veiled nomads, Barbara began to feel queasy. She had brought a hat with her, but Freda had been wearing it after her own floppy white sunhat had fallen to bits. Since Freda was still recovering from her bout of dysentery, Barbara felt guilty asking her for it back but, with the sun beating down on her head, she was beginning to pay for her British reserve. It was Peter who came to her rescue.

'You look awful,' he said. 'Why aren't you wearing your hat?'

'Freda's got it.'

Unabashed, Peter stuck his head in through the car window and told Freda that she ought to give Barbara back her hat.

'But she never wears one,' Freda said.

'She would if she got the chance.'

Freda handed it over meekly.

'Here we are,' Peter said.

Barbara took it, grateful this time for the boy's gauche behaviour.

After a brief lunch – eggs, corned beef, beans, bread, mangoes and tea, as Peter's diary records – they set off at two in the afternoon. If nothing else went wrong, Agadès was only a couple of hours away.

Having recovered from the ignominy of failing to bring spanners of the correct gauge, Alan had once again assumed his role as chief entertainment officer. He taught the other three a poem. Line by line, he would get them to repeat it, in the appropriate accents until, as they drove into Agadès, they could recite the entire ode together.

His teaching techniques must have paid off. When he came to write it down later, Peter found he could remember every single word of Alan's poem:

> This is the story of Sara Snell
> To whom an accident befell
> And funny though it may seem
> Embarrassing in the extreme
>
> It happened as it does to many
> That Sara wished to spend a penny
> Entering with modest grace
> Into the proper appointed place
>
> Upon the railway station
> She sat down in meditation

Unhappily unacquainted
The seat had just been newly painted

And Sara came to realize
Her complete inability to rise
Her cries of anguish quickly brought
A crowd of every kind and sort

The station master and his staff
Were very good and didn't laugh
The crowd outside said, 'I'll be jiggered'
And stood and simply stared and sniggered

Up spoke an aged porter
'We ough'er soak 'er 'orf wiv wa'er!'
Their efforts proving fruitless all
They gave the carpenter a call

He said, 'I know what I'll do,'
And neatly cut the seat in two.
Sara arose, only to find
She had a halo on her behind

The ambulance soon came down the street
And bore her off complete with seat
It took that poor unfortunate girl
Straight to the nearest hospital

The doctors all came on parade
To render her immediate aid
And taking her by 'and and 'ead
They laid her face down on the bed

The surgeon said, 'Upon my word
Did you ever see anything so absurd?'
Up spoke a pupil, unashamed
'Often, sir, but never framed.

TWENTY

ENOUGH TO MAKE YOU CRY

THE most impressive landmark of Agadès is its mosque. Peter took a photo of it as they approached the town; rising high above the maze of single-storey mud dwellings, it is silhouetted dramatically against the bright sky like a giant cactus.

It was a testimony to simple engineering. First, a timber framework had been erected, 100 feet tall and tapering at the top. Next, blocks of mud and straw had been placed to create an elongated pyramid, with the ends of the poles protruding through the four sloping walls at regular intervals. The entire building had then been sealed with a slip of brown earth, which had baked solid under the kiln-sun. Essentially, it was little more than a glorified sandcastle. Peter's comment in his diary mirrored the thoughts I'd had when looking at the photographs: 'amazing it doesn't fall down or dissolve in the rains.'

The four travellers were directed to the Trans-Saharienne Hotel, an inexpensive, friendly place where they would sleep in proper beds one last time before undertaking the main stretch of the desert.

'Give me your shirt, Peter,' Barbara said as they were unpacking. 'I'm going to be doing some washing.'

'I'd rather be dirty,' Peter snapped back.

Barbara looked up at the boy, but said nothing. Sometimes she couldn't make him out at all.

He was, without doubt, the most thoughtful person on the trip, she realized. If she was leaning back against the car, Peter would be the one to pop something under her head as a pillow. In the mornings he would roll up her sleeping bag and carry her heavy bags to the car. Barbara admitted to me that she disliked being helped: the disability resulting from her cycling accident had made her both independent and hypersensitive to people patronizing her physically. Peter never made an issue of helping her. He would simply note that there were certain things she could not manage and do them for her. Yet he could be so truculent. Barbara went over the words she had used: 'give me your shirt . . .' Maybe it had been her tone, evoking the response his mother received to her instructions. Maybe he reacted against offers of help the same as she did. There was nothing she could say now that wouldn't make him dig his heels in even more obstinately.

'Alan, do you want me to wash your shirt?' she asked.

'Oh, rather,' he said, leaping at the offer with obvious enthusiasm. 'Got to look smart for the Commandant.'

While Alan was off seeing about the car and regulations for crossing the desert, Peter went into Barbara's room. He held out the filthy shirt.

'Is the offer still open?' he asked.

With electricity not yet installed, the hotel had been built to give maximum coolness without the help of either fans or fridges. A large, central room was surrounded by a narrow, unroofed courtyard, around which was a square block housing the small double rooms. Each bedroom had two narrow beds, a chair and a dressing table. The walls, made of earth and chopped straw, kept it relatively cool inside, while a tall earthenware pot, designed to let moisture condense through its

202

porous sides, provided guests with chilled water day and night.

That evening they ate at one of the four tables in front of the hotel. The food was excellent, the wine was included in the price, and a lively atmosphere was provided by soldiers from the local French garrison.

'So, what did the Commandant say?' Barbara asked.

'He was very helpful,' Alan replied. 'He's going to get one of his mechanics to look at the car tomorrow.'

What Alan failed to add was that they had also discussed the hazards of the desert at some length. He had been told to report to the police to have the car checked over: if any of the official prerequisites could not be satisfied, the Morris would not be given authorization to attempt the crossing.

Apart from the visas and vaccinations, there were other requirements which travellers had to fulfil. A refundable deposit of £50 per person was required for the possible use of French troops to recover a damaged vehicle or injured passengers: a contract had to be made with the Société Africaine des Transports Tropicaux, (SATT) to ensure that in the event of a breakdown, mechanics would be sent out. In addition, they were expected to carry:

1   A reserve of 50 per cent petrol and oil, according to the normal consumption of the car.
2   A reserve of 5 gallons of water per person in addition to the normal daily ration of a gallon per day per person.
3   Also a reserve of twice the radiator's capacity.
4   Railing or wire netting to overcome the sandy tracks.

As far as Alan was concerned, the most significant phrase of the document he had been given came in clause 5 relating to vehicles: 'Vehicles should be in perfect mechanical order.' Even if the engine was repaired, even if they could sneak through without all the spares and supplies they needed, the car was still hopelessly low on the ground, and lack of sufficient clearance would automatically fail the Morris.

'What did you think of the shower, Freda?' Alan asked, changing the conversation.

They all laughed. Apart from a steel bucket suspended from a hook in the ceiling, the bathroom was bare. A handle attached to the bucket was there to control the flow of water through holes which had been pierced in the base.

Freda had been the first in. She soon discovered that the bucket was empty. On enquiring at reception, she had been given a lecture about how this was neither France nor England but the Sahara desert which, by definition, was a dry area, and that they should be exceptionally frugal with water, the supply in Agadès being particularly low at this time of the year.

For her part, she spent a considerable time trying to convince him that although she knew the Tuaregs never washed – and that, yes, the dye from the material that stained their skin must indeed make them look extremely beautiful – she would nevertheless be happier with a little water. Finally the receptionist weakened, and she managed to wheedle out of him half a bucket of water per person.

'I think I did rather well,' she said.

'You certainly did,' Alan agreed.

In relating her tale, Freda had not been complaining. For her, the makeshift washing arrangements were all a part of the exquisite romance of the desert – even if now, the Camay she hadn't managed to rinse away scented every mouthful of her dinner.

While they were still eating, a tall youth with a massive horned headdress balanced on his head emerged from the shadows and stepped sinuously towards them. He was followed by a dozen boys, all dressed in long robes, all decorated with bones. Accompanied by their own mournful chanting, they performed a mesmeric swaying dance before the travellers and soldiers.

'Don't ask me why,' Barbara said, 'but I suddenly feel homesick.'

The others didn't need to ask. They knew exactly what she meant. There was something about the plangent crescendo of voices which, although quite new, was evoking emotions which were all too familiar.

Before the dance had reached its conclusion though, the hotel owner burst through the door. Yelling something in French, he shooed them away furiously.

'Oh don't . . .' Alan started to say.

But it was too late. The boys had already scampered off. Perhaps the man had thought the dancers were annoying his guests. Perhaps the display would have been followed by aggressive demands for loose change. Or perhaps the sadness of the song had also affected the hotel owner, prompting memories he would have preferred to leave forgotten. Whatever his reason for chasing the boys away, the abrupt termination of their song troubled Peter.

Looking back on it, he was to write, 'I often wonder if this had any connection with what followed only one week later.'

Early the next day Alan and Peter drove the car over to the army workshop where it was immediately jacked up above the pit. The engine was still spewing acrid smoke that stung the eyes, and the mechanic confirmed that the shells on the third cylinder had gone again. He set about replacing them.

'We may as well change the oil while we're here,' Alan said.

'No oil here,' the Frenchman said.

'No oil?' Alan repeated incredulously. 'But this is a garage.'

'All must come through supply depot,' he explained.

Alan sighed impatiently. 'Peter,' he said, 'I don't suppose . . .'

'Yes, I'll go.'

There was a Shell garage directly opposite the hotel, but that was over a mile away. Even though it was still not ten o'clock, already the temperature had risen to around 110 degrees. With his eyes set on the tall spiky minaret ahead of him, Peter trudged along the scorching road. The sun beat down so fiercely that his thick protective hat might as well have been made of lace. The mosque did not seem to be getting any nearer.

'Have you got anything for a headache?' Freda asked.

'Veganin do?' Barbara said.

'Perfect.'

Freda's ailments persisted. The sprained ankle, the exhaustion, the dysentery, the headaches. How she would cope with the desert, Barbara couldn't imagine. Freda poured herself a glass of water to help her swallow.

'I just can't seem to shift the pain . . . just here, behind my eyes.'

'You mustn't let yourself get dehydrated,' Barbara said. 'You need one pint of liquid for every ten degrees. That means eleven to twelve pints per day in this heat.'

'It seems a lot,' Freda said.

'It is,' said Barbara quietly as something occurred to her. Would the quantity of water they were to carry be sufficient for the entire crossing?

Having bought the oil, Peter decided that he would ignore Alan's 'come straight back' and check out the view from the top of the minaret.

At ground level a doorway in the hall led him into a large hall where people would congregate and worship during festivals. Now it was empty and, as he walked over to the flight of stairs at the far side, his footsteps echoed. Up he climbed, round and round as the staircase spiralled to the very top of the tower. When he approached the narrow opening of clear blue sky, the space narrowed and he was forced to crawl the last few feet on his hands and knees. Emerging on to a tiny platform at the top, he straightened up.

'Gosh,' he muttered involuntarily.

The view was awe-inspiring. Surrounding the mosque below him was the patchwork of brown-red buildings. If he half closed his eyes, they became invisible, returning to the earth from which they had been fashioned. Looking up and round, the insignificance of this outpost became shockingly apparent: it was a mere pimple on the smooth, arid skin of the desert.

Standing there, above the town in the heat of the mid-day sun, Peter was experiencing something mystical. He tried to describe how he felt, but the words proved inadequate.

> A strange feeling came over me as I stood there, under a boiling hot sun looking at Agadès and the dry plains that surrounded it. This must be one of the worst places in the world to have to live in, yet I realized I had fallen in love.

Peter hadn't 'fallen in love': the three words trivialize his emotions. Yet when I read the simple description, a clear image formed. A boy, away from home, atop a mosque at the edge of the known, tingling with anticipation and wonder as he stared northwards across the flat, featureless wasteland he was about to enter.

The mundane realities of the trip reasserted themselves

as Peter descended the tower. From the sublime to the ridiculous, he thought, trudging back along the road with the can of oil. Having checked the dipstick one last time, the mechanic pronounced the vehicle ready.

Provisions were bought and Alan got the others to pack up their luggage.

'I'll go and see the Commandant,' he said.

For Peter, the descent from the spiritual to the crassly material was completed when he walked into his bedroom. Someone had been there. His clothes were strewn all over the bed, his sunglasses had been broken, stamped on. He rummaged through the clothes for the one item he minded losing – an ivory bird he had bought in the Congo. It had been wrapped up in a jersey so that the delicate wings and fine legs would not snap. The jersey was on the floor behind the bed. The bird was gone.

'It must have just happened,' Barbara said. 'They couldn't have had time to go through our things.'

'Not that there's anything worth having,' said Freda.

At that moment, Alan came racing in through the door. He was hot, agitated.

'We've been cleared,' he said, 'but we've got to go now. The road's about to be closed.'

TWENTY ONE

MISREADING THE SIGNS

THEY drove out of Agadès in the late afternoon of Sunday, 8 May. The official guidebook advised them to get a local to help them on to the correct road as the chaotic spaghetti of lorry tracks made by game hunters left it completely indistinguishable.

'Don't worry about that,' Alan said as he followed the tracks that looked to him the most recent.

'We're going south,' Peter said.

'It's all right.'

'But look where the sun is,' he persisted.

They *were* heading south, but a couple of miles later the track veered round until the sun was back where it should be, on their left.

'Oh ye of little faith,' Alan said and laughed.

No one begrudged him his smugness. Peter noted: 'at last we are in the Sahara: the real test has begun.'

The word Sahara comes from the Arabic, *sahra*, meaning desert, wilderness, wasteland, empty place . . . The Sahara is empty. It is also expanding each year. At the last count it was reckoned to be about three and a half million square miles in area – roughly seventy times as large as England. The land is so barren that it can barely support the 2 million Moors, Berbers and Tuaregs who live there.

Although famous for its overwhelming dunes, the

Sahara is not primarily a sandy desert. Most of it comprises rocky plateaux and gravel plains. It was along the rockier western trail that Alan Cooper crossed the Sahara in 1933. This time he was planning to take the considerably sandier Hoggar Massif route via the mountain oasis of Tamanrasset. Although far more beautiful, the journey would be considerably tougher.

They stopped for the night 50 miles on. The clouds on the horizon had transformed the usual orange glow of sunset into a display of iridescent colour. Purple, lilac and maroon shimmered and shifted as the sun darkened through yellow to red. Ribbons of dazzling vermilion streaked the sky above the sunken sun, and as they gradually faded the moon arose from another part of the wide horizon. Already the air had chilled.

A few skeletal thorn trees stood near the side of the road. Alan drove into the middle of them so that, with the Morris conveniently parked to form a dividing partition, he created two 'rooms'.

Peter slept better that night. He lay in the campbed, drowsily thinking over the stretch of road between Agadès and their campsite, reliving every bump and swerve. The corrugations had been the worst so far; the oueds, treacherous. Alan had literally had to stand on the brake to stop himself driving into them. And then there had been the rocks and holes. Until you were right on them it was impossible to determine one from the other: in the blinding sun eyes play tricks and refuse to differentiate between convex and concave.

Tomorrow he'd be a better navigator, he promised himself. Tomorrow they wouldn't go crashing down into dips and gullies; they wouldn't risk ripping the sump open on another concealed rock. Tomorrow . . .

Everyone woke up aching. The intense cold had wormed its way into every joint, numbing, stiffening; time and again it had dragged them out of deep sleep and back to a shivering nap which had left them more tired the following morning than when they had gone to bed. Up and dressed, their attempts to overcome the cold by hurrying proved impossible. They were awkward and clumsy. Peter tripped on his campbed. Freda knocked over a jug of water.

'Whoops!'

'At least it's not whisky again,' Alan joked.

The previous night, while Barbara had been trying to get the fire going, Freda had kicked her drink over. She was always knocking drinks over. Even when she tried to keep it a secret, the involuntary 'whoops' gave her away. Usually it was her own glass, when there was just a little left at the bottom – 'she only does it to get a top up,' Alan had maintained.

Freda wasn't the only one being wasteful with the water, however. Peter and Alan both had a shave, flinging the frothy dregs away when they finished. The water disappeared into the sand instantly, leaving only a few stubbly bubbles on the surface. Barbara and Freda both washed as well as they could, soaping off the beauty cream and cleansing lotion they routinely applied to their faces each evening – much to the amusement of the men.

'No good shutting the stable door after the horse has bolted,' Alan had observed unkindly one evening after his tongue had been loosened by a little too much red wine.

Water was not a problem. They had gallons of the stuff in the back and they would soon be refilling their containers from the well at In Abbangarit.

The hot sun rose quickly and, to benefit from a light breeze, they packed and left without having breakfast. As the sun climbed up in the sky, Peter discovered that his plan for improved navigation was not easy to fulfil. The dazzling brightness flattens everything: rocks, troughs, ridges – they all disappear in the shadowless glare. Having no sunglasses compounded Peter's problem. All he could advise was that Alan drive slowly.

They came to the next place on the Shell map – or at least assumed they did. Called Teguidda n'Adrar, it consisted of a few scrubby bushes, no more.

'Hardly seemed worth naming,' Alan said.

'Perhaps that wasn't it,' Peter suggested.

Some while later they arrived at a wide river bed. With no run-offs, the annual downpours turned to boiling torrents which gouged their way deep into the flat land. For that week or so, the river was impassable, and huge jagged boulders had been laid across its width as a makeshift crossing point.

'We can't use that,' Peter objected. 'The tyres'll be ripped to shreds.'

'We don't need to,' Alan said, driving down the bank and following old tyre marks where the soft sand had been compressed.

Back on the main route, the number of holes increased. As they were so difficult to see, Alan had no option but to reduce his speed, and with the car travelling more slowly, the breeze dropped and the temperature in the car soared. It was a chain of events guaranteed to try the patience of even the hardiest of explorers. Only Freda seemed untroubled by the heat.

'There should be a village or a well or something along here called Fagoschia,' Barbara announced from the back seat.

Nothing appeared to break the monotony of glaring beige.

'That's the trouble with these desert villages,' said Alan, 'they keep moving them on.'

'Maybe they've started putting mirages on the map,' Peter suggested.

They did pass the occasional well. It was the huddle of

scrawny goats and cattle that signalled their presence. The filthy water being scooped out for the animals was undrinkable and there was never any sign of permanent human dwellings. It was only their arrival at Teguidda n'Tecum that confirmed they were indeed on the right road.

It was a small village – their first since Agadès – consisting of quaint conical huts with straw roofs, resembling beehives. There the similarity ended, however. There was none of the industrious activity of a real hive. The village was deserted: no trees, no shrubs, no animals, no people.

'May as well drive on.' The others merely nodded.

Shortly after Teguidda n'Tecum, the desert began to fulfil the travellers' expectations. Sand-dunes, mirages and an endless expanse of pale desolation – it was all picture-book stuff.

'It's . . .' Freda was at a loss for words. She gestured airily at the landscape outside the car.

'It certainly is,' Alan said.

Peter's description was unequivocal: 'Miles of nothing: flat as a pancake.'

A mild sandstorm had obliterated the previous day's tracks. No road was visible, no tyre marks. The surface of the desert was as featureless as a frozen lake. The travellers were forced to use the markers the French had strung out across the length of the central area. These were 44-gallon oil drums, or *bidons*, which had been cut in half, filled with sand and gravel against the savage wind, and painted black for clear visibility. Placed at 1 kilometre intervals, they were too far apart for two to be seen at the same time.

'If you keep your eyes on the one we've passed,' Alan instructed, 'I'll look out for the one ahead.'

Each kilometre, there was an anxious moment when neither was visible.

'There it is,' one of them would shout out, relieved to see the shimmering, black blob far away in the distance.

When it first came into view, each successive drum appeared to be floating above the surface of a swirling, glutinous pool. Only as they approached did it gradually resume its position on solid ground.

Driving was exhausting. The sun, almost above them now, was reflected and intensified by the sand. Even with sunglasses on, the travellers were forced to squint into the glare. The wind, far from refreshing them, roared through the car like a jet of flame. There was no respite. Mile after mile they continued, concentrating on keeping the bidons in sight, looking out for the holes, oueds and soft patches which were waiting to ensnare the little car.

The lack of shadows proved costly. The first anyone knew of the mound of sand that the car could not straddle, was when a soft grinding juddered up through the floor and the Morris lost power. Alan tried to accelerate out of trouble, but it was too late and the back wheels spun uselessly.

For the first time, they were stuck.

The full impact of the desolation hit them as they climbed out of the stranded car. Apart from their own tracks – two pitiful, parallel scratches – there was nothing to show that any human had ever passed this way. In every direction, as far as they could see, there was nothing but thick, treacly heat. Turning slowly through the 360 degrees, the view remained constant, resulting in the eerie feeling they all experienced of having come to a halt right at the very centre of the desert.

Alan examined the wheels. 'It doesn't look too bad,' he said. 'If you all push up and back, she should come out without much trouble.'

The heat was suffocating, immobilizing. It wrapped

itself tightly round the travellers like a huge electric blanket, and as they took up their positions against the bonnet, every movement was impeded by the crushing swelter.

'Now,' Alan yelled, and slowly he released the clutch.

Peter, Freda and Barbara pushed, and after a tense moment of flying sand, the spinning tyres gripped and the Morris lurched free.

With under 30 miles to go to the fresh water supplies of the well in In Abbangarit, they drove on. All round them, the panorama continued unchanged. It reinforced the illusion of being at the same central point of the desert, and they felt themselves to be anchored and motionless, even though logically they knew they must be moving – like Alice and the Red Queen, no matter how fast they went, they never seemed to make any progress.

If there was a village at In Abbangarit, the four travellers never came across it. All they saw, apart from the well itself, was one crumbling mud hut. Most likely, the crowd of men and women watering their animals were nomads, able to erect and dismantle their animal-hide tents as often as the urge took them either to rest or travel on.

They were Tuaregs, the desert wanderers who, in 1955, at a time when camel caravans were being superseded by convoys of trucks and fleets of aircraft, were already becoming curiosities, anachronisms. Tough and proud, with a reputation for ruthless ferocity stemming from the hand-me-down tales of how they would deal with their enemies, it was their legendary hospitality which Peter and Barbara remembered.

'Let's get everything filled,' Alan said, as the Tuaregs insisted on drawing the water for them.

'You're sure it's all right?' The recent bout of dysentery was too painfully fresh in her memory for Freda to take any risks.

'Safe as houses,' Alan said confidently.

They had no alternative anyway. The next stop was 125 miles further on at In Guezzam and their current supplies would not hold out until then. With enthusiastic drinking gestures, the Tuaregs assured them that the water from the 200-foot well was fine, and they pointed out the low mud wall built around it to prevent any person, animal or debris falling in and rendering it undrinkable. The radiator was topped up, the jerry-cans and chargals were replenished – even a couple of jam jars were filled, 'just in case'.

Peter checked the tyre pressure and Barbara took the opportunity to reposition a campbed which had been digging into her back for the previous hour. Alan and two of the Tuareg men were communicating haphazardly in pidgin Arabic. The problem was not so much the basic vocabulary or grammar as their mutually exclusive *Weltanschauung*: the Tuaregs had no concept of the cold wet country called England that Alan was trying to describe, while he was unable to conceive of all the subtle nuances of meaning their many words for 'sand' might convey. This was unfortunate: if he had understood, some of the ensuing hold-ups might have been avoided.

A third man approached them. He was carrying a large gourd full of camel's milk which he offered first to Alan and then to the others. It was very rich, slightly sour, but as Peter noted, extremely refreshing: whereas water always left them wanting more, they found the milk completely thirst-quenching.

'What's going on over there?' Peter asked, pointing to an animated argument taking place some 20 yards away.

'Don't know,' Alan said.

The Tuareg at the well came up with the explanation. It seemed that the man who had brought them the milk had obtained it from someone else's camel. The owner was remonstrating with him loudly; he yelled and gesticulated until he caught sight of Peter and Alan looking at him. Then he smiled, waved and all was forgiven.

'It's so much easier being generous with another man's belongings, I always say,' Alan laughed.

He pulled out a packet of cigarettes from his pocket and began passing them round. The men seemed very pleased with this gesture – even the women, who didn't smoke, grinned happily – and nomads and travellers parted on the best of terms.

'All in,' Alan said, 'unless you feel like staying, Freda?' he added as an afterthought and winked.

'Not quite wealthy enough, I'm afraid,' Freda replied, playing along with his teasing. 'I'm worth at least ten times the number of goats any of *them* have.'

'Look,' Peter said unnecessarily. Everyone was staring towards the horizon at the swirling liquid pictures. The mirage was the most magnificent they had seen so far; a mesmerizing display of cool colours it was impossible to ignore. A sudden jolt reminded Alan of the harsh penalty they would have to pay if he drove over a sharp rock or into a patch of soft sand. He stopped the car.

'Do you think it'd come out on cine?' Barbara asked.

'Yes,' Alan said. 'Or maybe not. Is it just an optical illusion or is it really there?' He continued to watch the shapes heaving, breathing, flowing one into the other. 'Do you think animals can see them?'

'I think so,' said Barbara.

'Perhaps it will come out on film then. I don't know how similar the lens is to the eye.'

'Only one way to find out.'

It did come out. Sitting in Mrs Simpson's lounge, we watched the projected mirages shimmering on the wall. It was fascinating to see the curious forms, and yet the experience was somehow incomplete. Looking at the heat without feeling it was like watching a singer performing with the volume turned off.

In his diary, Peter described what he saw as 'colossal lakes with boats and elephants'. Barbara saw birds becoming fish becoming otters, shifting forms as they flowed through the turquoise and grey. On the wall, I saw something else again. It was a deep lagoon surrounded by dark, shadowy trees, reflected in the water below them. Hidden between the branches were animals, staring towards me, visible only by the occasional silver flash of their eyes.

Much has been written about the djinns of the desert. The Tuaregs believe implicitly in the evil spirits which dazzle you, disorientate you, lead you to your death. Visible from a distance, they are at their most dangerous when, unseen, they fill your head with troubled confusion. The djinns, of course, are the heat of the desert itself. In Mrs Simpson's cool lounge they had no power over those seeing them. Only in the desert can they exert their influence, hypnotizing travellers with their overwhelming, psychedelic beauty and then tricking them into doing something fatally stupid.

'I used to stay in a cottage in the Lake District,' Freda said as they continued northwards. 'A friend and I would drive there for weekends before the war. We were up there in the late summer of '37 or '38 – I forget now. Anyway, we saw the most incredible display of the Northern Lights.'

'The aurora borealis,' Peter chipped in.

'That's it,' said Freda. 'Like huge red and orange velvet curtains filling the entire sky. It looked so warm and cosy.'

'And yet here, the mirages all look so cool,' Peter said.

'Perhaps we see what we want to see,' Barbara suggested.

'I've heard that a particularly spectacular Northern

Lights is meant to herald something awful,' Alan said.

'Well, that's right,' said Freda, 'that's what my friend said. And then, of course, not long afterwards the war started.'

Everyone fell silent. Suddenly the mirage which, until a moment before, had been nothing more than a beautiful diversion, became a fearful portent; another omen.

As they continued along the shores of the illusory lake, Alan started singing about how much he liked to be beside the seaside. The others joined in with the nonsense, and the tension in the air relaxed, the spell was broken. Tiddly om pom pom. Away on the horizon, the mirage was fading fast.

Maybe what followed could have been prevented if Alan had properly understood the Tuareg's descriptions of the sand they should avoid. Maybe it was a simple case of misfortune. Or maybe there really are malevolent desert spirits, and while the four travellers had been watching their own interpretation of the mirage, the djinns had worked their mischief. Seen or unseen, real or imaginary, whatever the cause, the next decision they took was to be their worst yet.

TWENTY TWO

THE HEAT OF THE DAY

A T noon the sun was at its highest and hottest, beating down on the Morris with a searing ferocity. It was debatable whether the roof that Alan had painted white actually reduced the temperature inside the car. No one could imagine it being any hotter.

'Anyone else hungry?' Alan said.

'You bet,' said Peter.

Apart from the camel's milk and a couple of dry crackers, they had eaten nothing all day. Stopping was a matter of weighing up the pros and cons of filling their empty stomachs versus being baked alive on the shadowless wasteland. When the two lone trees came into view it seemed that, for once, the gods were smiling on them.

'Not much shade from them,' Freda said, looking at the thin twisted branches. If they were still alive, it had certainly been years since they had last borne leaves.

'We can rig up the tarpaulin,' Alan said.

As the Morris approached the trees it became clear that they were a good half-mile off the track. The AA guide had stressed how important it was, on these unimproved pistes, to follow the tyre marks left by previous users. On the couple of occasions the car had been temporarily bogged down it had been caused by

Alan ignoring this advice and following the bidons too closely. On his 1933 trip across the hard stony plateau to the west, this had undoubtedly been the best thing to do, but in the sandy desert drifting takes place near any obstacle, and driving too near the drums was hazardous.

The siren call from the trees proved too seductive. It had become exhaustingly hot in the car and Alan suggested resting until three o'clock, when the shadows would start to reappear. Barbara repeated the warnings from their guide, 'if anybody's interested!', but even she was being lured by the thought of three long cool hours spent lying in the shade.

'It'll be fine,' said Alan, turning the wheel. 'The sand's really quite firm.'

'Let's just hope it stays that way,' Barbara muttered.

The picnic site was as good as it could possibly have been. After a couple of failed attempts, when the brittle branches cracked under the weight, Peter and Alan finally managed to tie the tarpaulin into place. They laid out mattresses and pillows in the shadow beneath, and used the cases as a windbreak. Even though the resulting shade was scarcely any cooler, it was kinder to the eye. Peter, in particular, was beginning to suffer from his lack of sunglasses: everything he looked at glared back painfully as his retinas struggled to make sense of the overload of light. A stabbing ache behind his eyes was becoming more persistent.

Barbara was, by this time, doing her bit to raise the temperature still further. With her face red and gleaming sweatily, and her mousy hair sticking to her forehead, she leant forward to pull the saucepan of water off the fire.

'Hot drinks are said to be more refreshing than cold ones in the sun,' Freda said.

'Sounds like an old wives' tale to me,' said Alan.

'No, really, I read it somewhere,' she persisted.

221

'A Christmas cracker?'

'Christmas,' Freda repeated quietly, 'snowdrifts, frozen ponds and icicles.'

'Stop it, stop it,' Peter exclaimed, rolling over on to his front and burying his head in the mattress. 'I can't bear it.'

'I never thought I'd ever look forward to winter,' Freda continued. 'Crunching across the frosty grass; drawing in the ice flowers on the window.'

'Here,' said Alan, handing her a mug, 'drink your tea and stop torturing us.'

'Lunch is ready as well,' said Barbara, ladling an impromptu soupy-stewy concoction into their bowls. 'Bread?' she added, wielding the loaf.

'Looks like it to me,' said Alan.

'Ha, ha! Would you like some, or not?'

'Pass it over and I'll cut it.'

'The one especially nice thing about winter,' Freda was saying, 'is that there are no creepy-crawlies. Unlike here,' she added, punctuating the words with a sudden slap to her legs.

It might be tempting to assume that there are no insects in the middle of the Sahara. Surely, in that burning emptiness, there is nothing for them to eat, nowhere for them to shelter. But this is to underestimate the tiny creatures which, in all likelihood, will survive Armageddon, whether through nuclear holocaust, global warming or industrial pollution. As if in training for that barren future, insects have not only colonized the most inhospitable areas of the world but thrive there.

'What the hell do they live on?' Alan said, as he flapped away the cloud of flies buzzing round his spoon.

'Sand,' Freda said authoritatively.

The others laughed.

'Like us,' Peter added as he crunched through a mouthful of bread.

'Perhaps they were stowing away on the roof rack,' Alan suggested.

'Too many,' Peter said. 'We'd never have managed to move at all if we'd been that weighed down.'

'I read somewhere that a tick can wait months for some poor mammal to walk past before it gets its next feed,' Freda said.

'And they never eat between meals,' Alan said.

'Ow!' Peter yelped, and rubbed at his elbow. 'They bite.'

'Naturally,' Freda said, lighting up a cigarette and disappearing into a cloud of smoke she hoped might prove impenetrable.

It wasn't only the flies. There were large spiders with plump bodies and long, thin legs. Conditioned to cocoon everything edible they came across, every time anyone moved, sticky, glistening threads broke off and drifted through the air.

Then there were the ants. Neither black nor red, this desert variety was silver-grey. At first, Peter had thought the wind was blowing the top layer of sand granules over the surface: it was only when he lay down that he saw that the ground was alive.

No one slept that afternoon. It was too hot, too windy, too uncomfortable. Even Alan, who would always become drowsy after his midday meal, was prevented from drifting off to sleep by the insects tickling, nipping, stinging. By 2.30 he'd had enough.

'Shall we be making a move?'

'Oh yes, come on,' Peter said eagerly, and clapped his hands together in an unconscious imitation of Alan himself.

If they had convinced themselves that the shade offered by the tarpaulin was useless, they realized how wrong they had been when they stepped into the direct sunlight. The blast of heat was unbelievable. They felt as though every exposed bit of skin was being instantly charred. But Peter wasn't bothered. He was happy to be back on the road – or track – and hurried along, whistling something tuneless, getting everything together.

He helped roll up Barbara's sleeping bag for her and pushed it inside the bedding sack. He looked at her twisted arm and realized how much he admired this woman who refused to let anything beat her. And it wasn't just admiration. He liked her: she wasn't nearly as bossy as he'd first thought. He wondered if they would stay in touch when they got back to Kenya.

When Alan tried to set off the rear wheels spun powerlessly. The thin sandy crust they had crossed over cracked under the weight of the parked car and, as he released the clutch, the wheels broke through the surface and buried themselves deep in the powdery sand. There was a soft crunch as the bottom of the car came to rest on the ground. The two women in the back stopped talking. Alan glanced at Peter.

'Let's hope it's not too bad.'

The situation was worse than anyone had dared imagine. The rear axle was buried deep in the sand and the back wheels, suspended above the ground, could be turned by hand. They would prove useless in any attempt to drive the car out. With no spades or shovels, they had to try and scrape away the sand with their one tool, a broad-bladed Kenyan panga. That and their hands.

They emptied the car of everything. Even the spare wheel was removed to make the car that couple of pounds lighter. Though stripped to its minimum weight, the task of freeing the stranded workhorse proved exhausting and frustrating. The sand was like water: no sooner had it been scooped away than it trickled back underneath. After their previous experience trying to jack the car up, Alan had picked up a flat piece of wood in Kano, to use as a base. Even this proved useless. The board see-sawed, taking on sand with each turn of the jack, and gradually sinking. Several times they were forced to start from scratch.

The lack of shade began to take its toll. Barbara sat down dizzily by their pile of belongings. Freda sipped a glass of water.

'Pass me the tarpaulin,' Alan called to Peter.

Peter made a move, but evidently not quite quickly enough.

'Now!' Alan barked.

The relentless furnace-blast of heat was wearing down their energy, their confidence, their patience. It was too hot, illogically hot, so that even breathing became a torment as the burning air scorched the inside of their nostrils.

It took more than two hours to prepare the car. Alan was aching with tiredness and dripping with sweat when finally he managed to slide the doubled tarpaulin under the rear wheels. Before leaving Kenya, he had been warned that, despite the generic term, 'sand-mats', neither sacking nor carpet would offer the support necessary to free a car from the sand. What was needed was a pair of narrow metal sheets which would not sink under the weight of the car – they could have been attached to the underneath of the roof rack. Characteristically Alan had smiled, nodded and ignored the advice.

It was gone five before the car was ready to be pushed. Peter, Freda and Barbara stood at the front, their palms resting on the burning-hot bonnet, waiting for Alan to shout out. At this prearranged signal, the three of them were to lift and push simultaneously, while Alan would gently release the clutch.

'Go!' he yelled above the sound of the revving engine.

The car shuddered, but instead of moving backwards,

the turning wheels began to sink. The tarpaulin was proving to be as ineffective as Alan's detractors had claimed it would be.

'LIFT and push!' he yelled.

Called to do something physical, the three of them were just discovering to what extent the heat had sapped their strength. The Morris was simply too heavy. Yet they had to try – no one wanted to give up while the car was still stuck, and there would be time enough for resting at In Guezzam. Tapping resources they didn't know they possessed, all three heaved and shoved in unison. The car reared like a panicked stallion and leapt out of the dip, skidding on the soft sand and coming to rest on the hard sand twenty yards or so further back.

No one clapped; no one cheered. All their energy had been expended on trying to free the car. The relief they felt as they achieved their task was instantly superseded by an overwhelming sense of fatigue. The car still had to be loaded.

While they were resting, Barbara added a little more to the travelogue-letter she was writing to her friend, Mavis.

> And then we came on to find this lunching place. We got stuck in the sand ... and had our first experience of pushing and putting the tarpaulin (very heavy) under the wheels.

At this point the letter stopped. It was resumed further down the page. I read on.

MORE THAN A WEEK LATER
And what a week! The last time I wrote was really the beginning of the end.

TWENTY THREE

KISS OF DEATH

No one spoke as Alan drove away. The incident had proved too unnerving. For the first time, the sheer scale of their task had hit them. This was no mere Sunday afternoon jaunt; this was the crossing of the Sahara. Behind them, the churned-up mess of footprints and tyre marks bore witness to how easily the desert could simply swallow up those who refused to accord it respect. Whereas before, the virgin expanse of sand in front of them had enhanced the feeling that they were pioneers, now it scared them. They felt isolated, insignificant, and as they drove on, the nagging feeling persisted that the centre of the desert was travelling with them and that they would never manage to escape.

Peter blew on his smarting fingers. The hours spent clearing the sand had raised angry blisters which had burst as he was helping Alan carry the heavy chop-box over to the car. Rikki, the mongoose, jumped down from the back of the seat and rolled round in his lap. Sniffing at the stroking hands, it began licking at the watery sores.

'I don't think you ought to let it do that,' Freda said, looking at the animal disdainfully.

'He must be thirsty,' Peter answered, and smirked to himself as Freda shuddered.

Alan gradually increased the speed until they were racing across the smooth, firm surface parallel to the bidons. There was no vibration in the car; only the hissing echo of the tyres indicated that they were moving.

'The sand's much better here, isn't it?' Peter said.

At that moment, there was an abrupt loss of speed. Everyone knew what had happened and kept their fingers crossed that they'd make it to the other side of the soft stretch. Alan, however, had insufficient experience of sandy conditions. Even if the engine had been twice, three times as powerful, the result would have been the same. By the time he decided to shift to a lower gear it was already far too late. The car had almost stopped and depressing the clutch served only to remove traction just when it was most needed. In a desperate panic to remedy the situation, he then completed the set of classic mistakes for novices by accelerating wildly. The wheels spun and sank. They were stuck again.

'As if by magic,' Alan muttered under his breath. 'As if by ruddy magic. Peter speaks and instantly . . .'

'Sorry,' Peter said sheepishly.

It was true. His clumsiness had been replaced by something altogether more sinister. Any comment he would make worked like the kiss of death on the subject of the remark. 'The road's improved' he would say, and immediately it would deteriorate; 'the roof rack's fine now' and immediately it would slip; 'the sand's much better here . . .'

They climbed out of the car to inspect the damage. On this occasion the lifting and pushing routine worked without even having to use the tarpaulin.

It wasn't, however, the only time they ground to a halt. Even though Peter kept his lips clamped tightly shut, Alan never managed to master the conditions, and the further they went, the more frequent the stops became. In part, this was due to his own obstinacy. Despite constant reminders from both Peter and Barbara, Alan insisted on driving near the bidons.

In his diary, Peter noted down the number on the clock each time they ground to another halt: 6366, 6373, 6375 – the familiarity of the task made it no easier to push the car out. The next stop came one mile later: 6376, and as Peter's diary entry confirmed, Alan had still not learnt from his mistakes: 'we were stuck a few yards from a drum.'

'It's getting dark,' Barbara said.

'You mean you think we should stay here for the night,' Alan said sharply.

'Well, it wouldn't be such a bad idea.'

'Right,' he said, yanking the tarpaulin down from the roof rack and throwing the bedding material on to the sand.

The others busied themselves and tried to ignore Alan's increasingly agitated behaviour. Barbara unpacked a couple of items from the chop-box while Freda wandered off in search of any small burnable bits and pieces for a fire.

'Where are you going?' Alan demanded.

'To get some wood – if there is any here,' Freda answered.

'Waste of time,' Alan said. 'We should just go to bed – make sure we're fully refreshed for the morning.'

'Without something to eat?' Barbara asked.

'We don't need it,' he insisted.

Barbara looked at him strangely. He hadn't been wearing a hat for most of the day. Had he got a touch of sunstroke? With all that digging out in the open sun, it wouldn't surprise her.

When Barbara dished up the bread and soup, Alan ate as enthusiastically as anyone else. They had coffee and biscuits and shared a tin of grapefruit.

'Some water, please,' Alan said.

'We're down to about 4 gallons,' Barbara said as she filled his cup.

Alan didn't respond. His lips tightened and he looked up towards the rising moon. The *bon vivant* who had kept them all entertained and cheerful seemed to have resigned his post. He looked deeply troubled, but the others could only guess at the reason. Perhaps it *was* sunstroke. Perhaps the strain of being responsible for leading the trek was becoming too great. Or perhaps it was that Alan had begun to doubt himself. He, who had lived an almost charmed life, emerging from so many skirmishes unscathed, was possibly beginning to sense that his luck might be running out. At any event, it was Freda, not he, who got everyone laughing – albeit unintentionally.

'Oh, I do so love the African night,' she rhapsodized. 'And the full moon – look at it. Didn't I tell you there were more of them here, Barbara?'

'You did,' Barbara nodded, remembering their conversation in Maiduguri.

'Well, there you are,' she continued. 'It was full moon last night, it's full moon tonight. And how many do we get in England? One per month – at most!'

'At most?' Peter repeated, and started sniggering.

'Oh, the very outside,' Freda said. 'You probably only get to see about three or four a year.'

'But that's because of cloud,' Barbara laughed.

'Seeing is believing, that's my motto,' said Freda, smoothing down her skirt.

Barbara looked from the bowed figure of Alan to the bidon and the embedded car. Better than not believing what you can see, she thought bitterly.

The campbeds had been placed in their usual position – the two men on one side of the car, the two women on the other. It had been their most exhausting day so far, mentally as well as physically, and the four travellers fell asleep instantly.

The drop in temperature was vicious. As if the desert itself were ill, the daylight throbbing fever had dropped to a dark shivering chill. Barely above freezing point, the spiteful wind intensified the cold, making tired joints ache and troubling much-needed sleep. Peter thought he was dreaming when he felt the hands shaking him.

'Wake up, wake up,' he heard, and looked up to see Alan, already fully dressed.

'But . . .'

'Come on,' he said urgently. 'It's nearly dawn. Get up and let's push the car out.'

'What on earth's going on?' came an irritated voice from the other side of the car.

'The sun's coming up,' Alan said. 'You can sleep on if you want, but we're going to shift the car before it gets any hotter.'

Barbara emerged from her sleeping bag. 'Look where the moon is, look at your watch,' she said. 'Nearly dawn! Good God, it's a quarter past ten.'

Alan held his watch up to his ear.

'I thought it had stopped,' he said weakly. 'The moon must have woken me and . . .'

'It doesn't matter,' said Barbara. She could see how upset and disorientated Alan was, and it worried her. She did not want to make matters worse.

'See you in the morning,' she said.

'And not before,' Peter muttered drowsily.

Alan was not the first up when morning came. Thriving on the challenge of adversity, Freda was feeling more energetic than ever before. While the others were still sleeping, she had dressed, lit a fire and made a start with breakfast.

231

'Wakey, wakey, rise and shine,' she greeted them each in turn, handing out a mug of steaming tea.

'Anyone heard the weather forecast for today?' Peter asked, sitting up in his campbed.

The others smiled and shook their heads.

'Blisteringly hot periods interrupted during late morning by burning intervals,' he said.

'And there could be scattered outbreaks of clear blue sky and scorching sun this afternoon,' Barbara said, joining in.

After a light breakfast, they packed up all their belongings and arranged them in a neat pile. The items which hadn't been taken out of the car the previous evening were now removed and everyone inspected the car to see how deeply bedded in it was.

'Come on, then,' Alan said.

Everyone clapped their hands together, mimicking Alan's familiar gesture, and burst out laughing. Everyone, that is, except for Alan himself. Increasingly lost in his own thoughts, he no longer seemed inclined to see the funny side of anything.

They managed to push the car free without trouble. The cold night had formed a crust across the surface of the sand strong enough to bear the weight of the empty little Morris. If they loaded it up, however, the wheels would crack the surface and sink back down. They had no option but to drive on to a harder stretch of sand, even though that would mean repeating their exhausting task of humping all the luggage to the car afterwards.

As she was the smallest and lightest, Barbara was chosen to be the driver. She got in and pulled the door gently to.

The desert was at its most beautiful; cool and hazy, with the sun hovering tantalizingly out of sight below the horizon, tingeing the distance with a blush of pink.

The sallow pallor gave way, minute by minute, to peach, to coral, to crimson, as the vast, lifeless plain was warmed and resuscitated. The wind had dropped. There was no sound. Footsteps were hushed on the sand and even the clatter of plates and cutlery was muffled by the cocooning silence.

The noise of the engine ripped through the stillness as Barbara turned the ignition key. It seemed to echo to the farthest reaches of the desert, perhaps beyond.

'They probably heard that in London,' Peter said.

As Barbara eased her foot up, the others gave her a gentle push to be on the safe side. She drove off, keeping an eye both on the road ahead and, by leaning out of her door, on the sand underneath her. A couple of times she slowed right down, but the tell-tale cracking of the crust of sand persuaded her it would be wise to go that little bit further.

Peter, Freda and Alan watched the Morris disappearing into the distance. As the sound of the engine diminished and they were once again wrapped in the thick silence, their isolation struck them with renewed force.

'She's going a long way,' Peter said.

'Trying to find a firm enough patch of sand, I expect,' Freda said.

Although he knew that this was precisely what Barbara was doing, Peter found himself growing irrationally uneasy. What if it had occurred to her that though four could never make it, one just might? What if she'd realized that she'd be better off going it alone? What if they'd been abandoned?

His fear was recorded in his diary:

She kept going!! We thought she was running off . . . Surely she was not going to abandon us! . . . We were all greatly relieved when she turned and headed back, eventually stopping several hundred yards away. Of course, our fears were completely unfounded, but then the desert plays strange tricks on people's minds.

The walk across the sand to the car was exhausting. If they'd been able to carry everything in one go, it wouldn't have been so bad, but there was such a lot; too much luggage, too many individual items. They each had to go there and back three times.

The sun had wobbled its way above the horizon. Dark red and insubstantial, its pleasant warmth became intolerable within minutes. As it rose, it intensified, and by the time Alan and Peter returned for the last object, it was burning down with a numbing ferocity.

'We should have taken this first,' Peter said.

'I know, I know,' Alan answered resignedly. 'Right hand or left?'

'Right,' said Peter. 'We can change over in a minute.'

It had been a mistake leaving the chop-box till last. With the sun up, every yard they had to cover had become an effort – and not merely because of the heat. Since leaving Kenya they had become gradually acclimatized to the increasing temperatures. As the sun rose it began to dry the surface of the sand and now, with every third or fourth step, they broke through the fragile crust. Jolting downwards, their spines jarred and it felt as if their elbows and shoulders were being torn out of their sockets.

'Doesn't seem to be getting any nearer, does it?' Peter said as they changed round again.

'I wouldn't look if I were you,' Alan advised.

It would have been better, perhaps, if the sand had given way with every step; then they could have got into some sort of rhythm. But the firmness of the crust was impossible to judge and the Russian-roulette uncertainty continued right up to the hard shelf where Barbara had parked the car.

The last ten yards were the most arduous of all. They reached the car, let go of the steel handles and doubled up with exhaustion, panting. Peter pushed the plastered hair away from his eyes and sat down on the box. His knees were trembling.

'Well done, both of you,' Freda said.

'I couldn't stop any nearer. It was just too soft.' Barbara took Peter's wrist and inspected the raw blisters on his hands which had begun to throb viciously.

'They look painful,' said Freda.

'Could turn septic. I'll get you some ointment,' Barbara commented more practically.

Peter remained seated on the box, blowing gently on his hands while Barbara went to fetch the small first-aid box.

'Let me see.'

He held out his hands like a child proving that they were clean enough for the dinner table. Barbara squeezed some ointment from the tube.

'It's been a hard day,' she said.

'And it's only a quarter to six now,' said the seventeen-year-old philosophically. 'I suppose it can only get better.'

TWENTY FOUR

MAD DOGS AND ENGLISHMEN

IT was clear from Peter's diary that things went anything but well that Tuesday. If the four travellers had
hoped that the next time they got out of the car would be
on reaching the well at In Guezzam, they were to
be disappointed.

> 6376 Left: 6379 Lorry on left (broken). Body only and cab
> – as a warning . . . 6392 Stuck. 6393 Stuck. 6396 Stuck for
> 1 hr . . . 6402 Stuck for 10 secs. – but all pushed it out.
> 6413 Stuck . . . 6422 Stuck again. Only gallon water left
> . . . Time stuck 10.15 a.m.

Morale, however, was still high. There was no despair,
no panic, and certainly not even the faintest suggestion
that they might have to turn back.

The thinning crust of sand and the overladen Morris
proved to be a fatal combination. Even when the car
sank only a little, the clearance was so minimal that they
would find themselves bogged down once again. The
drill for extricating the car became automatic and was
carried out with military precision. Two would leap for
a rear wheel each and begin clearing away the choking
sand. Then either a campbed or the tarpaulin would be
eased underneath to provide the wheels with something

to grip. While the third person was checking water, oil and tyre pressure, the fourth would clear the front wheels, taking care to ensure there was neither a bump nor a concealed hole to ensnare the car a second time. An unsuccessful first attempt meant serious trouble as it embedded the wheels still further.

The procedure however, was susceptible to Sod's Law: if something could go wrong, it would.

'How's it looking?' Alan called from the front of the car.

It was their third stop and so far none had followed the textbook pattern of extrication. The first time, when Alan had accelerated, the tarpaulin had wound itself around the axle and jammed tightly on the U-bolts of the springs. It had taken the best part of an hour to wrench, bully and tease it free again. The next time, memory of this experience made them place the tarpaulin too far back and the spinning wheels merely spat it out and buried themselves even deeper.

'Nearly ready,' Peter replied.

'Give us a shout when you are.' Alan climbed back into the driver's seat.

When Peter was satisfied he stood back and signalled to Alan. Carefully and steadily, Alan released the clutch. The other three held their breath as the car lurched. Alan tried again, and this time the Morris glided smoothly out of the sand.

Freda patted Peter on the back.

'Why can't it always be so simple?' he asked.

'What, and take away all our fun?' Alan laughed.

Later that morning, the wind began to strengthen. Like the blast from an industrial furnace, there was something faintly metallic about its scorching heat. It whipped up the loose grains, sending airy sand-snakes zigzagging across the surface, before whirling them round and round into a hazy cloud that penetrated the tiniest opening. If Alan had sealed the car as he'd promised, it wasn't apparent. Even with the windows tightly closed, little drifts built up on the sills, on the dashboard, on the laps of the four travellers.

'Oh no, not again,' Barbara sighed as the sudden loss of speed signalled yet another stop, another back-breaking attempt to free the car, another exposure to the formidable elements.

Alan was the first out. He looked down at the wheels and winced.

'Doesn't look good,' he admitted, his voice whipped away on the wind. Whereas on the previous occasions only one, or maybe two wheels had stuck, this time all four were deeply entrenched in the soft sand. It made the job of getting the tarpaulin underneath impossible.

'Now what?' Barbara asked.

'Well, we can't stay here all day,' Peter said.

Alan was already down on his knees, anxiously shovelling the sand back with his bare hands. It was a hopeless task. The sand simply poured back into the hole he was making. He sat back on his ankles, closed his eyes and took a deep breath. Peter watched the older man and recognized the signs of fearful resignation. He reached into the car for the panga.

'Come on,' he said, encouragingly, 'it can't be as bad as all that.'

The sun was by this time nearing its zenith. Breathing in burnt the delicate skin inside their nostrils, causing them to lose precious water as tears. The swirling wind was howling round the car, whisking the sand up off the ground. It cracked their lips, lashed their skin, stung their eyes and, as Peter knelt on the ground, scraping around the wheels, the fine grains began to drift against his legs. It was not possible to free the car in these conditions and he was forced to abandon his own feeble efforts a few minutes later.

'We'll wait until it's cooled down a bit,' Alan shouted into the wind.

'Should we get back in the car?' Freda asked.

'I think it'd be best. It's hot, but at least we'll be out of the wind.'

Alan refused to heed his own advice. While the others sat in the suffocating heat of the car he paced back and forth in the scorching storm. They were down to 10 pints of water. The well at In Guezzam was still 60 miles away. He looked down at the wheels. If the storm didn't abate, the Morris would remain stuck. Alan found himself unable to make light of the practical problems any longer. He was frightened.

Sitting in the stifling car was not as dangerous as remaining outside. There, the strong wind, which dried the sweat instantly as it formed on the skin, would lead to rapid dehydration. Barbara knew this, and it was at her insistence that Alan finally climbed back into the car.

'Warm out,' he said and grinned.

The others smiled back weakly. They had been trying to sleep, to obliterate the present, but it proved impossible. They were condemned to experience every suffocating moment of their entrapment. Once again, Freda seemed to be tolerating the intense heat the best. Glistening with a mixture of cosmetic cream and perspiration, it was she who tried to rally the troops.

'Is this the worst situation you've ever been in?' she asked Alan.

'The worst?' he repeated. 'It's certainly the hottest. The worst . . . No, I suppose the worst was a couple of years ago . . .'

He and the Outram twins had been conscripted into the security forces in the face of increased Mau Mau activity. They had been sent from the Nandi district to Karatina where terrorists were suspected of hiding out in the forested uplands. The three of them were positioned by a fork in the road where it was rumoured that the wives would leave food and provisions for their menfolk. They dug a trench and settled down for the night. At over 8,000 feet it was cold, very cold, despite their greatcoats. They tried smoking, cupping their hands round the glowing tip to avoid giving themselves away. It was about 5.30, shortly before dawn, when they heard the footsteps.

'I jumped out of the trench,' Alan laughed. 'Stupid really. I couldn't see a thing. They could easily have shot me, but that didn't occur to me. I think it just felt good getting out of that freezing hole.'

Ignoring his shout of 'Halt!', the men continued running. Alan stepped forward, raised the Patchett automatic rifle to his eye and fired a semicircle of bullets into the darkness.

'We more or less gave up our watch then and lit a fire,' he continued. 'It got light soon after that, so we packed up and started back down the track to the village. We hadn't gone a hundred yards when we found a body. Then another. And another. All three with bullet holes right through the forehead. I'd scored a hat-trick.'

Despite the gory details, Freda couldn't help being impressed.

'Three,' she said. 'My goodness. And what happened to the bodies?'

'Not very pretty, I'm afraid,' Alan said. 'They carried them down to the railway station and left them on the platform as a warning to others.'

Peter found his mind wandering. The words 'warning to others' began to circle around his head ominously. He remembered the bleached bones they had passed. He remembered the skeleton of the tree trunk. But it was too hot to concentrate. Too hot to work things out. It was too hot even to breathe.

'Don't pant,' Barbara said gently.

'I . . .' he started to say. She was right: he had lost control and was panting like a dog.

'Take slow, deep breaths of air,' she instructed. 'Nice and slow. Otherwise you'll lose your body liquid far too quickly.'

It wasn't only Peter. The others also found that if they stopped concentrating on regular breathing it speeded up of its own accord, until they too were noisily puffing and blowing. Talking helped. Although paying attention to the other person's voice was tiring, it was impossible to pant and talk at the same time.

Peter remained quiet. He stared out of the windows into the hazy expanse of shimmering heat. It was how he'd imagined the surface of Venus would look. He tried to apply logic to the bizarre situation they were in.

They were about 60 miles from In Guezzam. They had 10 pints of water left between them. They would remain stuck in the sand until the temperature dropped. The problem was like a primary-school arithmetic puzzle: if it takes a Morris 4½ hours to do 46 miles, how many pints of water will four people need to reach the well? Or some such. As far as Peter could determine, there was only one answer to their predicament.

'I think we could get out now,' Alan said.

There was a lengthening shadow along the right-hand side of the car. What was more, the shade coincided with shelter from the wind. Freda and Barbara crawled out and sat down. Alan went to the front of the car and began checking under the bonnet: oil, plugs, radiator – it would be humiliating if after freeing the car the engine wouldn't start. Peter seized his chance. With the wind still howling, his words to Alan would remain private.

'I want to go for help,' he said simply.

'You what?'

'I want to go and get help.'

Alan stared at him incredulously.

'You think you can make it over *that*?' he asked, his arm sweeping round the horizon.

In Peter's head, the plan had been straightforward enough, but scanning the desert he had to admit to the magnitude of the task. Apart from the parallel tyre tracks which led from the edge of the circle to this central point, there was nothing but featureless sandy plains in every direction as far as he could see. Thoroughly daunting though the prospect was, what other option was left to them?

'I'll be fine,' he assured Alan. 'I can go through the night, while it's cool, and be back tomorrow evening with help and water.'

Alan seemed to be mulling over the idea.

'You'd get lost.'

'I thought about that. The moon's still almost full and it should be up at around nine tonight. I could follow the drums.'

Alan turned back to the car and fiddled with various wires and connections, ensuring that none of them had been shaken loose on the rough piste. Peter took his silence as permission to go, and he sidled away to plan the finer details of his rescue mission.

He would take his share of the water in one of the chargals, which he'd wrap around his waist. And then there was the small flask of whisky – for the cold night. His big hat was essential, as was a torch. He also decided to include a pencil and some paper to record the number of drums he passed. As long as he could cover the main stretch by night, everything should be all right.

There was only one other potential danger he could imagine. In something he'd heard or read, he had come across reports of packs of mad dogs which would attack the nomads, the camel caravans, anything that moved. But he couldn't let them stop him. If he was unlucky enough to stumble upon wild dogs – or vice versa – then it was fate taking a hand, and there was nothing anyone could do to counter that.

As Alan approached, Peter knew at once that his plans had been for nothing. It was plain from his expression precisely what he was going to say.

'We've, um . . . not been making particularly good progress,' he started, 'and I think it . . . I've decided to go and get help.'

'Where?' Freda exclaimed.

'In Guezzam.'

'But that's miles away. You'll never make it,' she protested.

Alan proceeded to outline the plan: taking his ration of water, walking by night, following the moonlit bidons . . .

'But that's my plan!' Peter exclaimed furiously. *I'm going for help.'

'You can't, Peter,' Barbara said.

'Why not? I'm much younger and I've got far more energy than him.'

'Alan's got more stamina,' Barbara contended.

'How do you know?'

'All that army training up in the Aberdares. He's bound to have.'

'It's very brave of you to offer,' Freda said. 'But I do think they're right. Older men have more staying power.'

'I should cocoa,' Alan laughed and winked at Freda. Even his humour was becoming desperate.

'Apart from anything else, it's Alan's responsibility as expedition leader,' Barbara said.

Peter turned away sulkily. It was obvious that nothing he could say was going to change their minds. Alan, not he, was going to seek assistance.

Peter's headstrong determination to walk to In Guezzam and rescue his companions interested me. It was classic

243

Boy's Own material and I wondered if he'd pictured himself in the romantic role of devil-may-care macho man. I asked him what kind of books he'd liked as a boy.

'Biggles,' he said with a laugh. 'I know what you're thinking, but no, I didn't want to be the big hero.'

'He's quite unassuming,' his wife, Margery, interrupted, 'but he doesn't like inaction. He needs to be actually doing something.'

'You see, we were stuck,' Peter said. 'That much was clear, and it would have been suicidal just to sit there and do nothing. It was obvious to me that someone would have to go for help. And I wanted to go.'

'You thought you could make it?'

'At the time, yes.'

There is a photograph in the album recording Alan's departure. The beleaguered Morris is to the right, with one of the empty chargals hanging from one of the quarter lights. Peter is sitting in the shade, looking down, still angry at how Alan's decision had been presented as a fait accompli. To the left are Freda and Alan. She is handing him the two bottles of water which were to last until he arrived at In Guezzam.

Recent research suggests that the regime of sipping rationed water at sporadic intervals is not only torturous, but also dangerous. A person sweats out more than he takes in by this method, leading to a net loss of liquid. It is far better to abstain for as long as possible and then drink until the thirst has been properly quenched. Yet it is the sip and suffer method of eking out water which every adventure-story writer imposes on his hero or heroine, adrift on the ocean or stranded in the desert. And if life doesn't copy art, it can be influenced by it. Peter may not have seen himself in the Biggles mould, but he and the others certainly employed Biggles' methods of survival.

In the photograph, Alan's pitiful two-bottle ration is

silhouetted against the vast desolate plains behind him. The sheer inadequacy of the amount is farcical, a feature mirrored by the man himself. He is standing there, a somewhat tubby man who could be a day-tripper reaching for a Thermos cup of coffee from his wife on the sands at Blackpool. He is wearing baggy knee-length shorts, a short-sleeved shirt, socks and shoes: on his head is a knotted handkerchief. There is a kettle in the foreground next to the ashes of a fire. Any second now they will all have a nice cup of tea and head back home before the roads get too busy.

It is altogether too eccentric. Four English travellers dressed in frocks and sandals, socks and shorts, attempting to cross one of the world's most notorious wastelands in an overloaded 8 h.p. Morris Traveller. How could they have presumed to undertake such a challenge so ill-prepared? The djinns would not tolerate such irreverence. The Sahara will be respected.

'Fine,' Barbara said as she handed the Brownie back to Peter.

'I think I'm just about ready,' Alan said. 'Got my torch, got my pen and paper, got my water,' he added, raising the two bottles.

'I still think this is madness,' Barbara said. 'Why don't we just wait for the Foreign Legion? We registered at Agadès – they're bound to come looking for us when we don't turn up at In Guezzam.'

'Belt and braces never did anyone any harm,' Alan said.

'But the whole point of registering with the French authorities is for emergencies like . . .'

'The French!' Alan said dismissively. 'You don't think you can trust the Frogs, do you?'

The sun was nearing the horizon when Alan finally set off. He'd be able to walk for an hour and a half before it became too dark to see. Then he could rest for a couple of hours until the moon rose. He shook hands with the two women, wishing them well. Peter he took aside.

'I'm leaving you in charge,' he said quietly. 'Look after them both.'

Peter nodded.

'Thanks, son,' he said.

'Good luck.'

They watched Alan walk off towards the nearest bidon. The wind had dropped and the sun was preparing for its palette display. Even if they hadn't noticed it sinking they would have known evening was near by the change of smell. As the searing power of the sun declines the ghost of the Sahara's once fertile past arises, as a warm, almost earthy scent laces the air.

They saw him reach the first bidon and continue. All three were still waiting for his farewell wave, but Alan never looked back.

TWENTY FIVE

THE LAST ILL-OMEN

ONLY when Alan was finally swallowed up by the murky gloom did Peter turn away. He looked around at the other two who had already started preparing for the night; connecting the inspection lamp, collecting scraps for a little fire, unfolding the campbeds. Routine had proved stronger than reality, Peter noted with a jolt: they had put up all four beds.

Seeing the place where no one would sleep that night filled him with a sudden apprehension. It was as though the desert was planning to pick them off, one by one. Alan had gone and the loss was like having a tooth extracted: while there, it is part of a group, but being absent imbues it with a disproportionate importance and the tongue probes round exploring the unfamiliar gap.

Peter probed into the gap that Alan had left. While the older man had been leading the trek, Peter had generally been willing to follow instructions, to do as he was told. As Alan had walked off into the distance, Peter's parameters had blurred. He'd been told to take care of the women, but how far was this possible? In 1955, his sex placed him automatically in a position of authority; his age, on the other hand, relegated him to junior status.

He neatly bypassed the conflict by stating that he was

247

going to get the car out of the sand. In this way he assumed responsibility for the group without having to give instructions to the two women.

'Can I help at all,' Freda asked.

'No, I'm all right,' Peter said. 'If you could make just sure the beds are well away from the car so I've got a bit of room to manoeuvre.'

Checking underneath with the inspection lamp, he was relieved to see that the car wasn't as badly stuck as he'd feared. Although the petrol tank was resting on the sand and the springs and front wheels were partly buried, it was only the rear shaft and axle that had been deeply embedded. Using Alan's folded bed as a base, he jacked up the first rear wheel as far as it would go. There was only a slim chance that his plan would work, but buoyed up by the thought of Alan's look of surprise when they finally caught up with him, he persevered.

'How's it going?' Barbara asked some while later.

'Fine,' he said. 'I'm going to see if I can get the mattresses underneath.'

'You think they'll do the trick?'

'I don't know,' he admitted. 'I'm filling most of the hole under the wheels with sand first. Just have to keep your fingers crossed.'

'When you're ready, we've made some supper.'

The break was very welcome. Sausages, broadbeans and mushrooms were washed down with a strong cup of tea which, as Peter noted, was made to last half an hour. He returned to the clogged wheels with renewed enthusiasm.

With the right-hand rear tyre up in the air, he pushed sand into the holes the spinning wheels had made and compacted it as much as the dryness would allow. Then, taking care not to knock the jack, which was balancing precariously on the frame of the campbed, he slid the mattress into the narrow gap he'd left. Scarcely daring to

248

breathe, he turned the ratchet of the jack and lowered the car gently. It made contact with the cotton ticking and slowly pressed into the soft wadding. Peter felt increasingly nervous as the wheel continued to descend without any sign of resistance from the mattress. And then it happened. The sand stopped shifting and Peter was able to let the car down completely without it sinking at all.

'Thank God,' he whispered, grinning excitedly to himself. If one had worked, there was no reason why the others wouldn't be as successful.

Freda had come over to ask if he was sure there wasn't anything they could do.

'No,' Peter said again. 'I'm happy working on my own, thanks.'

'As you like,' Freda said, 'but do give us a shout if you need a hand.'

'Why don't you get some sleep?' he suggested.

She nodded. Freda had been suffering since they had entered the desert. Not so much from the heat – she had coped with the temperatures better than anyone else – but from insects. Although she was markedly less jumpy with the creepy-crawlies than before, they still made her squirm with horror every time she found one walking across her skin. And there were many – huge glossy spiders, purple-and-black flies, and ants that seemed to get larger and larger the less hospitable the desert became. That morning her foresight had prevented a painful bite. As she had shaken her shoe before slipping it on, a scorpion had dropped out and scuttled away.

'They're meant to be rare in the sandy areas,' she'd screeched.

'There's one type in the northern Sahara that grows to over 4 inches long,' Peter mentioned tactlessly.

'I don't want to know that,' Freda said.

'*Buthus* something or other,' he continued.

'I don't want to know,' she repeated firmly.

If only this works, Peter thought, as he repeated the procedure of jack, sand and mattress with the second back wheel.

It did, and he stood back to inspect the car. It looked strange in the fiery glow of the red inspection lamp: a Morris in the middle of the desert with two mattresses protruding from its back wheels like two lolling tongues.

The front wheels were easier to prepare. As long as there were no large obstructions for them to stick on, the rear wheel drive ought to be powerful enough to pull the car free. All the same, anxious that nothing should go wrong, he checked under the car three times. If the tyres did slip, five hours work would have been completely wasted.

It was past eleven at night. Even though he'd been up since five that morning after an almost sleepless night, he couldn't retire before knowing whether he had managed to get the car out. He closed the bonnet gently and climbed into the driver's seat.

'Barbara, Freda,' he called out, 'stand by to push.'

The two women leapt out of their sleeping bags and were standing in front of him, eagerly awaiting his word a moment later.

'Don't do anything until I say,' he shouted over the revving engine.

Leaning out of the window so that he could watch the rear wheels, he eased out the clutch. To his horror, he saw in the light of Barbara's torch that they were beginning to slip.

It's not possible, he thought desperately. I checked everything.

He revved harder and lifted his foot a little lighter. The car suddenly lurched, throwing him hard against the steering wheel as it jerked backwards. At the end of the mattresses, the wheels slid gently on to the hard sand behind them. He continued to reverse until the whole car was out. Then he switched off the ignition.

There was a moment of absolute silence, and then the women began clapping and cheering.

'Bravo!' Barbara yelled.

It had been an exhausting day, but despite the fact that they were now down to one pint of water each, spirits were high. Tomorrow, if things went well, they would be reunited with Alan, and the four of them could complete the trek they had set out to do.

As always, before turning in, Peter filled in his diary. 'Girls so pleased I was allowed one glass of good water. More hope now!'

Barbara's alarm woke them at 3.30 the following morning. It was long before dawn and, as if maliciously contrasting the scalding heat of the day to come, icy cold. Their fingers were awkward and slow as they packed everything away.

'Here's a wee dram,' Barbara said, passing round a small glass of their remaining whisky. 'Get the circulation going.'

'That's better,' Freda sighed as the warming spirit slipped down her throat.

Drinking whisky was probably the worst possible way they could have prepared for their day. Alcohol absorbs water, dehydrating the bodies of even healthy drinkers. In their already dehydrated state, Barbara, Freda and Peter were effectively reducing the paltry two pints of water still further.

When the rising sun lightened the sky enough to see a couple of hundred yards ahead, they set off, following Alan's footprints. It was Wednesday, 11 May. A mileage of 6422 was on the clock. They had come 3,882 miles since their departure almost a month before.

The going was good at first. The chilly night had

solidified the surface crust of sand and it was clear which patches were hard and which should be avoided. At the wheel, Peter coped with any deceptively soft areas by putting his foot down and straining the engine no matter how loudly the damaged big end knocked in protest.

As they drove on the sand gave way to the infamous *feche-feche*. This fine mixture of dust and gypsum, the powder under the fragile top layer, would cling to the tyres as resolutely as mud. The area was made more treacherous by the presence of jagged black rocks which, as Peter noted, 'sprang out of nowhere'.

It was one of these rocks that they struck after only 8 miles. The sickening grinding of stone on metal was horrifyingly familiar. They were only too aware of what had happened the previous time they had struck a rock.

Please let the sump be all right, please let it be all right, Peter prayed to anyone who might be listening as he climbed out of the car.

The sump was fine, but the rock was digging into the petrol tank.

'Do you think if we tried to lift it as Peter drove off, it might work?' Freda suggested.

'We haven't the strength,' Barbara said miserably.

Peter drove forward slowly. The grating noise at the bottom of the tank scraped over the rough surface of the rock was worse than any dentist's drill. With their teeth grinding together in sympathy, Freda and Barbara tried willing the metal not to give way. An eternity passed as they waited for the rock to emerge behind the exhaust pipe.

'Let's have a look,' said Peter, jumping out. The car was far too low now for him to crawl underneath. He could see that the tank had been badly dented but, fortunately, none of their precious petrol was escaping.

It took three hours to complete 17 miles, and Peter's

diary records the relentless grip the desert continued to exert over them. '6433 – stuck on a rock. 6435 – small stuck. 6439 – stuck three times!'

Before they became utterly demoralized, however, they arrived at a better stretch. It was an area of the rocky *hamada* that had characterized so much of Alan's 1933 crossing to the west. Peter soon had the car up to 35 miles an hour and, for the first time in two days, they felt the benefit of the cooling breeze coming through the open windows.

'He's going to be so surprised to see us,' Freda said. 'I can't wait to see the expression on his face.'

'I hope he hasn't come across any mad dogs,' Peter breathed softly.

'You and your mad dogs!' Barbara laughed. 'Where on earth did you read about them? Even if they do exist, the chances of both mad dogs and an Englishman out in the same midday sun are highly unlikely.'

'I did read it somewhere,' Peter said defensively, glad all the same that Barbara had made light of it.

Peter had been following Alan's footprints across the sand. When the ominous change of colour in the surface loomed immediately in front of them, there was no time to brake. All he could do was to accelerate as hard as he could and hope the momentum would get them across to the other side. They were within feet of the edge when the Morris gave up the struggle and sank into the loose sand. The rear of the car buried itself up to the bumper.

Peter began scrabbling away at the sand like a man possessed. They couldn't be bogged down again. They couldn't spend another day under that merciless sun.

'Leave it,' said Barbara placing her hand on his shoulder. 'You can't possibly get it out in this heat.'

'I can,' he shouted. 'It's not that bad.'

'Look at it,' Barbara shouted back. 'It's at least as bad as last night, and how long did that take you?'

Peter sat back and pushed the sweaty fringe of hair away from his forehead. He knew she was right.

They covered the car with blankets in an attempt to insulate it from the burning heat, but still the inside of the Morris was like a kiln. Peter sat fretting, the intolerable heat, the agonizing thirst, the tantalizing proximity of the edge of the loose sand . . .

'Couldn't I have one more try?' he said weakly.

'Out of the question,' Barbara stated.

In his diary Peter may have described the two women as 'girls', but effectively it was Barbara who was now in charge. She rationed the remaining water with single-minded inflexibility. They were down to a sip of water every two hours. Outside, glimpsed through the cracks between the blankets, the shimmering mirages of magnificent cool lakes mocked the risible supply they were struggling to prolong.

Peter noticed there was a stone under his foot. He vaguely recalled in something he'd read as a boy (probably *Biggles*) that a pebble had saved the hero's life. When sucked, it had produced pints of cool natural water which had quenched the most voracious thirst. Nothing ventured, nothing gained: Peter dusted it on his shorts and popped it in his mouth. The promised slaking failed to occur. The stone was soon coated with the same claggy scum that clung to his teeth and glued his swollen tongue to the roof of his mouth. He spat it out of the window in disgust.

'A little drop,' he begged Barbara.

'Just wait for a bit,' she insisted.

He turned away and silently cursed this tyrant who was torturing him so mercilessly. Wait for a bit, wait for a bit – the words went round and round on an endless loop. Time crawled by, hour after featureless hour. The water slowly diminished.

In a last-ditch attempt to preserve as much body

moisture as possible, Barbara told them to bandage themselves up. They secured handkerchiefs and towels over their eyes, their noses and mouths: it would prevent transpiration, she explained. Physically this may have been correct; psychologically it was almost to be their undoing. Locked in darkness and silence, their brains intensified the one sense of which they would willingly have agreed to be deprived.

The heat was insufferable. It burnt them not only from outside, but also from within, as if their very core was in flames. It made no sense. Confused and disorientated, Peter wondered what he was doing there, sitting in the blistering darkness? What crime had he committed to be condemned to this fiery void? Panic stirred as, forgetting the blindfold, he reasoned that the heat had stolen his sight. He couldn't talk. He couldn't even breathe, he realized with sudden numbing terror. He was being suffocated, smothered; someone's hand was over his mouth, choking him . . .

He ripped frantically at the blindfold rags and gulped lungfuls of acrid air that scraped his throat, rasped his uvula. In front of him was the mirror image of the horror he had felt. Freda too had torn away the pieces of cloth. Her face, contorted by agonizing thirst, had renounced its human qualities, abandoned the veil of manners and decorum. She was panting shamelessly and curious guttural noises were emanating from her gaping mouth.

'Wha'?' Peter croaked.

She repeated herself, and nodded through the window. Peter looked but saw nothing.

Time hadn't ground to a complete standstill after all. Imperceptibly, the sun had been crossing the sky and was now down near the horizon once again. Barbara looked at Peter, who looked in turn at Freda. They all smiled. They had made it.

Once the sun had set the temperature plummeted, and with the sudden chill both their energy and their dignity returned. They were able to sip the water without feeling the need to drain the cup in one greedy gulp.

'Civilized behaviour is difficult when one is so hot,' Freda commented.

'Perhaps we should write a paper on the subject,' Barbara said, and laughed.

The embarrassment they had all been feeling passed. They were once more able to look one another in the eye, knowing that no one was about to mention their individual lack of control.

'I'll have another go at the car,' Peter announced.

'We'll get some supper ready.'

While the bitter cold descended, the previous night's procedure was repeated to the letter. Peter used the mattresses once again to free the car; Barbara and Freda lit a fire and made a light meal. At half past ten, the car lurched up on to the hard stretch of ground they had only just failed to make twelve harrowing hours earlier.

Similar though the two nights had been, they were not identical. The day had taken its toll. Peter could no longer crouch and stand and walk and bend as he worked on the wheels. He hadn't the energy. Now, as he kept his meticulous check on every aspect of the recovery, he had to crawl on his hands and knees. And whereas the night before, they had poured away the slops from their cups, today they drank every last drop of tea, spitting out the chewed-up tea leaves when there was no trace of moisture left.

Although the car was out of the drift and on the hard surface once again, the heady joy of the previous night was also absent. Not that they weren't pleased. Nor because they knew they could easily get stuck again a hundred yards on. In fact they had let out a brief cheer as the car had clambered up on to the rocky plain. A moment later, however, one of them had noticed the tiny heap of matted fur lying in one of the tyre tracks.

When the car had jolted forward, Rikki the mongoose had lost its balance and tumbled down from the open window on to the sand where, still semi-paralysed from the accident in Maiduguri, it hadn't been able to drag itself away from the oncoming wheel. The three of them stood around the little animal, despondent and anxious. In his diary, Peter subsequently wrote:

> . . . in the process of getting unstuck I killed Rikki. So we recorded our first death and buried him in the sand. Sailors are very superstitious as regards killing an albatross and I often wonder if the death of Rikki could possibly have had any connection with what later followed.

TWENTY SIX

WHO DARES WINS

'We should try and get the weight of the car down,' Barbara said as they were packing up the following morning.

'You mean leave some of our belongings?' Freda said.

Two weeks earlier the thought would have horrified her. Now it made perfect sense to do everything possible to increase the clearance under the car, to give that fragile crust of sand as light a load as possible, and she went on to sort out a case of cosmetics, clothes and shoes, and souvenirs she would just have to describe when she got back to England.

If she ever got back to England.

They left at 4.30 in the morning as the pastel blues and yellows in the sky were streaked with red. Behind them lay a heap of possessions – the foldaway chairs and campbed bases, cooking pots, mosquito nets, Alan's bundle of anti-Mau Mau tracts, Barbara's soda syphon and duffel coat, and the wireless that had failed to keep Freda up with the news – testimony to their last desperate bid to free themselves from the brutal hold of the Sahara.

The sand proved unimpressed with their attempt to lessen the weight of the Morris. It sank before they had driven a mile. By now every heave and shove counted, as their last reserves of energy rapidly drained away. Half a mile further on and they sank again. The heat had already returned with a vengeance.

'I can't,' Freda muttered.

'We've got to,' Peter said. 'We'll never last another day under this sun.'

'How much water is there?'

'Less than two pints.'

Bowing to the inevitable, Freda lowered her shoulder to the car and began pushing. The third time they got stuck, she started crying. Not from self-pity. Not from fear. But from uncharacteristic rage and frustration at the sheer cussedness of the desert.

She wiped away the tears. 'Waste of good water,' she said, and smiled wryly.

When they ground to a halt for the fourth time, it was immediately clear that they were going to have considerable difficulty freeing the car. They were right in the middle of a vast patch of soft sand. Looking back at the two deep furrows the tyres had made, it was hard to imagine how they had got so far into it.

The milometer confirmed the worst. They had covered a mere five miles. In Guezzam was still 30 miles off – at their current rate of progress, that was still a day and a half away.

'Push! Push!' Peter muttered rhythmically in an attempt to coordinate their efforts.

The Morris rocked forward a little, but a ridge of sand which had developed at the front shoved it back again. With the gangly thrash of a drunkard, Peter stumbled to the front of the car, dropped to his knees and began stroking the sand flat. For a moment he was back on a Zanzibar beach with his ayah, patting the walls of his sandcastle into shape. With a painful jolt, the desert was back in place. Peter leant against the car to pull himself up.

He looked ahead. Giant glass monsters were striding across the plains, one after the other, always avoiding his direct gaze. It's just my eyes playing tricks, he told himself. Optical illusions. But he knew that wouldn't make them go away. He could see close up, the car, Freda, Barbara; he could see the far horizon, but there was nothing in-between. Simply emptiness, an abhorrent void which his brain refused to acknowledge and his eyes filled up with visions, however unlikely.

'What's the matter?' Barbara asked him.

'Nothing,' he replied as he continued staring in front of him. Something had caught his eye, something solid in the shimmering haze. But there couldn't be anything there. It was one more of the desert's cruel deceptions. Thirsting travellers see cool oases with date palms and orange groves; stranded merchants see glistening towns with white walls, mosques and slender minarets. Peter's mirage was more modest. He was seeing an approaching truck.

He turned away. Mirages hate to be ignored. It was still there when he looked back. It was still there!

'Look!' he screamed as loudly as his parched throat would allow. 'Something . . . over there!'

Barbara squinted into the distance. 'Don't tease, Peter,' she croaked. 'It's not fair.'

'There is,' he insisted and reached into the car for the binoculars. His hands shaking, he struggled to focus the glasses.

'Let me have a look.' Barbara held them up to her eyes. She lowered her arms slowly and let the binoculars dangle from their strap.

'What is it? What is it?' Freda asked. 'Is there anything there?'

Barbara couldn't say a word. She was sobbing uncontrollably.

* * *

The distant speck became a dot. And the dot became a blob which, like some mutant amoeba from a Hammer horror film, split into two as it wobbled towards the three eagerly waiting travellers.

'It's like a watched pot,' Freda said.

'You mean a watched lorry never arrives,' said Barbara.

'That's right,' Freda smiled, and turned her back on it.

'There's a lorry and a car, I think,' Peter said a moment later.

He had no intention of missing a single second of their rescue. Keeping his eyes fixed on the approaching vehicles, Peter was savouring every moment as they zig-zagged across the treacherous piste, navigating their way round the patches of loose sand that would have halted the progress of the Morris.

'Hey,' he said. 'Let's finish off the water.'

'Why not,' Barbara said.

They gulped down all their remaining water. It was warm and stale, and tasted wonderful.

An eternity later the two vehicles finally stopped. Because of the softness of the sand, they had pulled up 600 yards away. It only confirmed the impossible task the travellers would have had to face in trying to free the Morris.

First out of the lorry-cab was a swarthy middle-aged man with dark hair and a black moustache. He waved and called them over. While they were walking towards him, the other door opened and a second man climbed down on to the sand. His hair was fairer, his skin light. It was Alan.

'He made it,' Freda gasped.

No one had mentioned Alan as the lorry was approaching. They hadn't dared. That all four of the travellers might be saved had seemed too much to hope for, particularly since Alan had broken the golden rule of

261

survival by refusing to stay with his vehicle. But there he was – dwarfed by the 3-ton Citroën truck he was standing beside – and very definitely alive.

It was only as they neared him that Freda, then Peter, and finally Barbara all registered the awful toll the walk had taken on him. Skeletally thin and almost unable to support his own weight, he was leaning weakly against the bumper of the lorry. His stubbled cheeks had hollowed out and deep lines extended down from the corners of his mouth; his eyes, sunk into grey circles, stared unfocused into mid-air; his skin was loose, leathery and deathly pale from the dusting of sand which covered every inch. They knew they were looking at someone who had escaped death by minutes.

'Alan,' was all they said.

They shook hands with him, hugged him, slapped him on the back, but nobody spoke. There were no words which could express their relief, their gratitude, their sympathy for the broken, barefoot man in front of them.

'You are more advanced than we think,' the Algerian driver, Georges de Zorzi, told them. 'Mr Cooper say you 30 miles more.'

'We managed to get the car out,' Peter explained.

'It is good we come now,' the Algerian said. 'The road becomes always more bad. But you have thirst. To drink, to drink.' And at a sign from him, his assistants leapt up on to the truck to get water for the three parched travellers.

There was certainly no shortage. As well as three 50-gallon drums up with the cargo, six chargals – whole sheepskins tied by their legs to a row of hooks – were hanging along the side of the truck. These contained a further 30 gallons of drinking water which, because the truck had been moving all day, was deliciously chilled.

'Not too much,' de Zorzi warned them as they reached

262

out for the water they'd been dreaming of for the previous two days. 'It can be dangerous.'

While they sipped at their drinks, Ali – de Zorzi's number two – ladled some of the tepid water from the barrels over their heads.

'Oh, that feels wonderful.' Freda shuddered as the water trickled inside her blouse and down her back. 'I never thought I'd ever feel cool again.'

The second vehicle meanwhile had drawn up beside them. It was a VW Beetle driven by Fredi and Heidi Saxer, a Swiss couple on their way to the Cameroons, where they were planning to study the local flora.

'You were already in the Cameroons?' Heidi asked.

'Passed through it briefly,' Barbara said. 'That's where all the problems started. We hit a rock and ripped the sump open.'

'I think it is not easy in such a car,' Heidi said, tutting sympathetically. 'Therefore we travel through the desert with a local driver. Even so we are having problems,' she added and nodded towards her husband.

Fredi, who couldn't speak English, was taking the opportunity to fiddle around with various connections in the engine. Since leaving Tamanrasset, the flow of petrol had been increasingly temperamental and he was determined to find out what was blocking the supply.

'And the sand,' Heidi was continuing. '*Furchtbar.* Terrible. The men of de Zorzi have often to push us out of the dunes, though we try to avoid. Even he was . . .' she mimed the familiar sight of wheels spinning uselessly in loose sand.

'Bogged down,' Barbara said.

'*Genau,*' Heidi said. 'He must used these things there.'

Swinging from hooks positioned along the side of the truck were two 3-metre sheets of metal. Above them were two shovels and a tow-cable. Peter couldn't help comparing de Zorzi's equipment with the paltry collection of odds and ends the four of them had had at their disposal. The jack that sank into the sand, the spanners that didn't fit, the tarpaulin which insisted on wrapping itself round the wheel axle, and on top of all this, a supply of water that the smallest delay rendered insufficient. They had never stood a chance.

'*Fertig*,' Fredi announced.

'He's ready,' said Heidi. 'We can go further.'

The Morris was also ready. De Zorzi's men had pushed it up on to the hard ground. Freda turned to Alan.

'Soon be back,' she said encouragingly. 'We'll get the doctor to give you a good going over.'

Alan's limp weak body suddenly stiffened. He turned round and glared at her.

'Back? Back?' he shouted. 'We're going on, not back.'

No one spoke. It hadn't even occurred to the others that Alan might still want to continue. They had been lost and nearly died, and now they were safe again. The chances of being saved once were remote: it seemed, at the very least, unwise to chance their luck a second time. Alan was adamant.

'This is my trek, my car, and it's my decision now. We get some water from de Zorzi and we go on.'

'We are not going on,' Barbara said firmly. 'Not alone.'

'I say we are,' he persisted.

'All right, go on then,' Barbara snapped, 'if you think you can do it then go, but we're not! We're going back with Monsieur de Zorzi.'

Alan looked to Peter for support. The boy shrugged.

'Barbara's right,' he said. 'You're in no state . . .'

'Right,' he interrupted furiously. 'As long as I know how it is. If you're all so dead set on going back, back we shall go.'

His crew had mutinied and Alan recognized that this particular battle of wills had been lost. He was damned, however, if he was going to lose the entire war. The opportunity for another assault arose almost immediately.

'You follow my truck,' de Zorzi was instructing Peter, 'drive in the tyre tracks where the sand is more hard. We stay together. If one stop, others stop. Is very important.'

Peter nodded. 'Do you think we'll make Agadès tonight?' he asked.

Before de Zorzi could answer, Alan had butted in once again. Apparently calm now, he explained that there was no need to return to Agadès; they would accompany him only as far as In Abbangarit, the well where they'd last filled up all their canisters, bottles and drums.

'We can stay in that little building we saw,' he continued, 'and wait for de Zorzi here to complete his business in Agadès and return. Then we can travel back with him to In Guezzam and on to Tamanrasset. After that, it's plain sailing.'

The others remained stubbornly unconvinced, but once again Alan seemed so sure of himself that it undercut their own self-confidence.

'Surely you don't want to give up now?' he added.

It was an unfair question. Of course they didn't, but having almost died, they at least were treating the trek a little more seriously than before. In the end it was Freda who spoke. With words she must have used a thousand times when trying to pacify the clamouring infants in her class, she managed also to calm Alan down.

'We'll see,' she said.

He smiled. The war had been won.

TWENTY SEVEN

IN CONVOY

Even though he was following in de Zorzi's lorry tracks, Peter found the going difficult. Time after time the little Morris would become deeply embedded in the sand and de Zorzi's men had to jump down from the back of the truck and push them free. Peter felt increasingly embarrassed, and the more agitated he became, the faster he seemed to find the next patch of ensnaring sand.

They had set off at eleven o'clock. Alan was once again sitting next to de Zorzi in the lorry and, having filled one of the gallon tins with water, the other three had settled back in the Morris. By 11.30 it was clear that the driving conditions were too much for the seventeen-year-old and, after their umpteenth stop, de Zorzi told his number two to take over at the wheel.

Ali looked no more than fourteen or fifteen, yet he knew how to cope with the sand. He seemed to sense intuitively when to follow the tyre marks, when to flick the wheel to one side and leave the track, and when to return. If he hadn't already discovered for himself how deceptive the surface could be, Peter might have assumed the younger boy was showing off, twisting the wheel this way and that for effect rather than purpose. His own experience, however, convinced him that Ali was a driver of consummate skill.

The next time they stopped it was not due to anyone becoming stuck in the sand. De Zorzi had noticed something by the side of the road and decided to investigate. It was the pile of belongings Barbara, Peter and Freda had abandoned earlier. At the time, they'd had no idea they would be retrieving them so soon.

'You had very bad problems here,' de Zorzi commented, seeing the deep tyre tracks and footprints.

'You're not kidding,' Peter said.

'It was well done to get out.'

From a man with so much experience of the desert, this was indeed a compliment.

'You know, it was luck I found you. And Mr Cooper,' he continued. 'The Volkswagen of the Saxers broke down and we must spend the night at In Guezzam – otherwise we are driving through yesterday.'

'Well, thank goodness the Beetle isn't quite as perfect as it's made out to be,' Barbara said.

De Zorzi laughed. 'Here, nothing is enough perfect!'

Apart from their more personal belongings, which they took back into the Morris, they loaded the rest on to de Zorzi's lorry.

'Free transport!' he said, and roared with laughter.

'It must lose something in the translation,' Freda whispered to Peter as they climbed into the car.

They drove on for several miles, retracing not only their tracks but also the churned-up patches of footprints and spinning wheel where they'd been temporarily bogged down. Seeing the reminders of the problems they'd had, Freda, Barbara and Peter were silently back there; sweating, straining, struggling with a situation they had been unable to escape.

De Zorzi had told them that the desert was constantly changing. The sand would shift, dunes would move, landmarks which were obscured on one trip would reappear on the next. Never two crossings are the same, he had said. He was making for Agadès on this journey, delivering supplies to the barren outposts of El Golèa, In Salah and In Guezzam en route. By the time he returned to Algiers, all trace of the awful problems the Morris had had to face would have vanished for ever.

Had they perished, the travellers too could have simply disappeared under an advancing crescent-shaped dune. The thought made them shudder and they all realized how at ease they now felt being a part of a convoy.

Unlike the others, Alan was far from happy with the situation. He felt that he'd lost control of his trek, and the fact that they weren't now even travelling in the right direction galled him.

At around 1 o'clock, de Zorzi drew up next to a lorry travelling in the opposite direction. It was being driven by three Europeans who were heading for the Mediterranean. Alan immediately saw them as the opportunity to return to his original schedule.

Any hopes he might have had were soon dashed. The driver must have considered the condition of both the Morris and its occupants as too much of a liability, and he flatly refused to have anything to do with them. Alan became belligerent.

'Come on,' he said. 'What's it to you? We only want to drive along behind you.'

'No,' the driver of the lorry repeated.

'You can't just refuse . . .' Alan shouted, evidently forgetting how dismissively he had treated Antoine Laugel. 'You can't stop us going wherever we want.'

The man simply laughed.

'Too much sun,' one of the others added, as they drove off.

What had been intended as an offhand remark was in fact true. Alan *had* had too much sun, and his erratic behaviour was a symptom of this condition. Although he had survived the ordeal of the desperate walk for help, he had not yet recovered from it.

Trudging through the night, the temperature outside was low enough to keep his body cool, but once the sun rose and he was unable to get away from its searing power, his body had rapidly overheated. The effects of this condition are serious. The *Oxford Textbook of Medicine* details precisely what takes place:

> If heat loss is insufficient, the consequent rise in body temperature leads to hyperventilation, to cerebral dysfunction involving irritability and confusion, and ultimately to cardiovascular collapse . . . and death.

When de Zorzi had first seen Alan, he was lying unconscious, spreadeagled on the sand. It was impossible to say how long he had lain there, but it was likely that damage to the large cells of the cerebellum and cerebral cortex had already taken place. This would account for the problem he was having with balance, voluntary movements and moods. 'Severe cases of heat stroke . . . if they recover, may show lasting cerebellar or cerebral signs.'

Ironically, his condition would have been accentuated by the fact that he was already acclimatized to the temperatures of the desert. People who have become used to the heat sweat more – a fact which would have speeded up the process of dehydration.

It is easy for a healthy person to diagnose both heat-stroke and water loss. The patient is irritable, confused and suffers from headaches. The eyes and cheeks are sunken, the skin is hot, dry, and has lost its elasticity. Alan was a textbook example of the condition and yet his fellow travellers failed to recognize how ill he was.

In part, this was due to ignorance: in part, to their own condition. They saw his sunken eyes and hanging skin, of course, but not the damaged cerebellum. Unaware that his irascibility could be a symptom of something serious, they assumed it stemmed from his frustration at being unable to complete the trek the way he'd envisaged. Nor could they judge the effect of the sun on themselves. For just as Alan's irrational determination to continue was a result of overexposure to the sun, so the two days' overheating and dehydration that the others had been forced to endure had lowered their own ability to reason and assess.

Had they been able to interpret what they saw a little more accurately, the catastrophic events which later ensued might never have taken place.

It was Georges Dante de Zorzi who understood Alan's condition best of all. The forty-two-year-old lorry driver had been crossing the Sahara for over two decades and had encountered travellers in various degrees of distress, from mild disorientation to complete collapse. Occasionally he had even come across the bodies of those who had given up completely. Every stage in the gradual disintegration of a person lost under the desert sun was familiar to him and he realized at once that Alan was a very sick man.

When he finally reached Agadès he made a statement to the police about Alan's health and state of mind:

About 60 kilometers south of In Guezzam I saw a white man getting up . . .

The man was wearing neither hat, sun-glasses nor shoes, and was dying of thirst.

I bathed him, gave him a little to drink and having placed him on the seat next to me, continued in the direction of Agadès.

270

The Englishman ... seemed no longer to be in possession of all his mental faculties.

Whereas de Zorzi could understand and sympathize with the way Alan was feeling, the deteriorating physical condition of his passenger was making driving increasingly problematic.

Rehydration must be done painstakingly slowly. Drinking too much liquid at once can be fatal and so small sips should be administered to the patient at regular intervals over a long period. At first, de Zorzi had been able to do this himself. But as Alan's body had gradually rehydrated, all the emergency reserves of energy he had tapped retreated and he had been overcome with fatigue. Time and again Alan collapsed with exhaustion, slumping to the floor, across the driving wheel, against de Zorzi himself. Even for the lorry the desert conditions were such that any lack of concentration on the part of the driver could lead to its getting stuck. It was becoming too much of a risk, a risk de Zorzi wasn't prepared to take.

'We must to rearrange the seating,' he announced once all three vehicles had stopped. 'Mr Cooper should lie down.'

It took some while to come to a decision and the final seating arrangement they agreed on was the usual mixture of compromise and chance. Initially, Barbara and Freda were to sit in the lorry next to de Zorzi, Peter would stay in the Morris, either sitting next to Alan in the back, helping him drink, or next to Ali who would continue to drive.

At the lorry door, however, Freda claimed that she was too tired to climb up on to the seat.

'Anyway, if I travel in the Morris, I'll be able to help Alan,' she said, 'as long as you don't mind travelling in the lorry on your own.'

271

'Not in the slightest,' Barbara said. 'It's entirely up to you.'

'It is too full, the Morris, I think,' de Zorzi said. 'Four people.'

'Well, I can take over the driving for a while,' Peter said. 'The going's easier here – and I've learnt a lot.' He grinned at Ali.

'We can try,' de Zorzi nodded.

The convoy that finally set off was as follows. The Morris was at the front. Peter was driving, Alan sat next to him while Freda was in the back. Behind them came the Saxers in their Volkswagen Beetle, and bringing up the rear was the Citroën truck. De Zorzi and Barbara were at the front, while Ali and the two other men were in the back, ready to push either of the cars free should they get trapped in the sand.

'You must to look in the mirror,' de Zorzi told Peter. 'If we stop, you stop. Always it is important in the desert to stay together. Do not continue if you lose sight of us.'

Peter promised that he would not.

'Here,' de Zorzi said, handing Freda a tin of Nescafé for Alan. 'Café frappé; tastes better than always water.'

Shortly before one o'clock, the three vehicles started their engines and set off on the stretch that they hoped would take them back to In Abbangarit uninterrupted. The road did improve and Peter managed to navigate the sandy areas far more competently than he had earlier. There was no wingmirror and the view through the rear-view mirror was partially obscured by the personal items of luggage in the back. It therefore fell to Freda to keep an eye on the vehicles behind them. Every so often she would lean out through the window and confirm that, yes, everything was still fine. An hour's driving left them less than 50 miles from their destination.

'I wouldn't mind a little more of that coffee,' Alan said.

'Strong or weak?' Freda asked.

272

'Oh, quite weak, I think.'

Peter could see why de Zorzi had needed to get Alan out of his cab. For a while he would be coherent and upright, able to talk sensibly and offer useful advice about the driving; then suddenly he'd collapse again. Flopping to one side or the other, he would mumble incoherently as if in a trance. It could take up to a quarter of an hour for him to come round each time.

Both Freda and Peter were extremely concerned. He was clearly more sick than either of them had thought.

'Here we are,' Freda said, passing Alan his cup of coffee.

At first, when she looked back through the window, she saw what she expected to see. There was the Beetle, there was the lorry: both where they should be. An instant later she realized she had been mistaken. In a sudden panic she slid over to the other side of the car and looked again. Perhaps they'd been in her blind spot. All she could see was dazzling white reflecting back into her eyes. From the hazy blur by the wheels away to the shimmering ivory satin billowing on the horizon there was nothing but sand.

'Peter,' she said, 'they're not there.'

'What?'

Peter braked immediately and climbed out. They were in a baking, windless area surrounded by low dunes. He ran up one to the right and scanned the horizon. There was no sign of the other vehicles.

'Why have we stopped?' came Alan's impatient voice from the front of the car.

'Can't see the lorry,' Peter explained. 'We've got to wait for it to catch up.'

'What on earth for?'

'De Zorzi's orders.'

'Oh, don't be so stupid,' Alan snapped. 'The road's fine here and we're almost at In Abbangarit. Let's drive on.'

'But de Zorzi . . .' Peter persisted weakly. He looked round at Freda.

When Alan had walked off into the desert, Peter had assumed responsibility for the group. It had been he who spent hours freeing the car from the sand. When Alan had returned, Peter was relegated to the position of junior partner once again. Seventeen years of learning to respect his elders and betters had left him unable to defy Alan, while Freda was incapable of opposing the man whom she held in such awe.

When Peter looked at her, wondering what he should do, she remained silent. It would have to be his decision.

'Are you sure?' Peter asked.

'Of course I'm sure,' Alan said. 'It's daft just sitting here.'

He seems lucid enough, Peter thought as he started the engine. And he is the leader after all.

Perhaps if Barbara had been in the car things might have turned out differently. Throughout the trip, it had been she who had challenged Alan, sometimes with success.

But Barbara wasn't with them now. She was in the lorry, and from her elevated seat she had watched as the Volkswagen had stopped: this time a plug lead had become disconnected. She looked ahead at the Morris, expecting it to come to a halt at any moment, but it kept on going. Both the Saxers and de Zorzi sounded their horns. Barbara screeched out of the window, but none of them were heard.

'I just couldn't believe it,' Mrs Simpson told me. 'I can still see it today. So clearly. That little car disappearing ahead of us. We kept thinking they'd notice, that they'd stop . . .'

TWENTY EIGHT

WATER ON THE BRAIN

THEY had come to rest on a gentle rise. Ahead was a long sandy hollow. Peter searched for any lorry tracks he could follow. There were none, and he began to wonder whether they had made the old mistake of following the bidons rather than the roadway. Just have to hope the crust holds, he thought as they set off.

The Morris made it up the hill easily and, at the crest, Freda looked all round. There was still no sign of the other vehicles. Remembering de Zorzi's advice, Peter decided to rush the hollow even though the surface looked hard enough. The first 100 yards went well. Then, without any warning, there was a crunch and everyone knew the wheels had broken through the crust. The car decelerated so quickly that there was no time to change down through the gears. A moment later the Morris gave up the battle with the powdery sand and ground to a halt.

Peter climbed out and looked. All four wheels had sunk and the bodywork was resting on the sand.

'Is it bad?' Freda asked.

'Awful,' Peter sighed.

It was far too hot to try to free the vehicle now. They had no option but to rest and wait for the others to catch up.

'Is there any more coffee?'

'We're out of water,' Freda said.

'But I'm thirsty, I'm thirsty,' Alan muttered dreamily and lolled back in his seat. If he were deprived now of his regular sips of water he would soon fall into delirium.

'The others'll be along soon,' Freda said encouragingly. 'You have a little sleep.'

Peter took the opportunity to write up his diary. Given the fact that they were immovably stuck in a patch of sand where the only tracks were their own; that they had no water; that one of the party was suffering from dehydration: given all this, the entry he made was remarkably optimistic.

We did very well up to here. Now we are 2 mls ahead of the lorry & stuck hopelessly with no water but we don't mind as we have had our fill. The lorry I hope will be coming on again at 3 after it has rested.

Knowing that de Zorzi was an experienced driver, they had assumed he would not drive during the hottest period of the day between midday and three. This meant he should arrive about an hour after that.

When four o'clock came and went, they began to make excuses for the delay. Perhaps they'd had an extra-long lunch break, perhaps the VW was playing up again, or perhaps de Zorzi was driving more slowly to make it as comfortable as possible for Barbara. At five, the reasons they'd contrived already sounded a little weak. By 6 p.m. it was clear that something had gone seriously wrong.

Peter felt the telltale tingles of panic racing up and down his spine. He breathed deeply, trying to keep his fears under control, but sitting still was hopeless. His imagination took over, projecting increasingly gruesome scenarios on the back of his burning eyelids. The only way he could remain calm was to keep busy, and that was dangerous. The more active he was, the more thirsty he would become. There was no water left.

'Just a little more,' Alan was moaning. 'A little drop of water. Surely that's not too much to ask.'

In the circumstances it was, and Alan's frenzied demands for water were making the other two all the more aware of their own thirst. Peter took a tin of pears and punctured the lid with the opener. Having first licked a stray drop of syrup running down the side, he passed the tin to Alan.

'Try this,' he said.

Alan sucked greedily, like a baby at the breast. It was the last of their fruit. Freda opted for some mushrooms in brine while Peter had to make do with the tomato sauce from a can of baked beans. Neither were refreshing and both contained so much salt that, to their dehydrated bodies, they might have been swallowing water from the Dead Sea.

As the sun set the three of them sat on the ground and leant back against the side of the car. It was cool in the shade and the sand was soft. Peter closed his eyes and wondered what Biggles might do in this predicament.

Of course, he thought and jumped up. The radiator. How could it have slipped his attention. Already, as he began unscrewing the cap underneath, he could see the gush of crystal-clear water pouring into the gallon can. Just to be on the safe side, he had a second container ready: it would be criminal to waste any.

His hopes ensured that he was bound to be disappointed by the amount the radiator held, but the thin trickle that emerged was insulting. There were barely two pints of metallic, lukewarm water.

'Beggars can't be choosers,' said Freda with a smile as

Peter poured her a cupful. 'And with a little bit of Nescafé you hardly even notice the rust.'

'Cheers,' said Alan, raising his mug. 'To us.'

'To us,' the others repeated.

The warm water and cool air revived both their bodies and their spirits a little. Peter had tried briefly to free the car but without much enthusiasm. After fifteen minutes or so he slumped back with the others to watch the sun going down.

'When did I try to walk to In Guezzam?' Alan asked, breaking the silence.

'The day before yesterday,' said Freda.

'Is that all? It seems much longer.' He paused. 'There was a nice sunset that evening as well.'

Peter looked at the older man. In those two days he had aged twenty years. His skin had lost its lustre, his eyes their sparkle, and though everything was more or less functioning as before, the inner flame that animates a human being was all but extinguished in the man. His cracked lips moved and a weak faltering voice began to recount his attempted walk to In Guezzam.

'I kept going until it was completely dark,' he said.

'You never turned round,' Peter interrupted.

'Couldn't,' he said. 'I didn't want any way of gauging how far I had to walk.' He took a long wheezing breath. 'Sat down by one of the bidons and waited for the moon to come up. It was all I could do to stay awake. I don't remember when she appeared. Nine, maybe. And I got up again. My whole body complained. It was cold and every joint seemed to be aching. I'd worked out that I had another 50-odd miles to do. Seemed feasible. Roughly London to Brighton, although the sand made it tougher going.'

He sipped at his water and looked up at the sky.

'It's funny, you know. I can't remember a single thing I was thinking. All those hours. Not a thing. I know I tried counting the kilometres off for a while, drum by drum. But that got a bit tedious. I'd keep my head down and try and fool myself that the next bidon was miles away, just for the surprise of suddenly arriving at it. Stupid really.'

After a pause he went on. 'I saw this cairn. It must have been around six the following morning. It was getting light, but the sun hadn't come up yet. I remember imagining the weather forecast. I thought, if I tried hard enough and concentrated on scattered showers, long periods of rain, stuff like that, it might not feel so hot.' He chuckled. 'At one point I was marching along shouting "O-ver-cast, O-ver-cast" with every footstep.'

He paused again and his eyes glazed over. Freda looked at him anxiously.

'Where was I?' he asked, coming round.

'The cairn,' Peter reminded him.

'Oh yes, the cairn. The bloody cairn,' he said, nodding slowly. 'The Foreign Legion use them sometimes,' he continued. 'Make a pile of rocks and put something under it, or near it. Some tins of food, raisins, sugar, that sort of thing – medical supplies sometimes. Just in case someone . . . well, for people like me, I suppose. So I went over to look. Bent down and moved the top rock. I was so tired by this stage everything was swimming in front of my eyes. And then the bottle . . .'

He sighed. 'I'd got it under my arm. Saving it for when I really needed it. I must have . . . I don't know. As I leant over it slipped. Bloody thing slipped.'

He looked close to tears and Freda patted him reassuringly on the back of his clenched fists. He took another minute sip of rusty coffee.

'If it had landed on the sand it might not have broken,' he said. 'But it hit the rocks. Smashed to bits.

'I tried sucking the wet sand. Useless, though. And, of course, there was nothing at all under the cairn.'

He snorted.

'It was getting hot by now. Worked out that I had only about 20 miles to go, but I knew I'd never make it in the heat. The problem was there was no shade anywhere. And I had to rest. I had to get out of the sun. In the distance was the next bidon. It seemed like the only hope I had, so I staggered on and . . . Oh, it was total lunacy . . . I pushed the bidon over and scooped the sand out. Then I crawled inside. It was nice at first. Cool. Dark. I must have fallen asleep immediately.'

'In the drum,' Freda said quietly.

'I know,' said Alan. 'But there was nowhere else . . .'

They all sat silently, thinking of the raging heat which must have developed in the bidon once the full strength of the sun started beating down on the black metal. The inside must have been like a furnace.

'The moon was up when I came round again,' Alan went on. 'I'd been out for eighteen hours or so. Couldn't find my shoes anywhere. I suppose I must have kicked them off – I don't know. But I did know that if I couldn't make those last 20 miles that night I wouldn't make them at all.'

He fell silent again for some while before continuing.

'I think I managed another ten bidons after that. I'd lost the paper and pencil. I can remember seeing the next drum in the distance and I put my head down and aimed for it, but . . . Whenever I looked up again it was way over to the left. Never getting any nearer . . . When the sun came up again that was it. I must have passed out. I . . . The next thing I knew was hearing a lorry. I tried to get up, to let them know I was there . . . but luckily they'd seen me anyway.'

He stopped talking again, reliving that moment of disbelieving relief as the driver had climbed down from what he thought might simply be another cruel trick his mind was playing. He turned and smiled weakly at Freda and Peter.

'The rest you know.'

It was dark by the time Alan had completed his story. Telling it had exhausted him, and he closed his eyes and fell asleep.

'Poor man,' Freda said as she covered him with a blanket where he lay.

'Brave man,' Peter said. He was going over the argument they'd had over who should go for help. He was so sure that he could have managed it if only they had given him the chance, but now he realized how wrong he'd been. If Alan hadn't been able to make it, nobody could.

Peter and Freda put the mattresses out and lay staring up at the stars. Sleep callously refused to take them away from the nightmare situation they were in.

'I think I'll try flashing the lights,' he said, finally abandoning any hope of repose.

'The lights?'

'Headlights. Someone might see them.'

'Oh, good idea,' Freda said, seizing on it enthusiastically. 'We'll take it in turns. Keep them flashing all through the night.'

Peter said, 'I'll have first go – you try and get some sleep.'

'I can't,' Freda admitted.

'I know.'

They kept it up till about three in the morning before exhaustion overcame them. Freda was on the campbed. Peter was in the car. He tried eating more of the baked beans, but without the sauce it was like chewing cardboard and, having extracted every drop of moisture, he spat the little pellets out on to the sand.

The sun rose with appalling inevitability around six. It

281

was Friday 13 May 1955: the twenty-ninth day of the trek. Peter's diary makes it clear how aware he was that it could be their last.

> Woke early . . . Made a 'tent' for the 3 of us using rocks to hold the tarpaulin at each side of the car. Almost no water now. If we are not found this morning or today we will have had it. Mr C. is in a very bad way. Freda is the only one with any energy.
>
> Thank goodness Barbara is safe. We are all hoping at the moment that she is doing something to help but no one here knows whether the lorry is in Abbangarit (having gone a different way from us) or behind us with trouble or what.
>
> If behind us it should be here at about 8. If in Abbangarit it should be here before 2. When these times come & there is no sight we will all know we are finished.
>
> Am writing to mother after 2 if no lorry.
>
> Thank heaven at least one the party will survive.

Barbara had watched the Morris driving on with a mixture of horror and anger. Why hadn't they done as they were told and kept checking behind them? Why hadn't she insisted that Freda get into the lorry while she stayed with the other two? She couldn't help suspecting that they had seen the other vehicles stop but that Alan had browbeaten the boy and the timid school-teacher into continuing. Whereas if *she* had been there . . .

But perhaps she was being unfair. Perhaps they had made a genuine mistake. With so much sun none of them was thinking straight. They had only to let their attention lapse for a minute and the consequences could be dire. All she could hope now was that they realized their mistake and rectified it immediately.

'Just stop,' she whispered, over and over, willing Peter to hear her.

The car was disappearing from view when Ali signalled that the Volkswagen was ready. De Zorzi jumped back into the cab and they sped across the sand in an attempt to catch up with the Morris.

A hundred yards further on they lost sight of the tracks. Although it wasn't particularly windy, there was enough of a ground-level breeze to send grains of sand hissing across the surface. They formed miniature drifts behind stones and pieces of bone, and filled in any dips, any holes – any tyre tracks in their path – transforming the piste, leaving it as flat and featureless as a sheet of glass.

'What now?' Barbara said, her voice betraying her anxiety.

'We carry forward,' de Zorzi said.

They drove on for another half-hour, and as the view ahead improved it became obvious that something had gone wrong. Somehow they must have passed the Morris.

'The only place is perhaps the testing area,' de Zorzi said.

Three miles earlier they had come to a fork in the road. Familiar with the route, de Zorzi had automatically taken the right-hand track but he conceded that, to the novice, both ways looked feasible. To the left was a stretch used by the French army for putting their trucks through the motions. Although it looked like an established track, it soon petered out in the unmapped area of shifting dunes.

'Perhaps they have taken that route,' he sighed. 'I hope not.'

As Peter had thought, the others did stop for a long lunch. Apart from the intolerable heat, the dazzling sunshine makes seeing so difficult that any search would have been pointless. At 3 p.m., when the shadows started to lengthen, they set out again. Back and forth they drove, scanning the horizon for any trace of the missing Morris.

'Do you think maybe they continue to In Abbangarit?' de Zorzi asked.

Barbara had to admit she didn't know. Although they had been travelling together for almost a month, she couldn't say that she really knew Alan. Of course, along the way, she had noticed his little quirks – what irritated him, what saddened him, what brought on that huge throaty laugh of his – but the inner man remained a mystery.

As they continued their search up and down the sand she remembered an anecdote he'd told them right at the start of the trek. He had once owned a 1924 Chevrolet with a dickie seat that his friend's children got to sit in as a treat. One afternoon Erica Boswell's young son, Timothy, had been riding at the back when a grinding crunch and thud had sounded from under the bonnet.

'What was that?' Timothy had asked.

'Oh, you don't want to worry about that,' Alan had replied immediately. 'This car's mummy was frightened by a fire engine.'

The story had confirmed Barbara's initial impression of the man. He was good with children because he was a child himself, a spoilt boy who had never grown up – and the trouble with children, however adorable they may be, is that they are unpredictable.

After three hours spent scouring the sands for any trace of the Morris, de Zorzi called a halt. The sun was sinking fast and he wanted to set up camp before darkness.

'We look again tomorrow,' he promised Barbara. 'Last look before continue to Agadès.'

True to his word, de Zorzi organized a final search of

the area early the following morning. Since the lorry was running low on fuel, he and Fredi Saxer went out in the Volkswagen. As they set off Barbara prayed that this time, please, they would find her friends and bring them all back safely.

TWENTY NINE

FRIDAY THE THIRTEENTH

THERE was a conical heap of sand and stones about 100 yards from the trapped Morris. Having rigged up the tarpaulin as a makeshift shelter and windbreak, Peter struggled to the top of the hillock with his binoculars. He raised them to his eyes and turned slowly, scanning the distance for any sign of life. Apart from the shimmer of scorching dust, there was nothing.

'See anything?' Freda asked hopefully on his return.

He shook his head. 'Nothing that I couldn't see from down here. I'll have another look later.'

'All right,' said Freda calmly. 'By the way, I found a tin of milk. I hope you don't mind, but I've given it to Alan. I thought his need was . . .'

Peter looked down at where the leader of their expedition was lying in the shade of the tarpaulin. Despite the intense heat, he was shaking involuntarily.

'No, that's fine.'

The 8 o'clock deadline he had set himself came and went, but Peter was too weary to scale the mound again. Every so often he would crawl out from the shelter full of good intentions, but the overpowering heat would hold him back. He simply stood 10 yards or so from the car and surveyed the horizon.

There was nothing. Why should there be any more to

see from the top of the mound? Yet he remained un-convinced by his own pessimism. Peter was not the type of person who could simply wallow miserably, no matter how hopeless the situation appeared. By 9 a.m., the anticipation of being discovered had reached such a pitch that he couldn't remain still any longer.

He tried to tell Freda he was going to look, but though his lips moved, no sound emerged. His tongue was swollen, his throat sore and his vocal chords had dried out like strips of raffia. When he tried again it felt as if someone were sandpapering his tonsils.

'I'm going to have another look,' he rasped painfully.

He sat down, wincing as the hammer blow of heat struck him painfully. Every day was noticeably hotter than its predecessor as the temperatures gradually built up and up to the day when the torrential, steaming rains would cool everything down again. With only a week to go till the skies opened, the desert was almost at its hottest.

He had gone only 5 yards before realizing that there was something there. It was the unmistakable ticking thrum of the Volkswagen engine that first alerted him. Could there be aural mirages? Looking up, he saw a dark rounded shape in the middle of the liquid plains of shimmering sand.

It was the Volkswagen, and coming straight for him.

'Freda,' he croaked. 'Freda, look!'

'What is it?' she asked, as she crawled from the shelter and hobbled towards him.

'There,' he said, and with his arm shaking furiously, he pointed to the distant puff of dust. 'They've seen us.'

'Thank God!' Freda whispered. Tears ran down her cheeks as the Volkswagen continued towards them. 'Thank God! I'll tell Alan.'

Peter remained staring at the little car as it drew nearer and nearer. Soon they'd be back with de Zorzi and his gallons and gallons of wonderful water. Soon they'd be back in Agadès, no matter what Alan said. The likelihood of cheating the desert a third time was so remote that he would refuse to cross it unless everything was a hundred per cent certain. A hundred and one per cent!

When the car first began to veer off, Peter assumed it was swerving to avoid an area of loose sand. But the car continued to turn.

'No,' he muttered, unable to believe that he'd been wrong; that they hadn't seen him after all. 'NO!' he screeched, the pain of shouting ripping through his throat. 'Here. Over HERE!'

They didn't hear him. A moment later the car disappeared behind a dune.

'Wait,' Peter whimpered. He ran to the hillock as fast as his weak, rubbery legs would allow.

The sand slipped as he stumbled up the crumbling slope. 'Just wait,' he repeated. 'Just a second.' But the ascent continued like a scene from a frustration nightmare – two steps up and one step back as the stones shifted and the sand collapsed under his feet. 'Please wait.' On his hands and knees now, he clambered up the last few yards to the top.

The whole panorama heaved and lurched as he wobbled to his feet, heart thudding, eyes throbbing. There was nothing. Nothing but the vast stifling emptiness of murderous heat. He remained standing there, scrutinizing every quivering square yard until he was forced to concede that the little car had gone. Then he looked again.

'Gone,' he whispered. And with it all his hopes of ever escaping the desert alive.

'Any luck?' Barbara said. De Zorzi shook his head.

'I saw tracks,' he said. 'I think maybe they drive to In Guezzam.'

Barbara looked at him closely. 'You're sure?'

'Not sure,' de Zorzi said. 'But I think. Best thing now if we get to Agadès and inform French authorities. They can arrange army search party – just in case.'

'What time do you think we'll get there?' she asked, aware that, if they *were* lost, the army would have to be mobilized as soon as possible for there to be any chance of finding survivors and not corpses.

'Maybe one, maybe two,' he said.

It was nine o'clock in the morning, which meant it would be five hours before the search could even begin. Barbara found herself hoping that they *had* defied de Zorzi and gone on to In Guezzam.

The sun had attained its fiery zenith above the Morris and sunk back down beneath the horizon. Another day was over; another night to come. No one had spoken since the Volkswagen changed its course and vanished behind the dunes. I spy with my little eye something beginning with S. Sand, sun, sky. There was no need for any other letters. The time had passed without idle conversation or silly games.

It is the trivial minutiae, however, that fix a day in the memory. Reflecting on that particular Friday, Peter could remember nothing to give him a clue as to how he'd spent the long burning hours. Perhaps he had passed out, he thought. Perhaps time is another mirage. The emptier a day is, the slower it passes, and yet when you look back it has flashed past in an instant. Peter's day in the desert had been featureless, anonymous, as minute after empty minute had gone by, each one identical to that which it replaced. In retrospect, it had been that single minute, infinitely repeated as a mirror image of itself, but no more substantial for that. Peter had no recollection of the time passing because nothing had happened. Memory is dependent on the day-to-day titbits for nourishment. When they are absent, the past ceases to exist.

'We made it,' he muttered to Freda.

'We did.'

It was all they had to grasp on to: the hope that as they had made it so far they could make it a little further.

'How are you, Alan?' Freda asked.

He nodded gently but his eyes remained shut. If he was in pain, he was certainly suffering with dignity. Freda took a cloth, dipped it in one of her jars of moisturising cream and wiped it round his eyes and lips. 'Nice and cool,' she said.

For the superstitious, Alan's trek was star-crossed from the outset. Even before he had set out, there had been the breaking of the *mchanga* – the charmed Baluya string of beads which was to keep him safe – and the killing of his favourite dog, a death which the African servants took as a fearsome forewarning of what could happen to its owner. Their lucky mascots had fared no better: one had escaped, one had been paralysed and finally run over. During the journey, the omens had been just as disquieting: near Koumra they had been cursed by the gnarled old woman in charge of the dancing girls, while in Agadès the mournful boys with their skull headdresses had been chased away. None of them knew whether this would add to the cumulative effect of the warning portents. None of them understood the hold that the sorcery and superstition of the dark continent might have over them. Yet they had all been affected by the mounting sense of foreboding.

There is no definitive explanation for Friday the thirteenth being considered so unlucky. Adam and Eve ate the fateful forbidden apple, and subsequently both died, on a Friday. Cain murdered Abel on a Friday. There were thirteen at the Last Supper when Jesus sat down with his twelve disciples. Jesus was crucified on a Friday. The increase in the number of accidents which research has indicated actually do occur on Friday-the-thirteenths is probably due to the self-fulfilling nature of an omen. Even if Alan could have ignored all the African fore-warnings and maledictions, the coming together of the superstitions of Africa and Europe was, like the conver-gence of black and white in its colonial manifestation, a recipe for disaster.

'It's getting cold,' Freda said, struggling to her feet. 'I'll get Alan a blanket.'

Peter rolled over on to his side and surveyed the pathetic scene, ghostly and unreal in the moonlight. The Morris, trapped up to its axles; Alan lying motionless on the sand; the skinny primary-school teacher hardly able to remain standing as she stumbled to the car.

As he watched Alan, he began to feel uneasy. He screwed up his eyes slightly to clarify his vision, but it made no difference. The gentle rise and fall of the man's chest had stopped.

Peter crouched down next to him to check whether he was still breathing. He felt for a pulse on the inside of his wrist, on his neck. The body was still warm but the heart had stopped beating. It was 8.30 p.m.. Alan had died.

'No, he can't be,' Freda said, losing the calm she had maintained for so many days. 'He can't be,' she repeated and, pulling the body away from the car, she shook his shoulders gently. 'Not dead. Not dead.'

There were still a couple of inches of whisky in the bottle. Freda had heard of St Bernards and the reviving properties of their miniature barrels of rum – and wasn't whisky the *water of life*? 'Not dead,' she mumbled again and tried and tried to force the neck of the bottle between Alan's cracked lips.

'Just a little,' she whispered. 'A little sip.'

A trickle of whisky ran down over his stubbled jowls and soaked into his shirt.

Freda sat back on her heels, exhausted. Even grief needs energy to be expressed, and Freda's energy was spent. She leant forward, brushed back his cowlick of hair and kissed him on the forehead.

The blanket was next to her in a heap. She laid it out over the body and slowly, mechanically, smoothed the creases away.

'God bless, Alan,' she said and closed her eyes. 'God bless.'

'Yes, it could have been seeing Alan's body that spurred me on.' Peter nodded thoughtfully. 'I think it brought home the finality of it all ... You stop breathing and that's that. No more chances.'

He was responding to my question about where he had found the energy to keep going. I had read in his diary that, once again, he had managed to free the car. It seemed almost inconceivable that having gone so many hours without water, so many days under the broiling sun, so many draining weeks on the road, he had still refused to concede defeat.

Evelyn Barnes had sent him off with the fond hope that the trek would make a man of her son; rather, it seemed to be turning him into a Superman.

'I remember it was an awfully difficult business. I was so weak.'

Peter relived those moments, crawling from wheel to wheel on his blistered hands and knees, jacking up the car one turn at a time – forced to stop after every movement, he knelt on the ground, head down, trying not to let himself pant. The old familiar routine, but painfully slower than before. Once the jack slipped and he wasn't quick enough to prevent the tyre crushing his hand. He'd looked around, but Freda was sleeping at last. It took a further wearying fifteen minutes to scrape the sand away and free himself.

With two wheels on the makeshift base, Peter tried to drive the car out of the drift. The rear wheels merely spun and the car sank. He would have to start all over again.

In the end Peter's dogged persistence paid off. His ultimate success was summed up with characteristic brevity in the diary: 'Got car out after struggle of 8 hours. First back then forwards, then back, then forwards.'

He lurched his way over to Freda's mattress and woke her. His head was spinning so fast that he was hardly sure whether he had spoken the words he wanted to say to her. She seemed to understand.

'That's wonderful, Peter,' he heard. 'I'm sure we'll come to water soon. I know we will.'

Peter didn't remind her that they had drained the radiator. Even if there was a well nearby, there was no guarantee the Morris would make it. They could but try, and although it was still two hours before the dawn they decided to leave at once rather than wait for the agonizing heat to return.

'What are you doing?' Freda asked as Peter got into the driving seat.

'I thought we were going.'

'But Alan?'

'Alan?'

'We can't just leave him here,' she said.

'There's no alternative.'

'There is, there is,' she argued, an edge of hysteria creeping into her voice. 'We'll take him with us. I can't leave him here for . . . for the vultures.'

'There are no vultures here,' Peter muttered dully.

He knew that Freda was far too distressed to give in, and he hadn't the strength to bury Alan's body. It was he who had no alternative.

The struggle with the body would have been comical if it hadn't been so painful. Even their combined strength was insufficient to lift it up. It was dragged across the sand, propped up against the rearbumper and heaved, one limb at a time up into the back.

'Don't hurt him,' Freda had whispered as the head rolled back heavily against the side.

With no water in the radiator, the engine started knocking violently the moment they drove off. Three miles further on, with wisps of steam oozing out from under the bonnet, they stopped to let it cool. This pattern was repeated until they had completed 12 miles. After the fourth stop the car refused to spring into action. No matter how hard, how desperately Peter pulled the starter nothing happened. The battery was too flat to turn the engine.

As if in a dream, he reached under the seat for the crank-handle. He put it in place. That was difficult enough, swaying back and forwards, unable to focus; turning it proved impossible. There was no strength left in his arms and he stood leaning on the handle, unable to press down, unable to straighten up.

A sudden blinding flash filled his eyes as the rising sun rose above a distant hill. It was at this moment that Peter knew he and Freda had reached the end.

THIRTY

TIME RUNNING OUT

THOSE last hours were confused. Peter drifted in and out of consciousness. Afterwards, all he had were scraps of memory, unfettered by the rigours of time, which he pasted into place like a collage in his attempts to recreate the missing day.

Three camels glided across the sand, their legs wading through the shallows of an imaginary lake. They are supposed to be inquisitive beasts and Peter had waved, hoping to attract their attention. Maybe they could be milked. But the camels had sailed away, oblivious to the thirsting humans.

Alan's body had started to decompose. It could not remain in the car. To be spared the sight of his dead friend, Peter ensured that the blanket was securely in place before pulling the body out through the back doors and into the shade.

He unbolted the back of the rear seat and lowered it. With the mattress in place, the car was as comfortable as they could hope for.

Down the side of the seat was a stray can. The label had come off.

'Let it be grapefruit,' he muttered as he pressed the point of the can opener into the shiny lid. It skidded on the smooth surface uselessly. He tried again, but his

295

arms were shaking and his hands far too weak to grip.

Whatever the contents of the tin might have been, neither he nor Freda were to discover. Still clinging on to the hope that a rescue plane might arrive at any moment, they rifled through the spongebags that Freda and Barbara had brought with them, looking for anything that might prolong their lives a few minutes more.

There was Optrex, which they used to swill out their mouths. There was cold-cream which soothed the burning rims of their eyes.

'You remember what Alan used to say?' Freda asked.

Peter nodded. Every night he would call out, 'Night girls. And don't forget to do your faces.' It had become a silly joke based on how frivolous he thought women could be. Now they were depending on the same lotions and creams to prevent that last essential drop of moisture from escaping.

There were bandages. However much they hated wrapping the suffocating cloths round their faces, they knew their lives could depend on keeping nose and mouth sealed from the parched air.

In one of the side pockets they found a vanity mirror. In sunlight a simple mirror can generate up to 7 million candle-power of light. The reflected beam can be seen even beyond the horizon. Peter leant his arm out of the window and watched spellbound as the sun ricocheted away, sending out their desperate mayday.

They were both sitting in the afternoon shade of the Morris when they heard the aircraft. A churning rumble of noise, approaching from the south. Despite themselves, they let their imagination go and saw a tiny Fokker Friendship landing on the piste in front of them, three men jump out and run towards them with sloshing buckets of chilled water.

As the plane appeared from behind them, it was

transformed instantly from the emergency rescue plane to a Boeing full of passengers bound for Europe. Freda waved anyway. Peter tilted the mirror to try and shoot the beam into the cockpit. The airliner was soon gone, leaving only a disintegrating line of wispy cloud.

'Why haven't they sent out a rescue plane?' Peter croaked, 'They must know we're lost by now.'

'I don't know,' Freda said quietly.

Three camels glided across the sand in the distance. Peter tried to remember if they were going in the same or the opposite direction to the ones he'd seen that morning. If it was the opposite direction, they could be the same three camels returning from wherever they had been. If the same direction, they were probably different – unless they were walking in gigantic circles.

Peter and Freda were still on the ground at dusk. Barefoot, buttons undone, panting under their gags, they watched the huge red quivering ball sliding impossible quickly below the horizon.

A large spider had been making its way up and down the rippled undulations of the cooling sand towards the promise of a warm night near the car. Coming to an area of soft material, it tested it with its front legs before deciding there was no danger and advancing.

'Spider,' Peter said, pointing to Freda's skirt.

She looked down.

'A big one,' she said and, calmly flapping the cotton cloth, sent the wingless creature flying off through the evening air.

On, off, on, off, on, off . . . The headlights flashed out across the silver sand for an instant before plunging the desert back into darkness.

'Best to shine them now,' Peter said. 'Before the moon comes up.'

'That's not for hours yet. Let me know when I should take over.'

Peter had nodded, but in the event he hadn't needed to. The silver had yellowed, and long before the moon rose, the tarnished beams had flickered and gone out.

Peter knew that there was still a small drop of the whisky left. He'd been saving it, savouring the thought of that delicious, burning wetness sluicing round his swollen tongue.

As the sun had scorched the ground, he'd leant back for the sand under the car and let the cool grains trickle down his back and chest. His skin might have been deceived into believing it was water. His mouth, however, was still crying out for something liquid. He reached for the bottle.

To his horror, he saw that Freda had finished it off. She had even forgotten to replace the cap, with the result that the very last drop had evaporated.

The legs stretched out in front of him looked curiously unfamiliar. The right one was worse. The calf had shrunk and a deathly pallor seemed to be shining through the tanned skin. The ankle resembled the bone from a Sunday joint of lamb wrapped up in brown paper. He fingered it lightly, and felt nothing. Scratching harder, he was still unable to break through the scaly numbness.

It doesn't even seem like mine, Peter realized.

The thought didn't frighten him. He was past that. It was with the detached curiosity of an old man mechanically turning the cards in a game of patience that he inspected his body, poking and prodding to see what else was beginning to dry out.

The sun was once again at its hottest and Freda and Peter were both sitting at the front of the immobile car, gazing out through the dusty windscreen. Tiny clouds were forming in the sky, clouds that would soon – though not soon enough – bring torrential rain to the desiccated plains.

In a panicked frenzy of activity, Freda had flung her hat away, torn at her blouse, ripped at her skirt. It had to be possible to cool down, to lower the temperature of her parched and burning body. But now she was still again. She realized that, like a fly trapped in a spider's web, there was no escape and struggling would only hasten the inevitable.

'If you could have anything in the world,' Peter asked in a hoarse whisper, 'what would you most like to drink?'

Freda smiled. 'I'd be perfectly content with a glass of water.'

'Nothing else?' he persisted.

Freda remained silent. The faint smile was still playing round her lips, but there would be no more attempted jokes from them now. Her sheikh had let her down.

It was 1.30 in the afternoon of 15 May 1955, and Freda was dead.

Peter closed his eyes. It was all too immense to comprehend. He had to shut it out, will it away, try to wake up from the nightmare that had him in its lethal grip. He saw himself sitting there, a bony seventeen-year-old leaning back against a useless car, his life evaporating. Behind him was the corpse of the trek leader who had abandoned him in the middle of the desert; beside him, the body of the woman whose surrender in her efforts to survive had left him alone. Alone to face his own death in agonizing isolation.

It was weakness that now prevented him dashing round in a futile, panic-stricken fever. The car was immovable; the water which lay deep below the surface, unattainable; help – even if it was on its way – could only arrive too late. It was too much to fight against. And yet, perhaps an aeroplane ... Peter was incapable of renouncing hope entirely.

The sudden image of Alan sprawling around under the collapsed heap of pews in the missionary church came back to him, and he smiled. Freda shooing away the hole in the blanket. The ridiculous complications he and Barbara had experienced buying those stamps in the Congo. It had been fun, great fun, he thought; but that simply made the tragic outcome all the sadder.

If only, he thought. If only . . .

He hadn't consciously noticed it at the time, but in her last hours Freda's breathing had been rasping and irregular. Now there was nothing. She looked so at peace, yet ironically it was her silence that reminded him that she was not simply sleeping. The calmness in her expression confirmed an article he'd read which said that those who die of dehydration feel no thirst at the end, only fatigue.

The sun had aged the boy, toughening his skin and burning off his innocence. But now the brutal initiation ceremony which should have signalled Peter's entry into manhood had gone too far. He had passed from youth to senility. Wizened, unsteady and suffering from a dehydrated parody of old age – so was the boy approaching death.

'I don't want to die,' he whispered. 'Not now.' It was a statement of fact. There was no emotion behind the words. The white hot sun had cauterized his feelings, just as it was now desiccating his body.

It was hotter than the day before. The sun poured down on him like boiling oil. He should get into the car and wait for the shadows to swing round – he knew that. But he couldn't move. One more second, he told himself. Then I'll make the effort.

He remained sitting in the dazzling heat, lifting hand-fuls of sand, one after the other, and watching mesmerized as the tiny grains fell in a glittering trickle. It was like a giant hour-glass, and the sand had all but

300

run out. If he could just keep a little in the air . . . He imagined the entire Sahara desert as a clock which, if he managed to invert it, would start the flow of time moving all over again.

Freda would start breathing, and he'd get into the driver's seat next to her and reverse to the place where Alan would revive. Then, all three of them could climb back into the car and return to the lorry where they would be safe.

He realized with a jolt that he had drifted off. Was this the sleepiness which preceded death?

Had there been a tree nearby, Peter might have carved his initials into the trunk – just to prove that he had been there, that he existed. There were no trees. There was nothing but the scalding shroud of shifting sand which, with its own special Midas touch, turned life to death.

'Got to let them know,' he mumbled, shocked at the sound of the cracked huskiness of his own voice.

He dragged himself up to his feet and stood, swaying, as his head hammered and swirled.

They should know, they should see, he thought and, answering an imperative to make his mark stronger than himself, he pulled the Box Brownie out of his case.

He staggered backwards, falling once, to a point where he could get the car centred in the awful desolation which had ensnared it. If only he could stop shaking. Holding his arms as rigid as possible, he stared down at the square and its inverted image which refused to come into focus. Stop shaking, he commanded himself.

'Just have to hope it's not too blurred,' he muttered, and pressed down on the button.

The photograph in the album is extremely moving. Although it is somewhat blurred through camera shake, nothing can detract from the impact of the scene. The little Morris is in the middle of the picture. The rear-doors are open and the tarpaulin is hanging limply down the back. Lying on the ground to the right is a small, rounded mound covered by a blanket. It is Alan's body. Freda is in the passenger seat at the front.

My eyes kept being drawn back to the number plate. KBY 779. The letters and digits look so incongruous in the centre of that vast, empty wasteland. Everywhere humans go, they name and categorize, sort, register and classify, bringing order to chaos. But here it is not possible. Here, maps could never keep pace with the shifting sands. Here, letters cannot cast their defining spell, and numbers count for nothing.

As the camera clicked Peter felt his strength drain away. He had left something for the future; there was nothing more he could do.

With the sun still directly above, there was almost no shadow into which he could retreat. He couldn't sit next to Freda in the car and he hadn't the strength to remove her. Instead, he lay on the ground next to the Morris, his head half underneath in the only patch of coolness for hundreds of square miles around.

He felt so wonderfully, wonderfully sleepy. Everything would be all right. As he lost consciousness the grains of sand, hissing over the surface crust, were already beginning to collect in his hair, in the folds of his shorts, to pile up as embryonic dunes against his legs.

THIRTY ONE

SOLDIER IN TEARS

THE vibrations that brought him round made no sense at first. They seemed to be emanating from the earth itself, as though the Sahara had fallen asleep with him and was now snoring loudly. The sound persisted and increased until Peter could no longer put it down to his imagination. Concentrating on every painful movement, he raised his head and peered into the distance. Two lorries were trundling across the sand towards him.

So close to death, this might simply have been another hallucination. I asked Peter if at that moment he had dared to trust his senses.

'No, I couldn't,' he confirmed. 'I dragged myself up by the side of the car with my arms. My legs wouldn't work at all, and I remember just staring at these two strange-looking trucks coming towards me. I couldn't believe it. I didn't wave. I didn't shout. I just stood there and watched.'

He went on with his account in a matter-of-fact tone. 'There were two or three French Legionnaires in each of the lorries. I remember they circled me for a while and parked a short distance away, as if they were scared of coming too close. Then, as one of the soldiers ran towards me, I collapsed. Another burst into tears.'

The men were soldiers of the Bataillon Autonome du

Niger Est. Following a request by Commander G. Feral, made at 1800 hours on 14 May 1955, a patrol of seven men in two lorries had been dispatched from Agadès at 0500, 15 May. They found the missing Morris at 17.30 the same day.

Leader of the patrol, Company Sergeant-Major Tourat, reported the scene which greeted them on their arrival. It was little wonder that one of the toughened Legionnaires had cried.

17 h 30 – In the dunes ... 381 kms from Agadès we arrived next to the Morris. It was pointing south and had come to a halt in recent lorry tracks.

At our approach, a man dressed in shorts stood up, acknowledged us and fell back to the ground. This was BARNES, Peter, Bruce, Robert.

In the car, stretched out and undressed, was the body of Miss Muriel TAYLOR. Lying with his face to the ground and covered with a tarpaulin was Alan, Norman COOPER. The corpse of the latter was puffed up and his face, which had been eaten away by maggots, was unrecognizable.

Finally Peter could allow himself to relax. The responsibility he'd felt for his friends and for himself had been taken away. He no longer had to struggle to stay alive but could leave it now to the professionals who would do it for him.

Tourat was rigorously efficient. Peter was soaked in water to bring his core temperature down and a civilian medico, M. Salembère, gave him an injection to replace the essential minerals his body had lost. Only then would he allow Peter to drink some water – one frustrating sip at a time.

When he was confident that Peter would pull through, Tourat organized the burial of Alan and Freda. They were placed in adjacent graves at 5.55' N x 18.40' W, and marked with simple, wooden crosses bearing their names.

This was still the Sahara desert, however. The colonial introduction of map references, rehydration programmes and Christian sacraments had done little to obscure the centuries of superstitions of spirits and djinns. For all their military precision, had it not been for the most bizarre coincidence of the entire trek, the Legionnaires would have been digging graves for three instead of two. Peter could not have survived another night unaided.

The Legionnaires had spent most of that Sunday travelling up from Agadès and there had been little time left to search the area before nightfall. At 16.15 they came across an encampment of Kel Rhela nomads. The leader of the tribe, Ounès, told the soldiers that he and his people had seen curious flashing lights in the sky, 20 kilometres to the north-west.

'All through the night, the troubled spirits of the dead roamed the dark air.'

'And you went to investigate?' Tourat had asked.

Ounès had shaken his head solemnly. 'Too dangerous, the spirits.'

The nomads worship the sun and moon, and light itself is venerated. At the point of death, the soul of the deceased returns to the sun: the fact that the lights had appeared during the night proved to them that their ancestors were either angry or distressed. The following morning, they would perform the necessary propitiatory rituals, but alone in the hostile desert at night they had shuddered with fear as the display of spiritual displeasure continued. The Legionnaires had known at once that there was a more practical explanation for the lights.

Ironically, both Freda's death and Peter's survival

resulted from the behaviour of the superstitious Kel Rhela nomads. If the light in the sky had had no religious significance for them, they would not have considered it worth mentioning to the Legionnaires, and Peter would have died. If however, their beliefs hadn't led to such blind terror, they might have investigated the source of the lights themselves. If they had, Freda would probably have survived.

As the injections and minute amounts of water coursed round Peter's body he was racked with sharp agonizing cramps. Limbs, muscles, organs, one by one they had all switched off, leaving his dehydrated body utterly numb at the onset of death. With the intake of water, sensitivity returned, and he was forced to endure the anguish from which his body had tried to protect him. The Legionnaires looked on with helpless sympathy as the boy writhed and groaned. Unable to give him painkillers for fear of damaging his liver or kidneys, they could only mop his brow and continue with the strict regimen of regular sips of the life-giving water which, despite the torture, was bringing about Peter's rebirth.

All night he was cared for. Occasionally the pain became so intense that he would fall from the bed and sprawl out on the sand. Strong invisible hands would lift him back and replace the thick blankets. Once, he tried to walk – he cannot remember why – but his legs had rejected the command and he collapsed in a broken heap. Again the hands took control.

The soldiers could have had little trouble picking him up. During his brief but interminable time in the desert, his weight had fallen from 11 to a mere 7 stone. Gradually, as the discomfort subsided, Peter squirmed less. As he wrote, however, he remained, 'as helpless as a baby'.

The following morning Sergeant-Major Tourat

radioed back to Agadès to report what they had found and to give their estimated time of arrival. He had tried to do this the night before but couldn't be sure his message had been received. The hiss and crackle on the line due to atmospheric conditions made radio contact almost impossible at the onset of the rains. Too late for either Alan or Freda, the weather was about to change.

The aim was to reach the military hospital at Agadès before nightfall. By ten o'clock they were ready to depart. At the front of the new convoy was one of the trucks, towing the crippled Morris. The radiator had been refilled and the engine cleaned of the choking sand, but the battery was still flat. Peter lay on a mattress at the back while Corporal Roger Rubillet steered the vehicle out of the treacherous dunes. The second truck brought up the rear.

'You're stationed in Agadès?' Peter asked, looking over at his driver.

'Yes.'

'Why did it take you so long to come and find us?'

Rubillet said nothing.

'We should have arrived at In Guezzam a week ago,' Peter persisted. 'Why didn't you come before? What went wrong?'

The corporal remained obstinately silent. He was clearly under orders not to discuss anything before his superiors at the garrison had questioned the survivor. Peter slumped back. Formulating the questions he had been wanting to ask for so many days had exhausted him. He felt the confusion returning.

Some while later they stopped briefly for the Morris to be uncoupled. The musky sourness of camels wafted in through the window, and Peter squirmed anxiously.

'Want, want,' he yelled out.

'What you want?' Rubillet asked.

307

'The camels, camels ... drink ...' Peter burbled up at the perplexed soldier.

In his returning delirium, the boy was convinced that if he didn't drink camel's milk he would never escape the clutches of the Sahara. The desert had tried to kill him; only the desert could now nourish him back to full health.

'Milk, want milk.'

'Du lait,' Rubillet exclaimed.

Gulping down the familiar creamy liquid Peter felt warmly content. Everything would be all right now. He fell into a deep sleep.

As the convoy continued southwards the weather suddenly worsened. With no warning, it turned from one moment to the next. The sky darkened and howling winds hurled themselves at the puny vehicles. Startled by an uprooted thorn bush crashing into the side of the car, Peter awoke to find himself alone in the motionless vehicle. He looked out of the window but saw nothing.

His first irrational thought was that he'd been abandoned once again. Then, as he peered into the air, thick with blinding sand, he was just able to make out the shapes of the soldiers, scurrying around, tying down the tarpaulins on the trucks, lashing the three vehicles together, staggering through the storm with massive rocks to place in front of the wheels – even with the brakes on, the huge Dodge trucks were being blown along.

Mixed in with the sand, hitting the car like a volley of bullets, were occasional bursts of rainfall. Sporadic and insubstantial though these first flurries were, Peter realized that the rains which might have saved his friends had finally arrived.

At 10 a.m. on Tuesday, 17 May 1955, Corporal Rubillet drove the Morris into the walled courtyard of the military hospital. Though still weak and semi-delirious, Peter was finally safe. The nightmare was over.

'Well, almost over,' Peter told me. 'I remember being carried from the car – to a bed, I thought. Hoped! And this doctor came up with the most colossal hypodermic in his hands. Well, I was still in a bit of a state, but I was *compos mentis* enough to tell them that no way were they going to put it into me.

'I kept pushing him away and shouting, no, no, no. He was trying to inject it just under my belly button and I could imagine exactly how painful that would be.'

'So what happened?' I asked.

'They were insistent, of course. But in the end I managed to get them to put it in my leg.'

He showed me the large angry scar where a 4-inch septic ulcer had formed. It had taken over six months for the abscess to clear up – including a month in Derby City Hospital – and even today it causes him discomfort.

'Perhaps the injection did save my life,' he said. 'What I do know is that at one stage it looked as though I was going to have to lose my leg.'

Peter was taken to his room. It was a tiny white-washed mud construction with two small windows and a door, stiflingly hot both day and night. The slatted bed with its tissue-thin mattress was torture to his gaunt and aching body and, though the Morris had been impounded by the French authorities, the Commandant – Gabriel Feral – gave permission for him to have a mattress, sleeping bag and pillows fetched from the car a week after Peter's arrival. During the day, when the sun was past its highest, the hospital staff would move the boy's bed outside.

There is a photograph of him, taken by one of the nurses. The spindly iron bed-frame is resting on the sand in the shade of a high mud wall. Peter, skinny but smiling, is propped up on one elbow looking into the camera. In his diary, he briefly described the long hours spent there. After the adventures of the journey and the horrors of the desert, he seemed content doing as little as possible, letting his body recuperate. 'I drink lots of wine – water to the French. Every morning I lie and watch masses of goats go past . . .'

The routine imposed on Peter's life was punctuated by four sets of regular visitors. First of these were the servants – and occasionally the chefs themselves – bringing him meals. They had evidently been given strict instructions to fatten the boy up, but Peter, whose stomach had shrunk to the size of a pea, was incapable of eating the seven-course meals they served up three or four times a day. With huge 'Tommy' gazelle steaks for breakfast, the pattern of the day's menu was established. Apparently, there was an oasis nearby, which meant there was no shortage of fresh vegetables.

Had a wizard lunch with *fresh* tomatoes today. Also 'tommy' steak, onions, leeks, peas, carrots, beans, potatoes, biscuits, custard – and the chef brought in some Lyle's golden syrup. Plus as much bread as I could eat. (Not very much)

The task of coping with this cornucopia of deliciously prepared dishes grew more acute. 'Today I was sick due to far too much food,' he wrote on Friday, 20 May. It was a problem which was not so much dietary as linguistic.

'Mangez, mangez, drink your soup, eat this, eat those, more, more, mangez tous, we bring you something else?'

And Peter wasn't proficient enough in French to explain that he had eaten all he could. 'Non, non, non,' he would groan as yet another overladen tray appeared. But his protests were misinterpreted.

'Malade?' the chefs asked, and felt his brow for fever.
'Pas malade, full, full,' Peter said.

But the chefs called the doctors anyway, just to be on the safe side. They would come, take his temperature, listen to his heart, inspect his leg, and prescribe more food.

The medical staff kept a close eye on Peter from the moment he arrived. That first day, the doctor had visited him every hour to check his heart and lungs, and as he slowly gained strength the visits continued. A selection of army nurses and medics would arrive at regular times to tend to his ailing leg. They would massage and manipulate it to stimulate the blood circulation, they would replace the dressings to the wound which his weakened body refused to heal. Once, when it was clear how septic the leg had become, the doctor who had first injected him cut away the top layer of skin, swabbed away the red and yellow liquid which had accumulated there, and painted it with a sealing plastic compound.

As well as the chefs and doctors, Peter received a succession of visits from well-wishers during those first idle days in the hospital. The Legionnaires who had found him in the desert, M. de Zorzi, local ex-pats, wives of the army bigwigs, the Commandant himself – all of them dropped by on innumerable occasions to hear the English boy recount his story of how he'd nearly perished in the desert. They brought him iced oranges and limes, chocolates and pastilles; they found English books for him to read and magazines to improve his French; and after the Commandant had allowed him access to his little suitcase, they would sit with Peter, looking at his souvenirs and photographs of the ill-fated trek.

Far more sinister than any of these visits was the daily arrival of two Frenchmen, one uniformed, one in a light-blue suit. Every day they put probing questions to him about the trek.

At first Peter could hardly reply. His tongue was still

swollen and in between brief periods of lucidity he would lapse back into delirium. Even when he had recovered physically, there were problems. His French was too poor to explain the finer details of the story and he had to rely on hand gestures and stick-men drawings to clarify apparent inconsistencies and discrepancies. At the end of every session, no matter how garbled Peter's replies had been, the two men would pat him on the back, enthusiastically encourage him to 'mangez, mangez,' and depart.

The following day they would be back with their note-pads, going over the same questions all over again. Peter had the feeling that he was under some kind of suspicion. Writing paper was refused him and, although several times he was assured that he could visit the Morris, the promised trip never materialized.

Barbara came to visit Peter first on Thursday, 19 May, and then every day after that until the Monday when she left for Kano, in British Nigeria, to deal with the bureau-cratic formalities of their predicament.

'They say I need British documents giving me the right to recover the car,' she explained to Peter. 'Otherwise the French will keep it impounded, so I'm going back down to Kano. I'll try and get some money from the embassy while I'm there too – for air tickets back to London.'

'But we've got money,' Peter said.

She shook her head. 'The money we paid Alan is all in travellers' cheques. In *his* name.'

Peter sighed: they might have been rescued from the desert but they were still effectively stranded.

'And that's not the only thing,' Barbara said.

While she was outlining what she had discovered, it suddenly became clear to Peter why the two Frenchmen were being so pedantic with their cross-questioning. They were attempting to establish culpability for the disaster.

'The lorry was running out of fuel,' Barbara explained. 'De Zorzi kept searching for as long as he could, but in the end we had to go on to Agadès. I think we must have arrived at eleven or thereabouts – on the Saturday morning – and we went along to see the Commandant some time after that. De Zorzi was furious. Wanted to know why no search party had been sent out; why five whole days had been allowed to elapse since we sent our original ETA to In Guezzam.'

Commandant Feral had looked at him blankly. He checked in his records and confirmed that, yes, a Mr Alan Cooper had paid a visit to the central office of the French Garrison – he remembered offering him the services of one of his military car mechanics. Apparently Alan had informed them then that they were planning to cross the Sahara and was told to report back the next day. It would be necessary to have the car checked over, to sign a contract with the emergency rescue services, and to obtain customs clearance – all that sort of thing.

Barbara took a deep breath and then went on: 'The only problem was he didn't do any of that. Nothing. He never went back to the Commandant at all.'

Peter could find nothing to say. He thought of all those hours he'd spent under the relentless sun, praying that the search party would find them. They would never have found them, he now realized. Since Alan had omitted to register their departure, no one knew they had left Agadès. No one knew when they failed to arrive at In Guezzam. No one knew they were lost.

Suddenly Alan's bizarre behaviour began to make sense. The little things which, at the time, he had dismissed as mere quirks of their eccentric leader, now took on an ominous significance. The way he had rushed in that Sunday afternoon, hot and flustered, insisting they leave immediately, although there was only an hour or so of daylight left. 'The road's about to be closed,' he had said. It had sounded strange at the time, but Peter had trusted and respected Alan far too implicitly to question either his decisions or his honesty. Then there had been their argument. No wonder Alan had been so determined to be the one to go for help. He had been spurred on by guilt. Because of his irresponsible deception, no external rescue was possible: he knew he would have to attempt to remedy the situation himself.

'He lied to us,' Peter said simply.

His feelings towards the dead man were ambivalent. A certain gratitude persisted that Alan had been prepared to sacrifice his own life to make amends for deceiving them, but even at the end he had failed to admit that he had ignored the regulations.

The sense of betrayal Peter felt was overwhelming. He had managed to survive his ordeal despite Alan, not because of him. If it hadn't been for de Zorzi, all four of them would have perished.

And no one would have known.

THIRTY TWO

ONE MAN'S WORD

THE questioning and cross-questioning continued. It was now clear to Peter why. Alan Cooper had claimed that he had informed the authorities of his impending crossing: the Commandant maintained that he had not. It was a case of one man's word against another, and the French military was determined that there should be no ambiguity as to where the blame lay.

On Tuesday, 24 May, representatives from the police and the army went to see Peter. By this time his friendly interrogators were satisfied they had examined the disaster from every angle, and exhausted all possible lines of questioning. Peter made a comprehensive statement about the trek and signed it.

As they left, the two men patted him on the shoulder and said that he should practise his walking as he was free to leave as soon as his leg improved.

Writing paper was made available soon after that, and Peter wrote a brief – though reassuring, he hoped – letter to his mother.

Dear Mum,
You will have heard what happened. Cooper and Miss Taylor died in the desert and I have been in the military hospital in Agadès for a fortnight now. I was rescued just

315

in time and at present am limping badly due to an injection they gave me to keep me alive.
Love, Peter.

Short and to the point though it was, Evelyn Barnes confirmed to me that it was the most wonderful letter she had ever received. Her own reply was to be more laconic still.

'You see,' she explained, 'a boy of 17 . . . if he'd given up then and come back to Kenya, he'd have thought that the whole trek had been a failure. That *he* had failed. I wanted to let him know that he didn't have to return. If he had, I'm sure he'd have regretted it for the rest of his life.'

She sent him a telegram.

'GO ON. DON'T COME BACK. REPEAT. GO ON!'

'The trouble is, you can't get much feeling into a telegram,' she added and laughed.

Peter never slept well in the hospital. Even when he had his own mattress on the bed, his leg kept him awake. Every time he rolled over the vicious stabbing pains reminded him that it was far from well. 'My leg at its present rate of improvement will be better in 12 months!' he noted miserably in his diary.

The discomfort prevented him from falling into deep sleep. Time and again, throughout the night, the ulcerous wound would drag him back to the surface of unconsciousness, where dreams were at their most active. Dreams which would return him to the desert he had fought so hard to escape, and condemn him to a night of jacking up the car. Over and over, he would turn the ratchet and raise the car, only to see it sinking back down into the soft sand at the vital moment. Back, once again, in the searing heat, his thigh was branded by the white-hot sun.

He would wake up in a sweat and lie there in the dark for a moment or two, completely disorientated. The temperature of the room which had fuelled his dreams continued unabated. His throat was raw. It was only when he sipped the chilled water from the earthenware pot by his bed that he managed to convince himself the nightmare was indeed over.

On Saturday, 28 May, the captain of the unit entertained Peter for the evening. He took him for drinks, introduced him to his wife, showed him his pets – a dog, a cat and an 8-foot baby giraffe that reminded Peter of all the gazelles which he had received from the Sultan of Zanzibar. It occurred to the captain that the boy was bored, and after dinner in the Officers' Mess he suggested that Peter might like to move in with the Legionnaires in the camp, rather than remain 'in solitary' at the hospital.

Peter leapt at the chance. As his novelty value had worn off, so the number of visitors he could expect in a day had also declined. He was bored.

There are a couple of photographs of the Legionnaires he got to know. Posing in front of a low mud wall, they do not look like the brawny, shaven-headed desperados who, by repute, join the Legion to sever links with a life of crime, depravity and abuse. It is said that there is only one question which is strictly forbidden: 'What did you do before you joined up?' Looking at the four fresh young faces, smiling into the camera, it is hard to conceive that any of them might have led the life of a hardened renegade.

There is Jacques Strohl, a thin angular German who had built an automatic shower in the barracks and trimmed Peter's hair for him. Next, is 'le Gros', the tubby cook. Roger Rubillet, the corporal who drove Peter back to Agadès, is next to him. A short dark man, he had inherited his fine features from his Indonesian father, who had met his French wife between the wars. Rubillet himself was married to a local woman with whom he'd had three children.

'But what'll happen when you're stationed somewhere else?' Peter had asked.

'Oh, I'll compensate her. Good sum of money. She'll be OK.'

'But you won't see her again?'

'No,' he said.

The fourth soldier in the photograph is another German. Peter could not remember his name, but the caption he wrote underneath states: 'The left-hand man was at this time going mad.' His eyes looked bewildered, the expression haunted by horrors he cannot come to terms with.

'Too much sun,' Roger Rubillet had said, and tapped his temple. Six of them had been sent out on patrol on camel-back and had become hopelessly lost in a desert sandstorm. The German had watched as the other five had died.

I looked at the photographs again. Peter's happy, smiling face contrasts so markedly with the German's expression of harrowed anguish. Superficially, at least, their experience had been similar, but whereas Peter's nightmare was gradually receding, the German was carrying with him the agonized images of death he had witnessed as a constant reminder of his own mortality.

Peter enjoyed his stay in the camp. His French improved, his letters got written and, as often as he could, he would practise walking. He was not, however, allowed to forget how close the murderous desert still was.

On 1 June he, Jacques and Roger went to the weekly picture show. Rows of camp chairs fanned out in semi-circles from the whitewashed wall the film was being projected against. With no air conditioning in Agadès, the outdoor cinema was the most pleasant place in town to watch a film. Until the wind began to blow, that is. Within minutes a gale was howling through the makeshift auditorium, lashing the soldiers with airborne sand that filled their ears and eyes and totally obliterated *Air Force* from the screen.

'You should see the rains,' Roger yelled in his ear. 'They last only five minutes, but the whole area is turned into a lake for an hour – 15, 20 centimetres deep.'

It did not rain that night, although the storm continued until the early morning. Peter woke to find himself covered with an even dusting of the sand.

Every day, he returned to the hospital for the medics there to check the progress his leg was making and to re-dress the wound. 'A couple more days,' they would inevitably tell him. Peter was getting restless. On Friday, 3 June, the captain informed him that he'd arranged a lift to Zinder for the following day. He was to travel with a French lorry driver called Donici.

'Leaving?' Peter said.

'Tomorrow,' the captain repeated. 'Donici likes to get an early start, so you should prepare everything today.'

Peter didn't need to be told twice. With Roger Rubillet assigned to be his chauffeur for the day, he chased excitely round Agadès getting things done. He was given a final couple of shots in his leg at the hospital, after which he went to Commandant Feral's office. There he was handed 2,000 francs and a letter for the British officials explaining who he was and what had happened. Next, he collected Barbara's luggage from the hotel and his own from the gendarmerie, where it had been kept.

After lunch he went to see the Morris at the army workshop. Standing in front of the tiny car, Peter was overwhelmed with a sadness he had never known before. It occurred to him that perhaps the authorities' refusal to allow him access to the car before had been for medical reasons, psychological reasons. Too many painful memories flooded back. He asked if he could try the car out but his request was refused. Peter was relieved. It was still too soon.

He slept badly that night, tossing and turning on the uncomfortable bed, impatiently willing the time to pass more quickly. The sun completed its unhurried journey round the underbelly of the earth and re-emerged low in the eastern sky at precisely the moment it was meant to rise, not a second early, not a second late.

It was the morning of 4 June 1955. Peter was soon up and ready to leave the French Legionnaires who had rescued him from the desert, taken care of him for the previous three weeks, and slowly nurtured him back to health. He would never forget any of them. When Donici arrived and Peter climbed up on to the driver's bench, Roger, Jacques, 'le Gros', the mad German and the captain were all there to wave him off.

'Next time you cross the desert, you go by truck,' Roger called out.

Next time? Peter wondered if there would be a next time. Certainly he felt disappointed at failing to reach Tamanrasset, the oasis settlement in the mountains at the centre of the desert. While he was being driven away in the opposite direction, regret sharpened his imagination, and the town assumed the cool seductive beauty of a sparkling jewel, so much more exquisite for being mounted at the heart of such dreary desolation.

Perhaps there would be a next time after all.

In London, a woman was lying in St Bartholomew's Hospital in the final throes of labour. Along the length of Fleet Street editors were passing up their dummy copies. From *The Times* to the *Daily Worker*, they all reported a story gleaned from a French West African newspaper based in Dakar, concerning two British subjects who had died of thirst in the Sahara.

On the day that Peter left the hospital, the news finally broke in England.

At 3.30 a.m., or thereabouts, as those first editions of the national dailies were rolling off the presses, the woman gave birth to a baby boy, who would be christened Paul Christopher.

That baby was me.

The trip south was slow and uncomfortable, and the drivers of both trucks were unfriendly. Peter wondered whether their sullen hostility stemmed from their having been ordered to take passengers against their will.

The weather deteriorated. At three o'clock they ran into a sandstorm that turned the air opaque. There were no side windows in the lorry and the wind whistled through the cab, lashing Peter and Donici with its stinging load of sand. They struggled on blindly for a couple of miles, hoping that the storm might abate, but it grew worse still, and Donici was forced to a halt.

There was a crash: the lorry behind had run into the back of the now stationary vehicle. Peter lurched forward, jarring his knee and badly knocking the septic wound. He fingered round the bandage lightly, worried that the jolt might have started it bleeding again: Donici inspected the back of his truck. No damage had been done to either.

'Sand clear now,' Donici said when the rain started. He was right, but the furious cloudburst was almost as impenetrable as the sand it had washed back down to the ground. They battled onwards through the mud, guessing at where the submerged road might be from the gaps in the trees, hoping they wouldn't hit a hole and wreck the chassis.

For 60 miles these conditions persisted. It became clear

that they were not going to make Zinder that day and, as the light failed, they set up camp on the sodden earth just north of Tanout. Peter lay shivering in his sleeping bag, keenly aware of how utterly dependent man was on the elements. He found himself unable to imagine the savage heat he had left behind in the Sahara.

By the following morning the water had drained away. They made Zinder by 1 o'clock.

'Barbara! I thought you were in Kano.'

She laughed; 'I've been travelling around so much I hardly know where I am myself.'

When Donici had dropped him off, Peter had followed the instructions he'd previously been given and taken a lift to the home of Mr and Mrs Bishop, an American missionary couple. He had emerged from their bathroom to find Barbara in the sitting room.

'So you've already been to Kano?' he asked.

Barbara nodded. 'I've got all the papers and documents. I'm going back up to Agadès to collect the car. Want to come?'

A stupid question! Peter's diaries confirm how eagerly he had jumped at the opportunity.

> She had permission to go to Agadès & get the car & equipment to Kano. Now I have to return again!
>
> Or rather, I didn't have to – I really wanted to for the excitement of the trip.

Barbara booked them on to a Trans-Saharienne lorry to Agadès which was scheduled to leave at 11 a.m. on 7 June. In the event, however, they were not to make use of it.

Shortly before they had gone to bed the previous night, the radioman informed Mrs Bishop that a mission plane would be arriving in the morning and that she should be there to meet it. Being one of the no-news-is-good-news school, she immediately began to fret that something had happened to her son, who lived in Kano.

The plane was due at around 10.30. An hour earlier, a Renault station wagon pulled up outside the Bishops' house and a man emerged asking whether a Peter Barnes or a Barbara 'Tuchy' or 'Duthty' were staying there. Finally tiring of the succession of rumours, lies and speculation, Fleet Street had decided to obtain a first-hand account of the survivors' trek. Their man on the doorstep was Gilbert Baker, a freelance reporter based in Nigeria who was representing the *Daily Mirror*. He was also, as it happened, stepson of the late Labour Cabinet Minister, Dick Crossman.

At first neither Peter nor Barbara could believe that anyone was interested in their story, but when he showed them clippings and extracts from the recently published reports of their ordeal they agreed to be interviewed – if only to correct some of the ludicrous inaccuracies.

'Listen to this,' Peter said and read from the *News Chronicle*. 'It's a quote from Freda's brother: "Why were the party short of water? They had water bottles and a reserve supply in a 40-gallon drum. Suggestions that they were ill-equipped are completely wrong. They had a station-wagon and a one-and-a-half-ton pick-up."'

'A what?' Barbara exclaimed.

'That's what it says – "a one-and-a-half-ton pick-up. Mr Cooper had been leading African safaris for 25 years ..."'

Eager to clear up the situation regarding the pick-up – to say nothing of the murder charges, exhumations, coloured porters and all the other editorial flights of fancy – they gave Baker the complete story, as well as the reel of film Peter had taken during those last days in the desert. Both of them liked the young reporter. He'd been in journalism for only a year, and his obvious lack of experience made him more sympathetic than his world-weary colleagues.

'You could use my car to get to Agadès,' he suggested. 'I've hired it for a week – or perhaps I could come with you, get to know you better, meet the authorities at the garrison . . .'

The arrival of the plane put paid to any plan of Baker's for writing an exclusive. On board were two reporters who had flown in from London, via Kano. Baker's face fell as he recognized Frank MacGarry of the *Express* and the *Daily Mail*'s T.F. Thompson.

Out of consideration and sympathy for Gilbert Baker, Peter tried to remain silent in the face of the immediate barrage of questions from the Fleet Street professionals. It was hopeless. He and Barbara had become public property. They couldn't avoid talking.

Peter and Barbara left Zinder at nine in the evening. They were heading for Agadès in Baker's car, where they would recover the Morris and drive it back to Kano. After spending the night at Tanout they continued early the following morning and made their destination by 2 p.m.

Seeing the car again came as a shock. The optimistic, if premature itinerary that Freda had neatly painted on the back door remained a poignant reminder of the tragedy that had taken place. Peter's head spun with fragments of memory. Kenya, where Alan's rambling farm would have to be sold up. Uganda, where they'd laughed till their stomachs ached as the dug-out canoe had capsized and sunk. The tropical jungle, the bread-fruit, the pygmies and their scrawny chickens in the Belgian Congo. The narrow sliver of the Cameroons they'd crossed, where that jagged rock had caused such catastrophic damage to the sump. And then the Sahara:

the part of the trek everyone had been so much looking forward to, the glittering desert which had claimed the lives of two of his travelling companions.

Spain, France, England – countries neither Alan nor Freda would ever see again. Without a word, the survivors packed their belongings into the car and set off for Kano at four o'clock in the afternoon. From there they would fly to London.

There are photographs of this journey – their final trip in the Morris. The rains had turned the roads to a boggy quagmire which, in places, were completely submerged under a lake of water. Progress was slow. One picture shows Barbara bent over the engine of the stranded car, up to her calves in water. It is the final irony.

EPILOGUE

NONE of the press reports was accurate; all of them sensationalized the desert tragedy. Although I found no evidence in the official documents that it might be true, the *Sunday Pictorial* was not alone in exploring the angle of foul play.

> Was it murder? That's the question the International Police in Paris are asking now about the two Britons who were at first believed to have died of thirst motoring across the Sahara.

This was very distressing for the relatives. Southport police had informed Mrs Mabel Moffat of her sister's death on Wednesday, 1 June. They had made no mention of murder, and the implications in the press provoked an angry response from her. The *Sunday Express* quoted her:

> My sister's ambition was to cross Africa by car.
>
> She was due here in the middle of this month to look after my corgi while I went to the Italian Riviera.
>
> Now I have cancelled that trip and may go to Africa instead.
>
> There has been no mention of what became of the two

326

coloured porters or the valuable luggage the party was carrying.

Other papers had contacted Freda's brother, Mr Albert Dawson Taylor of Wilmslow Road, Manchester. The tone of his remarks printed in the *Yorkshire Post* was similar:

I shall speak to the Foreign Office by telephone tomorrow and ask them to make investigations, if possible right away. There seems to be no reason why the trek should have ended in this way.

As I read through the articles in which unconfirmed reports were given as hard facts, in which rumour built on rumour created a totally false scenario, I was saddened. The gallant attempt of the four travellers to survive an ill-conceived plan to cross the desert was being cheapened by the press. Everything had become sinister. Everything was a mystery. The *Daily Sketch* reported the concern expressed by family members with the words: 'Relatives of 38-year old woman schoolteacher who died mysteriously of thirst while trying to cross the Sahara . . .'

Why *mysteriously*? Had she been reported as dying of thirst while sitting in a swimming pool, perhaps – but in the middle of the Sahara? And why didn't these relatives correct the age printed in the newspapers?

'38-year old Miss Muriel Taylor' (*Sunday Express*); 'Miss Muriel Taylor, aged 48' (*Daily Mail*); 'Miss Muriel Taylor, 52 year old teacher' (*Sunday Dispatch*). If there is a mystery, it is why Freda's brother and sister didn't know how old she was – or at least could not agree on the same age.

Muriel Freda Taylor, the experienced driver, the fearless world traveller: this wasn't the Freda I'd got to know through their journey. Freda had been quiet, uncertain, gentle, yet as the end approached, she had drawn on reserves of an inner strength which she probably never knew she possessed. I had grown both to like and admire her. The hardened, practical version of her which the newspapers chose to depict was a convenient but erroneous fiction.

While it was upsetting to read that her death might not have been accidental, at least Freda's family had been informed of their loss before the story reached the news-stands. Alan's relatives were less fortunate. The first Alan's sister heard of his death was when she picked up the paper that Saturday morning.

There followed a series of anxious communications between her, Alan's solicitor and the Foreign Office in an attempt to keep the news from his legal next of kin. At eighty-four, Alan's mother was in poor health. His sister believed that the shock of hearing about Alan's tragic attempt to visit would have killed her.

Since the events had occurred almost three weeks earlier, I was keen to discover why Cooper's family had learnt of his death in so unfortunate a manner. Certainly the French were not to blame. Details of the incident were sent from Agadès to the British Embassy at Dakar on 18 and 21 May. Various explanations were given for the news failing to get further. 'Agadès has only one telephone number, and that is out of action during the hot summer months.' 'Owing to the distance of Niamey from Dakar, the information we have received is somewhat belated.' 'The Whitsun holiday intervening has not helped matters.' Despite the litany of excuses Whitehall concluded that 'Dakar have been very remiss in not telegraphing the information on receipt of the French authorities' letter of May 21'.

The French were affronted by suggestions made in the British press that they, rather than the four travellers, had failed to observe the official regulations concerning desert crossings. They felt due for praise and gratitude on account of their prompt assistance to the stricken Britons, instead of which, they found themselves being held responsible for the deaths. 'Why was the expedition allowed to try a desert crossing?' the *Daily Sketch* had asked: 'Why did it take eight days to find them when their bodies lay beside their broken-down car only 125 miles along a desert track?' demanded the *News Chronicle*.

Already smarting from worldwide criticism of their foreign policy in Algeria and French Indo-China, the French were in no mood to tolerate these insinuations. The British Foreign Secretary was contacted and an apology demanded. At the same time the French official report of the incident was sent to the British Consulate in Dakar. It underlined Alan's responsibility for the tragedy: he had set out 'without sufficient water and without informing the French authorities'.

Peter and Barbara remained oblivious to these diplomatic wrangles. By the time their BOAC flight touched down at Heathrow on Thursday, 16 June, Fleet Street had already dropped the story and only the arrival of the two survivors temporarily rekindled interest.

When the aircraft came to a standstill, a stewardess asked Peter and Barbara to remain seated until all the other passengers had left. Looking through the portholes, they could see why. The tarmac was thronging with the men and women of the press, all eager for a story.

Finally allowed to move, the pair were shepherded towards the exit by an airport official. It was chaotic. Dazzled by camera-flashes, stunned by the clamour of insistent questions and shamelessly jostled, Peter and Barbara were bewildered.

As Mrs Simpson explained to me: 'As far as we were

concerned the trek had been a failure. We hadn't a clue why the newspapers might be interested in our story.'

They were taken through a side door without having to complete any of the usual customs formalities and ushered into a makeshift BBC studio. More photographs, more questions, and an interview which was recorded for that evening's TV news. After the emptiness of the desert, Agadès had seemed crowded; compared with the desert outpost, Kano had been a throbbing metropolis. Now, in London, the sheer number of people was making Peter and Barbara light-headed, disorientated.

Help was at hand. Mowlem's, the Kenyan company where Peter was employed, was a subsidiary of Unilever, and as Evelyn Barnes was a good friend of its head, John Westacott, a telegram had been sent to Lever Brothers UK asking them to give Peter all the assistance he needed. As he and Barbara emerged from behind the television cameras they were seized and whisked off to Mr Buckle's black Austin A70, waiting outside.

The pressmen were in no mood to give up without a chase. Buckle's chauffeur had not left the airport car-park before it became clear they were being tailed. The driver put his foot down in an attempt to shake off their pursuers. Once, he jumped the lights – the journalists did the same.

'They're still there,' Peter reported excitedly.

'We'll be OK,' said the chauffeur confidently as he pulled the steering wheel sharply to the left.

Speeding along the narrow side streets he soon managed to shake off most of those chasing them, though one car remained stubbornly on their tail.

'It's a Humber Hawk,' Peter said, turning back. 'Faster than us.'

The chauffeur snorted and whipped the wheel round to the right. Parked cars lining the kerbs had narrowed the road. There was barely room to get through – just enough for an Austin A70, not quite enough for a Humber Hawk, Peter noted gleefully.

'We've lost him.'

The chauffeur eased his foot off the accelerator and continued his journey at a leisurely pace. Barbara was dropped at the Aero-Club and Peter taken on to the Unilever building, where he was given lunch and a thorough medical examination.

That night, Peter stayed with the chauffeur and his wife in their flat in St James's Court and the following morning woke early. It was time for the very last stretch of the journey to his grandparents in Derbyshire.

They arrived at around 4 p.m. The calamitous trek was finally over. Of course, with all the excitement behind him, Peter's diary became abruptly sketchy. His return was marked with the words 'Everyone fine'.

There was a television set in the house, the first that Peter had ever seen. He switched it on just as the news was about to start.

'It's Barbara!' Peter yelled.

The airport studio was on the screen and he saw himself smiling into the cameras.

'It was madness,' Barbara was saying. 'We were fools to defy the desert . . .'

The newscaster went on to detail reports of 202 people who had died in Buenos Aires in an armed uprising against Juan Perón, but Peter was no longer paying attention. All those miles he had travelled and it was as if the desert had followed him back to England.

'Did you not say anything?' his grandfather asked.

'They must have cut it out,' Peter said, feeling slightly upstaged.

He paused and turned back to the screen. One brief news item and the whole incident was concluded – and they'd even managed to cut him out of that. Barbara was commissioned to write a couple of articles on the disastrous trek, but as far as he was concerned, that was that.

'Grandad,' Peter said slowly, 'do you think anyone'll be interested in my version of the trek some day?'

I asked Peter if his ordeal in the desert had left its mark. He spoke of hypertension and a loathing of cockroaches. (So it wasn't just Freda.) Peter's wife mentioned water: 'When we're travelling, Peter always takes at least twice as much as we could possibly need.' Peter added his 'obsession with cars'.

His house in Nakuru is full of the cups and trophies won while motor racing. Starting at the age of twenty, he first competed in an A40 Sports. In 1963, he helped found a motor club in honour of Independence: today the Kenya Motor Sports Club is one of the biggest in East Africa. Later still, he bought a Ford Taunus 17M, and after that an Escort RS 2000. The racing continued and the cups kept coming.

Initially I was surprised by Peter's passion for motor racing and yet, as I studied the diaries, I began to understand. The boy who had dispassionately recorded his own approach to death and who photographed the scene of his companions' demise had become the man who remained calm behind the wheel of a speeding car. Superficially, the Sahara had left him largely unaffected, but I remained convinced that Peter could not have escaped unscathed. The racing offered a vital clue.

In a letter to her friend, Barbara asked Mavis to get in contact with Evelyn Barnes and ensure that she knew her son was safe. She was writing after her reunion with Peter in the Agadès military hospital. The postscript is revealing, not only about Peter's state of mind so shortly after his last-minute rescue, but also as an indication of why he subsequently took up so dangerous a sport.

332

P.S. In case his mother is worried, Peter is quite normal mentally. The only thing is, he has possibly lost his fear of death.

POSTSCRIPT

I CONSIDER myself very lucky to have met Barbara Simpson and, subsequently, Peter Barnes, both of whom helped me with the writing of the book and, in the process, became good friends.

Barbara and I remained in regular contact. An active environmentalist, she played a significant role in saving part of Arabuko-Sokoke Forest from being cleared and established Turtlewatch, with the aim of protecting turtles in Kenya.

One of my fondest memories is when, on a trip to Britain, she visited me. At the end of an afternoon spent reminiscing over tea and scones, she asked whether I could help her out of her parking place. I assumed she wanted me to warn her if she was about to knock one of the other parked cars, but no, I was required to physically push the car away from the kerb while she steered.

'I'll be fine once I'm back on the open road,' she added cheerily.

Barbara died 30 March 2002, at the age of 87 at home in Watamu.

Peter, and his wife Margery, also communicate regularly. I am now the age he was when he received my first letter enquiring about the trek. During the years in between, Peter has continued with his motorsport and motoring events, though in an organizational capacity these days.

His mother – the indomitable Evelyn Barnes, who had first encouraged Peter to set out on the trek, and who had been so kind to me when I first visited – died in 2003 at the age of 90. I remain indebted to her for her insights into Peter's character – insights only a mother could have.

In 1995, at the age of 57, Peter had the first of three heart attacks. I asked whether he thought his health had been affected directly by his experiences in the desert. He replied that, since his grandfather and father had also had heart attacks – and at the same time in their lives – he thought that it must be hereditary. The difference, of course, is that medicine has advanced since then. Thanks to triple-bypass surgery, Peter is alive and well and working hard as manager of an estate, with idyllic views of Lake Naivasha, the Aberdares and Mount Longonot.

As well as the advances in medicine, technology has of course moved on in many other areas. My original research, for instance, would have been made considerably easier if the World Wide Web – then in its infancy – had been as extensive as it is today. Similarly, had global positioning systems and satellite phones been in existence when the four intrepid explorers set out on their journey across the Sahara, then the tragedy would, in all likelihood, not have taken place.

Politically, aspects of change have been slower. By 1989, all the countries that the Morris Traveller passed through thirty-five years earlier had already shaken off their colonial yokes, though the presence of the British, the Belgians and the French persisted linguistically.

Today in Kenya, Daniel Arap Moi's twenty-four-year rule is over and the new government is struggling to root out years of corruption; in Uganda, power is still in the hands of the military. The Belgian Congo in 1955, Zaire in 1989; the country has changed its name again, this time to the Democratic Republic of Congo, yet remains riven with conflict and internal strife. Nigeria, which was labouring under military rule in 1989, and which was to last a further decade, is currently experiencing its longest period of civilian rule since independence.

It is, however, Niger – the former French colony where the 1955 trek came to its tragic end – where least has changed. Following independence, the army of France was replaced by more than thirty years of home-grown military rule. Today, Niger is still one of the poorest countries in the world, a landlocked wilderness where arable land accounts for only 3.5 per cent of its total area, and a subsistence-based economy is often disrupted by lengthy droughts as the great Sahara tightens its merciless grip.

These days, it is possible to fly from Nairobi to London in eight hours, yet for those adventurous souls who – like Alan Cooper, Freda Taylor, Barbara Duthy and Peter Barnes – want a more interesting way to travel, crossing through Africa by car remains an alternative. But those who decide to would do well to remember it is as true today as it was in 1955 that, despite all man's technological advances, the Sahara desert continues to demand absolute respect.